They Made Their Own Law

They Made Their Own Law

STORIES OF BOLIVAR PENINSULA

BY Melanie Wiggins

Portraits by Keith Carter
Foreword by Ellen Rienstra

AN AUTHORS GUILD BACKINPRINT.COM EDITION

They Made Their Own Law:
Stories of Bolivar Peninsula
All Rights Reserved © 1990, 2000 by Melanie Wiggins

No part of this book may be reproduced or transmitted in any form
or by any means, graphic, electronic, or mechanical, including photocopying,
recording, taping, or by any information storage or retrieval system,
without the permission in writing from the publisher.

AN AUTHORS GUILD BACKINPRINT.COM EDITION
Published by iUniverse.com, Inc.

For information address:
iUniverse.com, Inc.
620 North 48th Street, Suite 201
Lincoln, NE 68504-3467
www.iuniverse.com

Originally published by Rice University Press

ISBN: 0-595-14191-9

Printed in the United States of America

for my sister Margaret

*The most valuable things in life are man's memories,
and they are priceless.*

ANDRÉ KERTÈSZ

Contents

Foreword xi
Preface xiii

THE PLACE
    1 / Indians 3
    2 / Intrigues in the Gulf 11
    3 / David Kokernot 20
    4 / Schooners Aground 28
    5 / Smugglers and Settlers 38
    6 / A Light on the Coast 47
    7 / Gulf and Interstate Railroad 51
    8 / The 1900 Storm 58
    9 / Oil Fever 66
    10 / Visions of Grandeur 79
    11 / The 1915 Storm 84
    12 / A Later Look 99
    13 / Crystal Beach and the Cowboys 104

THE PEOPLE
    Introduction 113
    14 / Louis George Hughes 121
    15 / Kate Hughes 137
    16 / R. C. Bouse, Jr. 147
    17 / Agnes Blume Stephenson 155
    18 / Dixie Bouse Shaw 161
    19 / Vera Shaw Miller 171

20 / Ernest Simpton   177
21 / Jim Bouse   189
22 / Stella Suhler   195
23 / Vernon Kahla   201
24 / Anne Broussard Mouton   211
25 / Mary Silva Dafonte   221
26 / Paulene Johnson Bouse and
    Barbara Johnson Brister   231
27 / Herman Johnson   239
28 / Monroe Kahla, Sr.   247

Notes   263
Bibliography   273
Index   279

Foreword

Bolivar Peninsula is a world unto itself. A narrow strip of land running parallel to the upper southeast Texas coast, bounded on one side by Galveston Bay and on the other by the Gulf of Mexico, it differs geographically from the rest of Texas and historically from other coastlands in the state. To this day it remains a definable entity with its own past, its own flavor, its own particular breed of inhabitant.

Beyond recorded history, the peninsula and its neighbor, Galveston Island, have coexisted, one anchored to the continent, the other embraced entirely by water. The island developed its own identity very early in the annals of Texas history, especially during the nineteenth century, when its sole city, Galveston, grew to be the state's most thriving port metropolis.

The peninsula, on the other hand, remained relatively unsettled, but still it holds its own in Texas history. The Karankawa Indians walked here, and before them ancient people who left no trace of their existence except an occasional arrow point or a sand-polished tooth or bone from the mammoths they hunted. Álvar Núñez Cabeza de Vaca walked here, and Jean Laffite, the Gulf Coast's gentleman pirate. Jane Long waited for her filibuster husband here during a winter so cold that Galveston Bay froze over. Outlaws, land dealers, immigrants from many lands, oil speculators, and countless others have walked here through the years in colorful succession, leaving behind a host of legends, memories, and ghosts. They have left their indelible footprints in the sands of the peninsula's history.

Captain Charles Taylor Cade, a former sheriff, land speculator, and cattle rancher from New Iberia, Louisiana, walked here, too. In the early 1880s Cade succumbed to the lure of Texas land and bought fifteen thousand acres at High Island. The land was available, cheap, and good for grazing livestock because of the abundance of marsh grass. Possibly, because of the area's peculiar geological configuration, he also planned to search for oil, which was already beginning to fire the imaginations of many. Although Cade made several attempts to find oil, he never succeeded. It was not until after his death in 1912 that "black gold" would be discovered on his peninsula property.

Bolivar Peninsula, this unique corner of Texas, deserves to have its story told, and no one is entitled to tell it more than Captain Cade's great-granddaughter, Melanie Speer Wiggins, lifetime devotee and sometime resident of the peninsula and now manager of her great-grandfather's still-vast holdings. This book—her book—is a history of the peninsula, the land, and its people. Here, in her words and theirs, is its story.

ELLEN WALKER RIENSTRA

Preface

In the 1880s when Texas land was a bargain, my great-grandfather, Charles Taylor Cade, Louisiana rancher and sheriff, bought a large section of Bolivar Peninsula, the narrow extension of land on the south end of Galveston Bay. For a hundred years the family held onto the ranch, though Cade came close to selling out in 1910 when he went broke. His wife, Elizabeth, hated Texas and stayed at home in New Iberia while he tended his cattle and hotel, the Sea View, at High Island.

"Grandma Cade wouldn't have anything to do with the hotel," my Aunt Betty says. "I imagine it was partly due to all the partying and drinking that went on there. She was very prissy, dignified, and straight-laced." Mother and her sister, Betty, Cade's granddaughters, refused to have anything to do with Bolivar either, saying they detested the mosquitoes, snakes, heat, and humidity.

Captain Cade's daughter, Kitty, married Charlie Holt, my grandfather, who looked after the Bolivar ranch for fifty years after Cade died in 1912. Charlie had an obsession for watching every square inch of the land, and he did it by constantly making surveys. His skinny figure, outfitted in khaki shirt, pants, and World War I canvas leggings, stalked through the marshes day after day, armed with a local helper and a knapsack of mustard sandwiches. He dug holes to hide the survey markers so neighboring landowners couldn't move them. In spite of his fierce dedication to the land, he was kind and generous to the local people; everyone on the peninsula knew and liked "Challie" Holt, as they called him.

Charlie's surveying helper, Monroe ("Pike") Kahla, said his boss arrived on the Bolivar ferry every morning in his Model A. In the marshes Charlie was merciless to his assistants; he outwalked them, ate practically nothing, and bragged about his endurance. Because he was a stickler for detail, he carried a pencil and tablet in his shirt pocket and noted all verbal agreements and marker locations. Later, if an argument came up and someone said, "Challie, you said such and such," he just pulled out the tablet and reminded them of the facts. "He was always right," Pike says.

Many years after Grandpa died, I became family land manager, a career I would never have imagined for myself in the days I studied art at college. Getting a grip on my new profession took time and many mistakes. In 1983 when Hurricane Alicia blew down the fences on a six-hundred-acre tract, I spent a fortune building new ones. I was really proud of the expensive, straight fence posts that looked much better than the old crooked ones. When I tried to lease the pasture again, local cattlemen informed me I should have put five wires, not three, to keep the cows in. Somehow, through trial and error and just plunging ahead, I learned about maintainers, limestone, muskrats, wolves, wild geese, and three-cornered grass, none of which had anything to do with Picasso or the Renaissance.

As my land education progressed, local people extended their friendship and confidence. Their acceptance of me had a lot to do with their fondness for Grandpa Holt, and some said I was a lot like him. I felt I had finally received their approval the day the goat ropers threw me into the Intracoastal Canal after I photographed their roundup.

Several High Islanders could remember the Sea View Hotel. When they described the old hostelry, I wondered why C. T. Cade spent so much of his time there. "It was out of this world," said Mrs. Vallie Gillman. "Pretty carpet on the floors and all the bedrooms had fireplaces. There was a hack to meet you at the station . . . and little horsedrawn coaches took you down to the beach." The world of High Island in the 1800s seemed so fanciful that I set out to write a book about C. T. Cade, who spent most of his life there.

My research started in High Island when I went looking for bar owner Barbara Mayfield, who owned an early photograph of the Sea View, one I had seen in the *Beach Triton* newspaper. Barbara lived with her aunt and uncle, Mr. and Mrs. Brannon, across the street from the old hotel site. The day I visited them, our conversation was cut short when Sadie Brannon spilled her beer on the family Bible. While we were cleaning up, Barbara arrived, listened to my request for her photograph and promised to get it for me. Several weeks later she was murdered by a drunken customer.

No one in High Island was old enough to remember Captain Cade, and I had given up hope of finding a picture of the Sea View, but a year later, after my mother died, I came across a snapshot of the hotel as I was sorting through her possessions. It was amazingly similar to Barbara's. With renewed enthusiasm I revived the search for Bolivar's past; ancient books, old newspapers, photographs, interviews with peninsula residents, and Captain Cade's collection of letters and documents began to recreate a picture of early life on Bolivar Peninsula. When I saw how many exciting stories there were to tell, I put aside my plan to write about Captain Cade so I could compile the anecdotes and tales of that remarkable corner of Texas.

Very special thanks go to Odessa ("Sis") Mouton, who convinced her friends and relatives in Port Bolivar to tell me their stories; she simply would not let them refuse. She walked me to neighbors' houses, started conversations, then left us to carry on, or she invited sisters and brothers to her home and served coffee and sweet rolls while we looked at old photographs and talked about family history. Sis helped me reconstruct Port Bolivar's past from shoe boxes, scrapbooks, and people's memories.

Many people shared their remembrances with me, and I want to acknowledge them for their help: Gertrude Standley, Bernard Guidry, Claud Kahla, Sadie Lee Brannon, Charles Faggard, Boots Faggard, Monroe Kahla, George Kahla, Bertha Kahla, Ernest Stephenson, Jessie Hughes, Harvey and Helen Carr, Ora and Arnold Kahla, Oca Bouse, Theresa Strimple, Dorothy Stephenson, Jessie Hughes, Eloge Broussard, Anartha Jenkins, Avril Rodriguez, Rev. Charles Perkins and Lorraine Perkins, Richard Rodriguez, Ora Fredericksen, Harry Hughes, and Frank L. Simpton, Jr. Benny Hughes's contribution of Samuel Hughes's diary added an unexpected first-hand account of settlers' lives on the peninsula.

The fifteen storytellers in the second part of the book, however, are the stars of the show. They graciously shared their time, friendship, and some incredible memories. They are Ernest Simpton, Agnes Stephenson, Kate Hughes, R. C. Bouse, Jr., Dixie Shaw, Vera Miller, Jim Bouse, Stella Suhler, Vernon Kahla, Anne Mouton, Mary Dafonte, Paulene Bouse, Barbara Brister, Herman Johnson, and Monroe Kahla, Sr.

A number of historians and scholars gave me invaluable information on Bolivar that, even in my most ardent diggings, I would never have found. They are Douglas Weiskopf and Will Howard of the Houston Public Library, Texas Room; Evangeline Whorton of Galveston; Casey Greene of the Rosenberg Library, Galveston; Kevin Ladd of Wallisville Heritage Park; Dr. Margaret Henson of Houston; James Glass of Houston, John Llewellyn of Alvin; Bill Hill and Dave Cantwell of Houston; Dr. Thomas R. Hester, University of Texas at Austin; Dr. Carl Lindahl, University of Houston; and Elinor Burrus of Crystal Beach. Ellen Rienstra edited the first draft, made suggestions, and goaded me on. Everyone offered me the enthusiasm, support, and interest to keep me going. The truth is, we did this book together.

THE PLACE

1 / The Indians

A beachcomber strolling along the Bolivar shore on a cool December morning could easily find a fossilized camel tooth, deer bone, or perhaps a broken Indian arrow point among the seashells and pebbles. Objects from prehistoric times wash ashore with the tides, giving the finder a collection of tantalizing clues to ancient life. Bison bones, mammoth tooth enamel, and Clovis points recall man's existence in 9,000 B.C. when roving people with flint-tipped spears hunted for huge beasts; they lived along the upper Texas coast forty or fifty miles seaward from present-day Bolivar. Arrow points and broken pieces of black pottery remind us of Indians, who inhabited the peninsula around 1200 A.D. Bits of blue and white crockery and square brown bottles come from early settlers' homes demolished by storms. A time span of eleven thousand years is represented by these relics of humans and extinct animals.[1]

At the end of the Ice Age, ocean levels crept higher; countless hurricanes and strong tides gradually changed the coastline, and Bolivar Peninsula was formed around four or five thousand years ago. Around 1200 A.D. Indians were roving around Galveston Bay and Bolivar using bows and arrows and crude tools, and collecting clams and oysters in the bays and bayous. Because they moved frequently, they left little evidence of their culture, and much of what we know today comes from the writings of French and Spanish explorers. The Spaniards found them in the early 1500s and gave them names but considered them "barbarous savages," having no understanding of their beliefs and customs.

In 1528 Álvar Núñez Cabeza de Vaca, member of a Spanish expedition in the Gulf of Mexico, left Florida with a small party of men to sail toward Galveston in crude boats. A storm demolished the fleet, and de Vaca with eighty or ninety men barely made it to the island and were stranded there—naked, hungry, and exhausted.[2]

Scraping together some driftwood, they built fires and tried to warm themselves in the icy November winds. A large group of native Indian bowmen (probably Karankawa) appeared and brought some fish and roots for them to eat; a few days later the Indians took the men to their cluster of huts.[3]

During that bitterly cold winter all but fifteen of the Spaniards died of exposure and starvation. There was nothing to eat but roots and fish. Five of de Vaca's group became so desperate that, as each one died, the others consumed the body. "The Indians were so shocked at this cannibalism that, if they had seen it sometime earlier, they surely would have killed every one of us," de Vaca said. Half the Indians died of dysentery spread by the shipwrecked men; the others wanted to kill the foreigners but refrained because they believed they possessed magical powers.[4]

"The people we came to know are tall and well-built," noted De Vaca. "Their only weapons are bows and arrows, which they use with great dexterity." De Vaca said the men had bored holes through their nipples and inserted thick stalks of cane through them; in their lower lip they wore a second and smaller piece of cane. The Indians wore no clothes, except that the women covered parts of themselves with "a wool that grows on trees" (Spanish moss), and young girls dressed in deerskin.[5]

De Vaca observed that from October to the end of February every year the Indians lived on the island subsisting on roots picked by the women and fish caught in cane dams. At the end of February they moved to other places in search of food.[6]

Three months of the year the Indians had only oysters and impure water. Wood was extremely scarce and mosquitoes plentiful. "Their houses are made of mats; their floors consist of masses of oyster shells. The natives sleep on these shells—in animal skins, those who happen to own such," wrote de Vaca.[7]

The Spaniard and his friends were forced to act as healers or be denied anything at all to eat. Sick or wounded Indians had always summoned the medicine man, who applied his cure, whereupon the patient paid him with all his possessions. The shaman's usual remedy for a wound was to make an incision over the site, suck the wound, and cauterize it, then blow on the spot as a finishing touch. The Spaniards, not knowing any other methods, blessed the sick, recited a Paternoster and Ave Maria and beseeched God for their recovery, then made the sign of the cross. This method worked well for the new physicians, and to reward them, the Indians brought presents of food and skins.[8]

After de Vaca had acted as healer for a time, the Karankawas began to treat him as a slave, and his life became unbearable. They forced him to do hard labor and grub for roots in the water until his hands were raw and bleeding. At that point he determined to become a neutral trader and escape from his captors. The area Indian bands were always begging him to go from one region to another to get things they needed, but their endless warring made it impossible for them to travel cross-country in safety.[9]

De Vaca chose as his principal wares pieces of sea snail, conchs used for cutting tools, sea-beads, and a fruit like a bean (from mesquite trees) used by the Indians as medicine and a ritual beverage. He traveled inland with his goods and returned with skins, red ochre to rub on their faces, cane for arrows, flint for arrowheads, sinews and cement to attach them, and tassels of deer hair.[10]

De Vaca survived with the Indians because of his ability to adjust to their ways and to identify with them. He and three of his Spanish compatriots managed to escape in October 1534, six years after they had been captured. According to de Vaca's accounts of Karankawa habits and customs, not only the Spaniards struggled for survival on the Texas coast, but the Indians as well.[11]

The Karankawas lived part of the year on Galveston and roved along the coast southwest of the island as far as Corpus Christi. During the next two hundred years their neighbors, the Akokisas, may have seasonally occupied Bolivar Peninsula and the bay area, and the Atakapas, who spoke a similar language, settled in a large strip of land beginning on the east side of Galveston Bay, up through east Texas and into southwestern Louisiana.[12]

"The Orcoquisas [Akokisas] are friends of the Attacapas and make their homes in the vicinity of the mouths of the Neches and the Trinity," wrote Spanish explorer Fray Juan Agustín Morfi in 1777. "These Indians have no fixed home; they do not cultivate the soil; they are few in number, and of little importance. . . . They never bear arms except against the wretches who are shipwrecked on the coast."[13]

Frenchman Simars de Bellisle accidentally landed on Bolivar Peninsula in 1722 when his ship went off course and ran aground. After the captain freed the vessel, Bellisle and four companions went ashore to find help, intending to meet up with the others later. They carried only a few biscuits, their rifles, and some ammunition, expecting to be there only four or five days—they believed they were near the mouth of the Mississippi River.[14]

For some reason the ship abandoned them, and after wandering for many miles down Bolivar Peninsula and around Galveston Bay, Bellisle's four companions fell by the wayside one by one. In spite of Bellisle's efforts to help them, the men collapsed and died of exhaustion, starvation, and despair.[15]

Bellisle, out of ammunition, now resorted to eating boiled grass and yellow tree worms. He waded out to an island in Galveston Bay in search of bird eggs and there came upon some Indians (Akokisas). They had arrived in dugout canoes from the north end of the bay to collect eggs. When they spied him, they drew back as though they had never seen a white man, then proceeded to march up boldly, take everything in his rowboat, and pull off all his clothing.[16]

The Indians took Bellisle with them to shore, and he spent the whole summer with them searching for food. "They possess no cabins or fields," he wrote. "That is why they travel in this manner. . . . The men kill a few deer and a few buffaloes and the women search for wild potatoes." He said that on rainy days none of them went to collect food; they drank only water, then threw it up and told Bellisle to do the same, that this was good.[17]

When winter came they began to treat him brutally, forcing him to go in search of wood and beating him with sticks. In reality Bellisle had become their slave and was forced to go naked with them on hunting and fighting expeditions carrying their heavy equipment, while the Akokisas traveled on horseback. One day with bow and arrow they shot and killed an enemy who was up in a tree, dragged his body away, cut off his arms and head, skinned him, and devoured him completely. Bellisle took this to be cannibalism; however, it is thought that the Indians believed they gained the enemy's strength by consuming their flesh.[18]

The Assinais (Hasinai or Caddo), who were allied with the French, finally rescued Bellisle from his miserable predicament by helping him make his way to the French fort in Natchitoches, Louisiana. His documentation of his experiences with the Indians is considered to be the first description of the Akokisa.[19]

A hundred years later, Secretary of State James Monroe sent George Graham to Galveston Island to advise privateer Jean Laffite to leave. On his long, difficult journey back to Washington, Graham traveled down Bolivar Peninsula by horse in June 1818 and mentioned nothing about the Indians of that region in his report to Monroe, which may mean that very few were left or that they were gathering food farther inland. Graham proceeded northeast and crossed the Sabine River, the present-day boundary between Texas and Louisiana; upon arriving at an Atakapa village north of Calcasieu Lake, he fell ill with acute dysentery.[20]

The Indians received Graham cordially and placed him in a vacant hut. The sides of the dwelling were made of poles interwoven with vines, and the cone-shaped top opened in the center so that smoke from the fire pit could escape. The hut had one door covered by a thick hide hanging from a bar, and the bed consisted of a slightly raised platform of driftwood covered with skins and moss.[21]

The shaman gave Graham hot concoctions of a red root, so astringent that he said he "felt his insides pucker up." The fire was kept going night and day, and the shaman poured water on the hot oyster shells of the fireplace, keeping the tiny room steaming hot. Graham said the steam and smoke kept him blind for days and his skin shrivelled, but he recovered rapidly on a diet of broth made from shellfish.[22]

Graham learned from the medicine man, who spoke a little English, that he could cure most ailments except the "white man's disease" (smallpox). He said that some years ago many of the clan had died before his medicine could take effect, and Graham noticed that several of the elderly members were pockmarked.[23]

The shaman refused to reveal the secret of the red root except to say that he had learned it from the Karankawas, and that it cured all bowel troubles.[24]

After he was up and about, Graham watched the Indians spearing fish. As their dugouts were somewhat frail, the Atakapas never ventured far into the gulf—they walked into saltwater lagoons and threw spears at ten-inch fish with unerring accuracy from twenty paces away. These spears tipped with bone were used for short distances and floated; the harpoon had a heavier tip and wooden floater attached with a thong, which enabled the fisherman to retrieve his weapon as well as wound and tire out the fish.[25]

Sometimes at night the Atakapas speared flounder with a short-handled spear that had a small bundle of fish bones on the end. Next day they cooked their catch in a pit, placed one on top of the other; smaller fish they stuck on the ends of reeds to dry, then smoked them over banked fires. Graham said they were tough and stringy, but another kind of fish with oily meat was quite tasty—these were an item of barter with interior tribes, who traded flint for them.[26]

Extensive trading went on among all the tribes of the Texas

coast—much more than the Europeans realized. When Cabeza de Vaca exchanged items with other groups, they had already traded them with neighboring tribes. By the time Jean Laffite was operating in Galveston, Indians and smugglers worked constantly between Louisiana and Texas exchanging goods. "The Orcoquisac carried their furs to Carcashu [Calcasieu] and Opelousas [Louisiana] to exchange with foreigners who live in those settlements," wrote Juan Antonio Padilla in 1820. Laffite often sailed to Calcasieu Lake to buy and trade for fruits, vegetables, and beef from the Atakapas and farmers.

When Laffite arrived at Galveston in 1817, the Karankawas were spending summers at the west end of the island near three trees hunting and fishing. According to one story, a shortage of females at Campeachy prompted several of Laffite's buccaneers to carry off one of the Indian women. Shortly thereafter a party of Laffite's men went on a hunting expedition near the three trees, where a band of Karankawas attacked them, killing several and wounding some. Laffite, upon hearing the news, mustered up two hundred men and marched against the Indians, numbering about three hundred, and fought them, resulting in defeat for the Karankawas. They stopped coming to the island.[27]

By the time Laffite departed from Galveston in 1821 the Indian population of Galveston Bay had been almost decimated, and by 1830 no Akokisas were left. It appears that by 1860 the Karankawa, long since extinct as an organized group, finally ceased to exist as individuals as well, and in 1908 nine Atakapas were still alive. In the interval between Cabeza de Vaca and Laffite, about three hundred years, the Indians of the upper Texas coast vanished. They died in large numbers from tuberculosis, syphilis, measles, smallpox and other diseases spread by traders, explorers, and missionaries; their hunting and gathering lands were taken from them, and they were killed in battles.[28]

Little evidence remains of Indian occupation of Bolivar and Galveston Bay except the remnants of a shell mound and a burial near Caplen, on the peninsula, and scattered clamshell heaps with occasional dart points and bits of pottery on the northern shores of the bay. Caplen probably was inhabited off and on and used as a cemetery from around 1200 to 1500 A.D. The shell midden at Singing Sands, about a mile away, seems to have been occupied by the Indians from somewhere between 1400 and 1600 A.D.[29]

At the Caplen burial site, a low knoll covered with oak trees, archaeologists found the remains of at least eighty-nine individuals. The bones were found in a flexed or semi-flexed state, with a few offerings such as lumps of red ochre, a tortoise-shell rattle, beads of bone and glass, a bone pendant, flint drills, and small projectile points of the Gary and Kent types. The reason for the flexed position remains a mystery; however, the Indians had only small shells and sticks with which to dig holes for the bodies, and a flexed body could fit into a smaller hole.[30]

On Galveston Island, nineteen Karankawas were buried on one of the high ridges now called the Jamaica Beach site, and thirteen more burials were found about three miles to the northeast. As far as we know, these few bones are all that remain in the area of a Native American people who first appeared on the Texas coast eleven thousand years ago.

2 / Intrigues in the Gulf

In 1815 Spanish Texas was the object of many schemes and plots to invade and take it from Spain. Anglo-American traders and adventurers, or "filibusters," envisioned conquering that vast realm for themselves, though they professed to be brave soldiers doing a noble deed for Mexico.

Two such opportunists, Henry Perry and Warren D. C. Hall, gathered about a hundred and fifty men and pitched camp near Vermilion Bay, Louisiana, with the idea of heading south to drive the two hundred Spanish soldiers out of Texas. In November 1815, Perry and Hall, with two small sloops and a schooner, transported some of their men, arms and supplies over to Point Bolivar, strategically located at the entry to Galveston Bay. They built a couple of cabins, then sent one schooner back to Vermilion Bay to pick up the rest of the men and munitions. As the schooner was returning to Bolivar, a dense fog set in, and the ship hit a sand bar; in less than half an hour waves battered the vessel to pieces.[1]

One man named Dougherty had found a spar and was clinging to it seven days later when Colonel Perry, crossing Galveston Bay in a rowboat, spotted him and brought him in; the man was near death from exposure and starvation. Perry at once sent out search boats to look for survivors. After a long trip along the bay shore and Galveston Island, the rescue party found eleven passengers on the eastern tip of Galveston. The survivors had drifted in on a small raft of ship's planks and were so weak from hunger they could not walk. One of the men, Samuel Davis, died on the raft trip, and the others ate his flesh to keep from starving. Out of seventy-one men and one woman on the ship, fifty-nine died.[2]

Besides the schooner, one of the small sloops was wrecked, but Perry, determined to go on with his plans, moved to a high bluff overlooking the mouth of the Trinity River in upper Galveston Bay. In March 1816, he joined forces with Louis de Aury, commodore of the Mexican navy and new governor of the province of Texas, who had just arrived at Galveston.[3]

Aury, with a crew of refugee Mexican patriots, outcasts and other followers, put up three or four huts of old boards, sails, and palmetto leaves and set in action an energetic and successful privateering business against Spanish merchant ships. Aury took many slaves from these vessels and brought them to Galveston for transfer and sale.[4]

The slaves were herded into stockades called "barracoons," enclosures with crude sheds covered with dried brush. Some were chained to posts and left exposed to sun and rain, and many were completely naked. The buccaneers often beat the blacks with snakeskin whips, and many died of loss of blood or pain. In winter pneumonia killed some, and malaria attacked them in summer; probably half the slaves survived less than two months.[5]

Once Aury had accumulated a sufficiency of blacks, he marched them in chained groups along Bolivar Peninsula to the eastern border of Texas. Lashed by trail drivers' whips, they trudged along an ancient Indian trail on the desolate coast, through snake-infested marshes, to the Sabine River. Slave dealers placed the "merchandise" in even more primitive barracoons to await purchase by agents of Arkansas and Louisiana plantation owners.[6]

On April 6, 1817, Aury sailed south on an expedition, leaving thirty or forty men at Galveston. Nine days later, Jean Laffite, who had been eyeing the place, swooped in and set up headquarters. The successful thirty-four-year-old privateer had lost his stronghold in southern Louisiana and was determined to continue his operations in the Gulf of Mexico. With fortifications on Galveston and Bolivar, Laffite could return from raiding forays to a protected harbor and capture vessels that entered the narrow strait.[7]

Laffite and his captains located a camp near Aury's old shacks, close to the eastern tip of the island, and formed a "government" with rules for division of stolen merchandise. The privateer built a two-story wooden house, painted it bright red, piled sand embankments around it, and placed two cannons in front pointed at the bay. His followers, a motley assortment of convicts, outlaws, and other fortune seekers with their mistresses and wives, constructed haphazard cabins with sand floors. Soon a couple of boarding houses sprang up, then a dock, several drinking establishments with billiard tables, and an arsenal. Laffite called the town "Campeachy," and by the end of 1817 the population was nearly a thousand.[8]

J. Randall Jones traveled to Galveston in 1818 to see Laffite about purchasing some slaves. "He treated me with the most respectful attention . . . ," said Jones. "I informed him of my business. . . . He informed me that he was out of Negroes at that time but he expected some before long."[9]

Jones said there were a number of boats of different sizes at Galveston—one a large vessel that Laffite had seized, loaded with sugar, cocoa, coffee, and wines, an armed schooner, and a ship from Boston trading potatoes and groceries.[10]

A young French Canadian sailor named Lacassinier joined Laffite on Christmas Day 1818. He was assigned to the *Rageur*, a small rakish schooner that attacked a vessel about twice her size near Merida, Mexico.

"It was early morning, and a slight mist hung over the water," Lacassinier said. "The commander of the *Rageur* fired a shot over the bow of the Spanish ship and ordered the blue pennant, emblem of the commune, hoisted. The noise of the discharge of the cannon had just died away when the railing on the deck of the merchant ship fell, and we could see scores of cannoneers ready to fire. In a few minutes a barrage of shots hit the *Rageur* causing her to stagger in the water."

Lacassinier said Laffite's cruiser was not seriously damaged and returned fire while moving out of range. The Spanish ship turned out to be a corvette of war and for some reason failed to pursue them. Lacassinier was hit in the leg with a wood splinter, which crippled him. Laffite later put him on his staff of "les sur fideles," or trusted men who accompanied shipments of silver and gold.[11]

Complaints of Laffite's activities were reaching Washington, D. C. President Monroe, tired of hearing Spain's protests, sent envoy George Graham to Galveston to investigate and ask Laffite to leave. Graham noted, "He observed to me that he had been called a smuggler a pirate & an enemy to the Country—that as to being a smuggler that was true, but that many who branded him with the appellation were not less guilty . . . that his captures had been exclusively confined to Spanish vessels. . . ." Laffite further told his visitor that he felt that the quantity of goods reported smuggled from Galveston had been greatly exaggerated—that, with the exception of the "Negroes," it had not amounted to much. He went on to tell Graham that all he asked was a reasonable time to call in his privateers and remove his property, and Graham assured him that he would have it. Laffite promised to depart in two or three months. This was in June 1818.[12]

Three months later Laffite's privateering continued undiminished, and he was making no motions to leave; however, a devastating hurricane hit in September 1818, flooded the island, and knocked down most of Campeachy, in addition to sinking three of his ships and beaching one. Laffite, ever determined, stayed on and rebuilt his camp.[13]

Early in 1819, James Long, a filibustering adventurer, raised troops at Natchitoches, Louisiana, marched to Nacogdoches, and declared Texas an independent republic, naming himself president. Long then sent two emissaries down to Campeachy to ask Laffite for his support in running the Spanish out of Mexico, and Laffite gave them a hazy though polite reply: "I see with infinite pleasure your disposition to embrace a cause that I have defended for eight years and shall never abandon. . . . For the munitions of war that you ask of me, I can provide you with very little at this moment, for we are awaiting the return of our cruisers.... However, I shall do everything for you that lies within my power." Although Laffite expressed sympathy for Long's ideas, he flatly refused to become involved in his enterprise.[14]

Hall met Jean Laffite for the first time that year and described him as follows:

He was six feet two inches high, a figure of remarkable symmetry, with feet and hands so small.... as to attract attention. In his deportment he was remarkably bland, dignified and social towards equals, though reserved and silent towards inferiors, or those under his command. He received visitors with an easy air of welcome and profuse hospitality.... wore no uniform, but dressed fashionably, and was remarkably neat in his personal appearance. He spoke English correctly, but with a marked French accent ... and entertained his guests with many amusing and entertaining anecdotes. He had a remarkable habit of closing one eye while in conversation, and many thought he had the use of but one eye.[15]

On Sunday, January 7, 1821, a warship appeared off Galveston at sunset. Laffite's observers thought it was a Spanish vessel, and one of the men went out in a rowboat to ascertain the flag colors. He returned to report that the *Enterprise*, a U. S. warship under the command of a Lieutenant Commander Kearny, had arrived.[16]

Early next morning Kearny came to shore and ordered Laffite to abandon and destroy his Galveston camp.

Lacassinier said Laffite had foreseen his expulsion and had already taken necessary steps to abandon the island. Some of his followers had deserted to join Long's army and were plotting to seize a large share of commune spoils for future expeditions. Knowing this, Laffite arranged for his friend Captain William Cochran to bring a schooner from New Orleans with a cargo of ammunition, rum, and forty men. That night, after they landed, Laffite gave a lavish dinner aboard the *Pride* with an ample supply of liquor.[17]

Among the guests that night was Jane Long, wife of James Long, who had gone to New Orleans to recruit men.

16 / THE PLACE

Mrs. Long told Mirabeau B. Lamar about her evening on the ship, and he later recorded her description:

> Laffite was not such an uncouth giant as she had imagined, but just the reverse. She had supposed he was ferocious in temper and in manners as rough and boisterous as the winds and waves . . . and was pleasingly disappointed on finding that he was just the reverse. . . . He had a pair of eyes as vivid as lightning and black as ebony. In conversation he was mild, placable and polite; but altogether unjocular and free from levity. . . . [A]ll attempts . . . to gain any important information from the host concerning his future operations were adroitly and politely parried.[18]

Just before dawn most of the buccaneers were unconscious when Captain Cochran and his crew went out to each ship in the harbor, drove spikes into the guns of all of them except the *Pride*, and removed the ammunition. They placed all war equipment from the ships and Laffite's arsenal, chests of gold and jewels, and a food supply in the *Pride*'s hold.[19]

When the drunkards awoke, the *Pride* had moved close to shore and commanded the commune with her guns. Laffite began tearing down houses and dividing merchandise, giving the mutineers their fair share and no more; Warren Hall received a substantial pile of wood to enhance his camp at Bolivar.[20]

When Laffite had demolished most of Campeachy, he ordered everyone to leave. On an afternoon early in May 1820, his men set fire to the remaining houses; flames and explosions crackled and banged as the flimsy structures disintegrated. Laffite and his crew boarded the *Pride* and sailed out of Galveston into the gulf.

An old Greek named Nicholas, captain of one of Laffite's schooners, said he accompanied Laffite on the *Pride* to Yucatan, where the buccaneer became a merchant trader. Nicholas claimed that Laffite died there in 1826 of yellow fever, but the real truth will never be known, for Jean Laffite disappeared.[21]

James Long, determined to continue his filibustering operations, stayed in his mud fort at Bolivar Point with his wife Jane, small daughter, and black servant girl. In spring 1821, Long departed with seventy-five of his men to strike at the most defenseless point in Texas, La Bahia (Goliad). He captured the fort, but several days later Spanish troops arrived, forced Long to surrender and took him to Mexico City.[22]

Mrs. Long, believing her husband would return, remained at Bolivar. Life was pleasant on the peninsula, and she had the company of fifty soldiers to protect her. For a few months everything went well, but no word came as to Long's fate. Two of his lieutenants packed their possessions and went to the Trinity River, taking a boat and some of the fort's tools. Soon others followed, and the food supply began to run out; the last soldiers to leave carried off the only barrel of flour. They begged Jane to go with them, but she flatly refused.[23]

Jane was now alone except for her small daughter and her thirteen-year-old servant, Kian. She had several muskets, a cannon, and some ammunition that the soldiers had left. To keep the three of them from starving she shot a few birds, gathered oysters, and fished. One day a large redfish swam off with her last hook and line, all her ammunition was used up, and they were forced to live mostly on oysters.[24]

The Karankawas, who lived on the west end of Galveston Island, made several attempts to cross the water to Bolivar in their canoes. Jane, when she saw them approaching, raised her red dress as a warning flag over the fort and fired the cannon; each time her shots frightened them away.[25]

During the winter months Jane, in the last stage of her pregnancy, had no help from Kian, who was critically ill. On the coldest night in Texas history, the wind blew off part of the roof, and snow drifted into the house as Jane gave birth to a daughter. Kian lay in bed, too weak to do anything.[26]

As soon as they could, Jane and Kian went out into the bitter cold and saw that Galveston Bay was iced over so heavily that they could walk on it. They chopped holes in the ice and collected some frozen fish, which they placed in an old barrel of brine and salt in the fort. While they were taking the fish, they saw a large black bear walking along the bay shore, and when Jane's dog began to chase it, the bear lumbered across the frozen channel toward Galveston.[27]

Next spring Kian, who had been out gathering firewood, came running back to the fort to tell her mistress that three white men were coming. Jane hastily put on her shoes and went out to meet them, but when the men saw her they fled. She pursued them for two miles, calling for them to stop, but they disappeared from sight. On her way back to the fort she found a large fish attached to a line, probably the one she had lost. The fish was their first food in three days.[28]

Several days later Kian announced to her mistress the approach of five ships. One of them landed, and the same three men who had fled from the fort walked up to Jane and spoke to her.

"You are Mrs. Long?" asked one.

"Yes," she said.

"What have you to eat, and how do you get it?"

"I have nothing but that redfish you see drying in the sun; I have lived on birds until my ammunition became exhausted, and now, having recovered my hook and line, I catch fish."

"Then," said one, "I will go to our vessel and bring you something." He left and came back shortly with a small amount of cornmeal, bread, and a few other things. One of the others walked out with his rifle to look for a deer and in twenty minutes came back with a fat buck for her.[29]

The men had no sooner sailed away when a pirogue landed with a Mr. Smith and his daughter Peggy from Calcasieu, Louisiana. He begged Jane to come with him up to his home on the San Jacinto River, but she declined, saying she would remain at the fort until her husband returned. Upon hearing her reply, he arranged for Peggy to stay with Jane and promised to send provisions when he reached his destination.[30]

The next day the captain of the ship that had stopped by Bolivar and later had landed at Galveston rowed from the island to Bolivar Point and told Jane he had read in a New Orleans newspaper that James Long would be unable to settle his business in Mexico short of twelve months. He offered to take her as far as Matamoros and give her money to get to Mexico City. She accepted his offer and had no sooner boarded the ship than she learned from a fellow passenger that James Long was supposed to be on his way up the coast. Immediately, she left the ship and returned to her old station on Bolivar.[31]

The next morning, Mr. Smith's son arrived with supplies and talked Jane into going with him back to his home on the San Jacinto River. They arrived at the Smiths' in March or April 1822, and on July 8 Jane received a letter saying that her husband had been shot in the chest by a Mexican sentry and had died. She and her children returned to her old home in Natchez, Mississippi, and later went back to Richmond, Texas, where she lived to a ripe old age.[32]

3 / David Kokernot

With Laffite's departure from Galveston, piracy and smuggling began to slacken, but still caused problems for the U. S. Coast Guard. Smugglers darted in and out the coastal fringes of Texas and Louisiana, waylaying merchant vessels, killing crew members, and taking cargoes. The New Orleans Customs Service began to bolster its forces against these outlaws in 1829 by adding more men and building larger revenue cutters. One of the men appointed as warrant officer was a twenty-five-year-old Dutchman, David Levi Kokernot. The New Orleans district customs supervisor told him to find "a good schooner of light draught and 150 tons burden and to charter same and report."[1]

Kokernot, born in Amsterdam in 1805, had sailed to the United States with his father in 1817. The young boy served as an apprentice ship's pilot in the Mississippi delta, then at seventeen worked as a crew member on merchant vessels traveling to New York, Amsterdam, and Hamburg, Germany.

At the age of nineteen, Kokernot went into business for himself. He bought three thousand dollars worth of flour, lard, and bacon and set out for the island of Santo Domingo (Haiti) in September 1824, on the *George Washington*. The weather was windy and squally, and a powerful gale drove the ship onto a reef near Santo Domingo. The ship went to pieces and all but three hands drowned.[2]

Kokernot and two others were thrown onto a rock and barely managed to stay there until the next day, when a passing revenue cutter spied them and picked them up. The captain and crew of the cutter were all black; they treated Kokernot and his men with great kindness, feeding them and giving them some "good old rum," Kokernot recalled.[3]

After two days the cutter left the three men in Port-au-Prince, Santo Domingo, a strange island inhabited by black people. Kokernot and his friends had only the clothes on their backs and not a penny in their pockets. "No tongue or pen can describe my feelings as I stood on the wharf in this forlorn situation," the young sailor said.[4]

Kokernot and his two shipmates went on board a French vessel to ask for jobs, and the French captain agreed to pay them four bits a day to load and unload cargo. The three went to work every morning in the blistering sun, thankful for a chance to earn some money.

After a month of grueling labor Kokernot met a plantation owner named Edward Brutus. Brutus, a tall, intelligent, and kindly black man from New York, lived in a magnificent stone house surrounded by hundreds of acres of coffee, sugar, and tobacco. Brutus took Kokernot to his home and offered to loan him as much money as he needed, but the young man refused it. "Kokernot, if you will not accept money, you can . . . go into my coffee plantation, gather as much as you wish, and sell it to supply yourself with clothing and such other things as you may need," Brutus said.[5]

So David went to work. The first week he picked three hundred pounds of coffee, lashed the sacks to a donkey, walked to town leading the animal and sold the coffee for five cents a pound. With his money he purchased clothes, boots and a hat, re-mounted the donkey and rode home feeling a hundred per cent better.

For eleven months Kokernot stayed in Santo Domingo working for Brutus. Then one day a vessel arrived from New Orleans under the command of David's old friend, James Spillman. Captain Spillman gave Kokernot passage on his ship in June 1825 to New Orleans, where the young man found his mother dressed in mourning. She had heard no word of his fate for two years.

Kokernot continued his career in shipping and earned an excellent reputation; he accepted the U. S. Customs Service offer and joined them in October 1829.

Kokernot's job was to discover smugglers' meeting places and secret routes; he knew that many of them sailed up Barrataria Pass to the Mississippi River above New Orleans, then shipped their stolen goods into the city. That year Kokernot claimed he and his men captured eight or ten sloops and schooners on the Mississippi.[6]

On March 18, 1831, David chartered the schooner *Julius Caesar*, took on a crew of ten men and twenty passengers, and launched a cruise from New Orleans to Galveston. Early on, two of Kokernot's friends piloting the ship strongly advised him to turn back. They told him a heavy storm was brewing in the gulf, but Kokernot ignored their warnings and continued the trip.

Two day later the *Julius Caesar* was sailing along with a good breeze, heading northwest, and at the end of the day had made a smooth run down the coast. At 7:00 P.M. the wind veered to the northeast, blowing "a tremendous tornado," Kokernot reported. About 1:00 A.M., the ship, with sails partially lowered, sprang a leak. Kokernot turned on both pumps, and the crew and passengers worked frantically to repair the leak, but they could not stop it. At daylight the storm kept raging; water was two feet deep in the cargo section and more was pouring in. "In all my travels and seafaring life I . . . never encountered such a storm," Kokernot said.[7]

The captain decided their only chance for survival was to head straight for shore. "At 7:00 A.M. we spied Sabine Pass; the breakers running mountain high," he said. Then Kokernot noticed two porpoises swimming toward land. He knew that porpoises always stayed in the deepest water and decided to follow them, then ordered all hands below deck except First Mate Thompson and two others.[8]

"We then ran for shore in the wake of the two porpoises, Thompson and one man lashed to the wheel, myself and another man lashed to the rigging," Kokernot said. The ship was running at fifteen knots per hour, and with such terrific speed the men feared the ship would capsize. Their only hope was to make the pass. As they came nearer the breakers, the wind changed to east-northeast. "When we struck the breakers the deck was swept clean and the last boat taken. But thanks be unto God we were all saved."[9]

The captain steered the schooner onto a shell bar near the Texas side of Sabine Pass and put out the anchor to keep her from sinking until everyone could get to shore. The crew cut down the mast and spars and made a raft; in a short time they transported all the passengers to the beach. The schooner was a total wreck.

"But now came our suffering. We were on a barren coast without water or any help; but plenty of mosquitoes, snakes, and alligators," Kokernot said. They could see no houses, farms or human beings in any direction. The men rescued a few barrels of food from the ship and collected most of the sails, which they fashioned into tents. Two of the crew, while looking around in the marsh, found a small dugout still in fairly good condition.[10]

Next day the storm had passed. Kokernot and a companion loaded several empty kegs into the canoe and started up Sabine Lake to look for fresh water and someone to help them. "After toiling all day we found the Neches and Sabine rivers. We pulled up the Sabine some thirty miles without finding a living soul," Kokernot said. They filled the kegs with river water and returned to camp exhausted and worried.

After resting a day, Kokernot and two crewmen paddled up the lake again and this time went up the Neches River. For twenty-five miles they rowed upstream, hoping to find a settler's house, but they saw no habitation on either side. "Downhearted and wearied out, we returned to camp, having filled our kegs with water," Kokernot said.

Two days later Captain Kokernot and three men—Redman, Morris, and Gill—took bottles of water, some scraps of food from the ship, a few other supplies, and set out walking along the beach toward Galveston. They had traveled three miles when they found an old deserted hut at a place called "High Islands." Later they learned that the small house once belonged to Laffite's old huntsman, Burrell Franks. "Here we dug a hole and found fresh water.... also killed a poor wild suckling sow. Finding an old broken salt kettle, we cooked part of our pork," Kokernot said.

After resting at "High Islands" that afternoon in the shade of some oak trees, the four men started down the beach again, hoping to find a farmhouse or someone to help them, but night came and they could see no sign of life.

Redman, at that point, said that if they struck out across the marsh to Redfish Bar, about eighteen miles away, they could wade across Galveston Bay to the mainland and get to the home of his friend, Amos Edwards, who settled at Dickinson Bay in 1830. At that time Redfish Bar was a series of tiny shell islands scattered across the shallow bay; cattlemen often drove their herds across it, as the water was only one-and-a-half to two feet deep.

The four set out wading through the marshes, making slow progress and growing more exhausted with each step. Several hours later they arrived at Double Bayou on the east side of the bay. "Our water was all out and we were very faint and exhausted. One of the men had a little water in a bottle, for which I offered him $500 in gold. He refused. During that time Mr. Gill had drunk so much brackish water that he became sick and died in my arms in great agony. I rolled the poor fellow up in my mosquito bar and laid him down in the marsh to sleep the sleep that knows no waking," Kokernot said.

The bay tide was high, the wind blowing from the southeast, and all of Redfish Bar was under water. There was no way to cross the eight miles to Edwards' house. The men felt wretchedly tired, but they retraced their steps through the marshes to the Bolivar shore.

"There, for the first time, we gave up all hope and laid down in the surf to die," Kokernot said. Morris, who had a little strength left, made his way back to High Island, filled all the bottles with water, and returned about midnight. He pulled the two men out of the surf, poured water down their throats, and brought them to life again.

Next day no one could move. Kokernot, feeling somewhat better, started walking westward along the beach to see if he could find help. As he left, he was certain he would never see the others again. He trudged about five miles feeling hungry, sick, and exhausted, thinking of his home in New Orleans, his wife and mother; he knew he was going to die in that barren place.

Kokernot had taken his gun and one last load of powder and shot. Suddenly he saw ahead of him a large group of cranes and headed toward them thinking, "Now is my time." Life or death depended on that one shot. He crawled up behind some driftwood, took aim, fired, and brought down one of the birds. "I ran up, caught it, cut its throat and sucked the blood, tore it asunder and ate one half of it raw. Rest assured it tasted extraordinarily well. The repast revived and strengthened me very much," he said.

Picking up his gun, he set out again and continued down the beach about seventeen miles until he saw a small house to the southwest, near Bolivar Point. Kokernot left the beach and headed straight for the house, wading as fast as he could through the sticky marsh. When he reached the house he was covered from head to toe with black mud. Standing on the front porch were three children who watched him approach and greeted him politely. The children, a boy of twelve, a girl about seven, and another small boy, belonged to Burrell Franks, Laffite's hunter.

"They were not afraid of me and brought a stool for me to sit on," Kokernot said. He asked them where their parents were, and they replied that the Franks had gone up the Trinity River to see some friends and purchase supplies. He told them about the shipwreck, and Elijah, the eldest, collected some bread, beef, and a jug of water, ran out, caught his pony, and went to find the other two men.

Kokernot asked the children if they had anything to eat, and they said, "Yes, plenty."

"The dear little girl gave me a large bowl of milk, which I greedily devoured. It tasted more delicious than anything I had ever tasted, but in a short time it made me very sick, throwing me into a burning fever," Kokernot said.

While Kokernot lay there suffering, the child sat by his side and gave him water for his parched lips. After a while she said, "I will make him well."

Kokernot looked at her in surprise. In his delirium she seemed to him more like an angel than a frail little girl. She jumped up, ran out into the prairie and gathered a handful of goldenrod, put the weeds in a quart of milk and boiled them. After adding some sugar, she served the concoction to the sick man.

"Drink it," she said. "It will make you well."

In less than an hour the patient suffered a profuse sweat, then slept soundly, and next morning felt completely recovered.

The second day after Elijah had gone in search of Redman and Morris, he brought them back, exhausted and starving, to Bolivar Point. They stayed at the Frankses' house for a week recovering, then a schooner arrived at the point, and Kokernot made a bargain with the captain to take him and his men to Sabine Pass, pick up the passengers and take all of them to Anahuac. Anahuac, once called "Perry's Point" because Henry Perry had camped there in 1815, was a Mexican customs garrison under the command of Colonel John Bradburn and a hundred soldiers.

On April 23, 1831, the captain of the schooner delivered the passengers to the Mexican military garrison where several Texas residents gave them a warm welcome. William B. Travis, Colonel James Morgan, William Hardin, and their friends helped the travelers find lodging and made them comfortable. Kokernot and his crew stayed in Anahuac for two months and at the end of July sailed back to New Orleans. "On the 30th we landed in the city and found all my friends in great trouble on my account, supposing that I had been lost with my schooner. When they saw me they were rejoiced, indeed," Kokernot said.

In 1832 Kokernot moved his family to Anahuac and joined Texas forces against the Mexicans. In 1836 they lived in Lynchburg, then moved to Gonzales in the 1850s. Kokernot never forgot the Franks children and in 1839 went back to Bolivar Point to see what had happened to them. Mary, the little girl who had fed him goldenrod soup, had married and moved to Corpus Christi, and William, the younger brother, had left. He found Elijah a young man of twenty, owner of his own ship and a successful Gulf Coast smuggler. (Elijah will be discussed further in chapter five.) Kokernot thanked him for his kindness years before and promised to help him if the need ever arose.[11]

When Kokernot was seventy-three, the *Gonzales Weekly Inquirer* published his memoirs, including a message to Mary and William Franks: "If either of them sees these lines he will know that I have neither forgotten them nor their deeds of kindness, and we may be certain . . . God has not."

4 / Schooners Aground

"It has been asserted that lands in Texas could be bought for 4 cents an acre, but such is not probably the fact at this . . . time," announced the *Attakapas Gazette* of St. Martinsville, Louisiana, in 1834. "It was understood that Col. [Stephen] Austin had been offered $25,000 for forty leagues of land . . . but the offer was refused. This, if we mistake not, would be at the rate of 14 cents an acre."

Anyway, the rush was on. In 1830 the Galveston Bay and Texas Land Company of New York bought several land grants in southeast Texas (Mexican territory) between the Sabine and San Jacinto rivers. Salesmen promoted contracts for a labor (177 acres) of land, tools, and one year's subsistence in return for settling in the Galveston Bay area and working for the land company two days a week the first year.

One of the earliest purchasers of Texas acreage was a young New York bachelor, name unknown, who made a trip to Galveston accompanied by a friend, to inspect his newly purchased property on the bay, check the title, and find out more about Texas. He wrote a colorful account of his journey in March 1831, called *A Visit to Texas: Being the Journal of a Traveler Through Those Parts Most Interesting to American Settlers with Descriptions of Scenery, Habits, Etc. Etc.* His two-week stay on Bolivar Peninsula is probably the first published description of the place.

The two young men (for the sake of convenience we will call them Frederick and James) sailed from New York to New Orleans, then boarded the sloop *Majesty*. Their ship followed the Texas coast past Galveston and up the Brazos River to Brazoria, where they landed and walked to Captain Cotton's inn, a log house on the river bank. "The general aspect of the country was verdant and agreeable . . . except in its total want of inhabitants. Not a dwelling, except the inn, was anywhere in sight, nor a single vessel, except our sloop," Frederick noted.[1]

The companions then made their way on horseback to Anahuac, which by then was a settlement of twenty or so crude huts, seven small shops, a customs house, and a barracks.[2]

In the 1820s a steady stream of American settlers had started making their way into Texas, to the dismay of the Mexican government, who passed a decree in 1830 to stop the flow. "The North Americans are taking over the country," said General Manuel Mier y Terán, commandant general of northwestern Mexico. Meanwhile, the Galveston Bay and Texas Land Company had sublet huge grants to other contractors who sold scrip for a few cents per acre to prospective settlers and speculators, who believed they were buying land.[3]

A shipload of thirty-four Germans had just arrived at Anahuac and were living miserably in leaky shacks and tents with their families. They had come with high hopes of starting farms or ranches, but the Galveston Bay and Texas Land Company ignored them because General Terán refused to recognize the company and would not allow distribution of any Coahuila and Texas territory.[4]

Frederick and James met two land agents in town, and the four decided to make a trip to Galveston to see how it looked. They bought provisions of bread, salt pork, and coffee, and sailed across the bay in a small boat.

Their impression of the island was that of "a sandbank of vast extent," and as they walked along the shoreline they saw a deer, killed a five-foot rattlesnake, and gathered "beautiful seashells." At the eastern end they discovered a hut flying the Mexican flag; inside they found several of Colonel Bradburn's soldiers from Anahuac making beef jerky.[5]

The hut stood in the vicinity of Jean Laffite's former settlement. Frederick had heard rumors that Laffite had buried some of his "ill-gotten money" near three trees and wondered where it could be.[6]

A few days later Frederick and James with the two agents, whom we will call Charlie and Richard, set out from Anahuac in a small boat to meet the ship *Climax* from New York, bringing more settlers and letters of instruction from the company. As they approached Point Bolivar from the bay, they spotted what resembled the masts of a ship beyond the peninsula in the gulf. They landed, walked across a flat grassy stretch, and came to the Gulf of Mexico. Standing on the beach they realized they had crossed the entire Bolivar Peninsula.[7]

Galveston Island lay on the right in the distance, and directly in front of them in shallow water they saw a schooner that appeared to have run aground on a sandbar. "On the beach we perceived a gentleman and lady, with no attendant and no boat, and were at a loss to imagine how they came there," Frederick said.[8]

The four friends introduced themselves to the couple, who gave their names as Mr. and Mrs. Burnet, from New Jersey. They had come on the schooner *Cull* to settle on the San Jacinto River and had run aground the night before. The captain had just brought them to shore and gone back to his ship to remove more passengers. When the Burnets had left the *Cull*, the other passengers were pitching everything they could find into the sea to lighten the ship and get it afloat.

From the Burnets' account of the ship's situation, the four men became concerned for the safety of the remaining passengers—they feared the enormous waves could knock the vessel to pieces in less than an hour.

Frederick and James with the two agents ran back across the peninsula, launched their boat, and rowed as fast as they could to the end of the point.

As they paddled through the shallows they noticed objects from the ship floating here and there, including two copper boilers pushed alongside their boat by the wind.

The men rowed for two hours to get out to the *Cull*, where they learned that the captain had taken a small group to shore, but those still on board were throwing out everything they could find. Suddenly the wind and sea subsided, and the danger seemed less threatening.[9]

The friends paddled back and landed not far from the point of the peninsula. Frederick picked a spot where most of the things thrown from the ship had floated to shore, and the group began to build a shelter for the night.

The men, using nails brought from the *Cull* and boards from the beach, put together a small shed. Somebody found several blankets in a trunk, and all slept comfortably in their makeshift house.

Next morning, Charlie spied something floating in the water and was delighted to discover several tin cups, a kettle, and other kitchen equipment from the ship. James and Frederick built a fire on the beach and prepared a meager breakfast for everyone.

By the first light of morning the refugees discovered to their joy that the *Cull* had floated off the bar and was sailing along toward Galveston Bay. The Burnets and other passengers said good-bye and rowed off to meet their ship, leaving the rescuers alone on the beach.[10]

As the day was calm and pleasant, the group explored a bit while they waited for the *Climax* from New York. "I may mention the appearance of a hog on the Prairie, to which we gave chase, hoping to obtain a supply of pork for our larder: but though we did our best to drive him towards the point with hopes of getting a shot at him, after many races and doublings he got off and we lost him," Frederick said.[11]

The hunters assumed that the hog had strayed from some nearby farm, as they thought the country must be inhabited, but they afterwards learned that there was not a human being in that region for many miles, and the animal had probably been wild.

Next morning Frederick and his friends saw a small schooner approaching the bay from the east, and after she got within the lee of Galveston Island, the captain rowed to Bolivar for a visit.

"He had chartered his vessel in New Orleans, for two hundred dollars, to two Frenchmen . . . they were going to Anahuac with a load of coffee, whiskey, and claret," Frederick said. "Just off the island [Galveston] they had fallen in with a clumsy boat belonging to General Bradburn, which he had sent, with a captain and four Mexican soldiers, to the Brazos River to see about cutting timber. As their boat was a dull sailer, they had got on board the schooner."[12]

During that night the wind roared, and the noise of the surf woke the sleepers in their shack. As soon as dawn broke, they saw the masts of the schooner barely above the rough water with a distress signal flying at half-mast, and none of the hull visible except a corner of the deck.

The sight of the foundered ship was terrifying, but the captain knew it was impossible to make a rescue effort because of high seas. The men were forced to watch helplessly for several hours as the crew struggled to get the vessel off the bar.[13]

Since they could do nothing to aid the distressed ship, the men decided to explore the interior of the peninsula. In a bayou they scooped up dozens of large blue crabs, brought them back to camp, and boiled them. "We had a highly relished feast, which seemed to restore me to health," Frederick said.

About two o'clock the wind and waves were calmer, so the captain and James rowed out to the vessel; but they noticed that the people on board were frantic to get to shore, so they kept at a distance for a while, wondering what to do.

The situation on the schooner was worse than the captain had thought. She had sprung a leak during the night and had sunk on the sand bar as low as she could go, leaving only a corner of the quarter-deck above water. Heavy waves had crushed the vessel in, and the exhausted crew had been working for hours in waist-deep water.

As the rowboat could hold only four, the captain insisted the two weakest passengers go off first. The crew chose the Frenchmen, owners of the cargo, both in a state of collapse.

The onlookers at the beach were anxiously waiting for the return of the rescuers, and when the rowboat arrived, everyone sympathized with the two unfortunate Frenchmen. One of them could say just a few words, while the other was so exhausted he could barely stand up.[14]

The rescue boat immediately returned to the schooner, while the three men took the Frenchmen to their hut, wrapped them in blankets, gave them a dose of whiskey, laid them near the fire, and rubbed their bodies briskly to restore circulation.

The patients began to recover, and in two hours had nearly revived. "It was affecting to see their expressions of gratitude, which they made by all the means in their power; our ignorance of their language not allowing much intelligible conversation," Frederick remarked.[15]

The boat came to shore again, rowed by the schooner's mate, carrying two more passengers. The mate had appeared strong and alert, but after standing near the fire for a while, he began to weaken, and when he tried to return to the ship, he could not hold an oar. His condition was so bad that Charlie and Richard walked him around for an hour. Later, the mate confessed that after the shipwreck the crew had discovered a bottle of whiskey in the hold and had swigged away at it until nothing was left.

The rescue boat brought two passengers at a time to shore until everyone on the ship was landed. A Mexican captain and one of his soldiers were so debilitated when they arrived that they were speechless.[16]

"We had . . . a large family to provide for, and though it was a light task to feed four, our number now being fifteen, it required forethought," Frederick said. By then the camp had a supply of food—flour, pork, and coffee. Oysters and crabs were easy to catch, and birds on the prairie could be shot any time. Teeming flocks of snipe, plover, and ducks filled the air, and shooting them was effortless because the birds, unused to seeing men, flew close by.[17]

Occasionally a deer would wander up and then leap off into

the grass as soon as anyone loaded a gun. Immense flocks of pelicans waddled along the shore single file, but the hunters had a hard time killing any because their weapons were equipped with small shot.

"We set the Mexicans to making bread . . . that we might learn something from them. . . . They made very thin cakes of flour and water, and laid them among the coals without regard to cleanliness; and these, with claret and whiskey for some, and coffee for others, formed our supper," Frederick said.[18]

In the morning the schooner remained in the same position. The sea was now calm, and five men rowed out to the vessel. After opening the hatches, they retrieved as much cargo as they could take in the rowboat: fifteen or twenty casks of whiskey, bags of damaged coffee, some of the Frenchmen's clothes, the sails and rigging, and a few other articles. By the end of the day camp supplies were considerably enlarged.

Next day no one had much to do, so Charlie and James began to build a flagstaff to help the *Climax* and other vessels in the gulf find the entrance to the bay. They found a forty-foot spar on the beach, nailed it on a board and added a piece of white cloth with several red handkerchiefs. After attaching to it a lanyard, they raised the flagstaff and planted it in the sand.[19]

A day or two later, the *Climax* appeared off the coast. Her crew had not seen the signal but realized they were near an inlet and sent a boat with five men to shore to check their position. They were approaching the beach when they saw the flag and headed toward it, landing about an hour after sunset. The refugees welcomed the sailors and asked about the vessel. As Charlie knew the entrance to Galveston Bay, he accompanied the sailors back to the *Climax*, but this turned out to be a mistake.[20]

The captain of the *Climax* did not see the approaching rowboat, and fearing the danger of shallow waters nearby, moved the ship out a little. Darkness set in, and the men on shore lost sight of both the ship and the rowboat. They began to worry that the six men would have to spend the night on the water with nothing to eat and one jug of whiskey to drink.

The wind increased to gale force, and nothing was known of the fate of Charlie and the sailors until three o'clock the next afternoon. Suddenly Charlie came walking up the beach from the east and reported that they had spent the night in the rowboat. After losing sight of the vessel the evening before, the men had headed toward Bolivar, they thought, had had a drink of whiskey, and then had lain down in the boat. At dawn they could see neither the *Climax* nor land. Several hours later they drifted to shore, not knowing where they were.

Charlie thought he recognized some of the driftwood of the peninsula, so he set out on foot searching for the camp, while the others remained at their boat. After a three-hour walk the worn-out agent made it to the hut, and the others followed shortly afterward. A few hours later the *Climax* appeared offshore and anchored.

That night the wind began to shake and batter the hut. The sleeping group woke occasionally, listened to the screaming wind and crashing sea, but feeling they were safe and could not help the ship, went back to sleep.

In the morning the sea had risen three or four feet and had almost reached the cabin door. Five-foot waves rolled across the beach and rushed across the green grass along the edge of the dunes. Torrents of rain blew with the wind; everything seemed to melt into a vast fluid world. "We naturally concluded, when we contemplated the scene, and considered the force of the storm, that the ship must have inevitably wrecked," Frederick said.[21]

At daylight Frederick, James, Charlie, and Richard left in a heavy rain walking eastward, presuming from the direction of the wind that they would find objects washed ashore from the *Climax*. They walked along the beach for several miles but found nothing. Just as they decided that all was well and the *Climax* safe, they discovered a barrel, then a box of bottled cider and two strings of onions. The barrel was filled with vinegar, so they opened the cider and gulped it down.

The thought of a wrecked ship caused the four to begin their search again, and as they walked along they found other things—tables, chairs, and various objects thrown from the *Climax*. Suddenly the searchers spied the ship in front of them, sitting upright on the beach, almost up to the grass.[22]

"Her masts were gone, but her hull apparently safe and sound. The sea was still very rough and she was surrounded by choppy water. . . ." They decided she was sitting too high to be demolished by the waves. Sailors and passengers, in a state of panic, were hurling barrels, trunks, and furniture into the water. When they noticed the four men on the beach, the crew shouted to them, but the noise of the surf and wind made their voices too faint to hear.

"We called to them that they were on the mainland, on the borders of a rich country, and not far from our temporary habitation . . . but they could not distinctly hear us," Frederick said.[23]

To demonstrate how shallow the water was, Frederick walked into it, intending to wade up to the vessel. After a few steps he sank in water over his head and had to swim back to land. The currents had cut deep channels on each side of the ship, and the vessel's weight had sunk her into the sand.

The captain said there was no way to save his vessel and proposed they build temporary quarters on the beach, then find a way to get to Anahuac, their final destination.

Frederick and his three friends returned to the hut. "In a short time we set off again for the wreck, leaving the Mexicans and Frenchmen, as we thought they could do no good. . . . "

By a stroke of fortune there were two excellent carpenters with their tools among the passengers. The *Climax* had brought building materials for Anahuac, and within half a day the carpenters had constructed tents and lean-tos made of sails and planks. The ship's cook, a large black man called General Midnight, worked diligently to provide meals for the starving travelers.[24]

Three days after the wreck of the *Climax*, two boats arrived at the peninsula camp with several Galveston Bay and Texas Land Company men from Anahuac; they had been looking for the four men, missing for two weeks. The search party was relieved to find all safe and greeted the group with handshakes and embraces.

One of the search boats belonged to the land company and the other to Colonel Bradburn, who had built it at Anahuac and sent it to Bolivar under the command of one of Laffite's former pirates. The appearance of the two boats was a happy sight for the ship's passengers, but their joy soon died when they discovered that they would have to pay a high price to get to Anahuac. Colonel Bradburn demanded twice as much as they had paid to come from New York, so they refused his offer.

The travelers, assisted by the two carpenters, built their own boat in three days and sailed to Anahuac. When they arrived, no one welcomed them to Texas, and the new general agent of the land company, who had come on the *Climax*, was so disturbed by the rugged living conditions in Texas that he took the first ship back to the United States.

Frederick and James resumed their journey through Texas, and the Burnets, who had traveled aboard the *Cull* on their honeymoon, sailed up Galveston Bay to their seventeen acres of land near the San Jacinto River. Burnet wrote later to Samuel May Williams: "We struck a sand bar and were compelled to throw many valuable things overboard, but we saved the [sawmill] engine and its appurtenances." The huge boilers, thrown overboard from the *Cull*, had been driven along by the wind to the north shore of Galveston Bay, where Burnet found and installed them in his lumber mill.[25]

Although his business failed for lack of competent workmen and settlers to buy lumber, attorney David G. Burnet succeeded in politics and became the first president of the Republic of Texas in March 1836.[26]

5 / Smugglers and Settlers

Gail Borden, newly appointed customs collector at Galveston in 1837, sat in a tiny office pondering his duties. With quill pen he wrote in the customs house records: "Smuggling will be carried on at the rolling over place unless means are employed to prevent it. The Schooner *Mary* wrecked at that place on the fourth ... had hauled her cargo onto the bay shore and shipped a part of it to this place on the sloop *Reindeer* without the knowledge of any person in the custom house."[1]

The "rolling over place," near the east end of Bolivar Peninsula, was six hundred yards wide. Ship captains, to avoid paying customs duty at Galveston, were in the habit of pushing barrels of cargo across the isthmus at night and loading them onto vessels headed for the Texas interior.

"I had, however," Borden continued, "learned from a man on Point Bolivar whom I had authorized to board vessels and to keep a 'lookout' that suspicious vessels were in that vicinity, and had not the *Reindeer* entered this port should have dispatched a suitable person yesterday to reconnoitre in the water, as I consider I have a right to do so on the bay side. . . . I would wish to know as soon as convenient if I shall be authorized to extend my authority over vessels and goods found on the Gulph side of the rolling over place."[2]

The *Reindeer*'s owner, Elijah Franks, was the son of Burrell and Mary Franks of Louisiana (mentioned in chapter three). The Frankses, in 1819, had claimed 640 acres of land inside the neutral ground (a haven for outlaws governed by no one) on the west bank of Calcasieu Lake at Hackberry Island. The land lay along one of Jean Laffite's routes up the Calcasieu River, where he bought meat and vegetables from the Atakapas and sold slaves to plantation owners.

Jean and his brother Pierre knew Burrell Franks well; his fame as a marksman intrigued them. When they offered him a hunting job in Galveston he agreed to move there and to furnish birds and game for Laffite's table. This was an easy task, for fields around the bay teemed with ducks, snipe, geese, wild turkeys, squirrels, wild hogs, and deer.

Mary Franks built a boarding house in Campeachy near one of Laffite's storage sheds and noticed hundreds of rats running around. She said there were so many that Laffite's house was lined with tin to keep them out.[3]

Burrell Franks rode through Anahuac one day on a hunting trip and met "Frederick," the New York writer traveling through Texas in 1831. "He was one of Laffite's men," the writer said, ". . . . above six feet high and remarkably expert in shooting a rifle." Franks gave a shooting demonstration for him by placing a friend down the street with a board, then shooting a hole through it.[4]

After Laffite's departure from Galveston, Burrell Franks claimed land near Bolivar Point and settled there with his family. As mentioned previously, son Elijah, by 1837, had learned to sail a ship and navigate the treacherous waters around Galveston and Bolivar Peninsula. His ship, the *Reindeer*, based at Sabine Pass, became so notorious for smuggling that he sold it in 1839 for a thousand dollars; three days later he purchased from his old friend David Kokernot *The Lady of the Lake*, with all furniture and equipment, for the same price.[5]

In June 1840, a Galveston grand jury indicted Elijah Franks and his brother Russell for grand larceny and made them post ten thousand dollars bond. Martin Dunman, part owner of the *Reindeer*, put up the money; however, results of the Franks brothers legal problems never came to light.[6]

Elijah had for several years carried on smuggling activities at Bolivar's narrow point and in 1841 claimed ownership of 1,476 acres at "the Rolling Over Place." He sold his father one-half interest and, two years later, obtained title from the Republic of Texas for the property.[7]

The customs collector's 1837 sketch of his problem zone identified Bolivar Peninsula as "Tory Land." Tories were mostly cattle owners from Louisiana (including the Franks family) who had settled under Mexican law and during the Texas War of Independence felt they owed allegiance to that government, much to the disgust of their fellow Texans.[8] In 1830, Mexico had banned American emigration to Texas, and General Terán had ordered George Fisher, a Hungarian opportunist, to set up an office at Anahuac to collect customs and to erect offices and living quarters at Bolivar Point to control the smuggling of goods into the Texas interior. Terán appointed Lieutenant Juan Pacho Fisher's assistant and promised him a regular guard of surplus troops. While waiting for the troops, Terán tried to set up a collection post at the mouth of the Brazos River, but after lengthy delays, he gave up and told Fisher to take over customs collections. Fisher issued a decree demanding that all ship captains obtain clearance papers at Anahuac, forcing them to sail one hundred miles from the Brazos River up to Anahuac or make the difficult overland trip from the gulf to Anahuac.[9]

Fisher's customs requirements, plus the unpopularity of Colonel Bradburn, created so much animosity that in June 1832, a group of armed Texans from the Brazos River region marched to Anahuac and forced Bradburn out. This violent action led directly to the Texas War of Independence, which broke out in the fall of 1835 and lasted about seven months. General Santa Anna took the Alamo by storm on March 6, 1836, leaving only one defender alive.[10]

Upon hearing of the slaughter, William Hardin, alcalde of Liberty, wrote a letter on March 21, 1836, to John McGaffee of Sabine

Pass, Joseph Dunman, Burrell Franks (of High Island), and their neighbors:

> Gentlemen:
> We received only yesterday an express from our Army giving an account of the defeat and probable massacre of Col. Travis and his force of 180 men and also it is expected that Col. Fannin shared the same fate.
> Our army has retreated to the Colorado where they intend to give the enemy a fight. We are called on in the most urgent and pressing manner to turn out and go immediately to the aid of your friends and fellow citizens.... Don't fail to report to Liberty prepared to march for our army as soon as you can possibly get there.[11]

The appeal fell on deaf ears except for Joseph Dunman, who despite his brother Martin's opposition, went into the army as an express rider and brought Travis' plea for reinforcements from the Alamo to Liberty. Men who failed to cooperate with the Texas army were included in a "Tory" list of 1836 and included Martin and James Dunman, Burrell Franks, and Elijah Franks, all of Bolivar Peninsula.[12]

The Texans defeated Santa Anna on April 21, 1836, and by December President Burnet had 300 Mexican officers in a prisoner-of-war camp in Galveston and no way to provide for them. He sent seventy-one prisoners by schooner to William Hardin's plantation near Liberty; they were suffering from hunger and exposure, having lost their shoes and most of their clothing. Hardin built barracks, shared what little food he had and allowed them to visit town.[13]

One of the officers, Captain Pedro Delgado described their situation in a report:

> Judge Hardin relieved our bitter condition by all means in his power, retaining for himself the worst of his houses, in order to appropriate the two others for the sick.... He kept two sentinels at night, relieving them in day-time and allowing some of us to walk about town.... Even in the stormiest weather Hardin would shoulder his rifle and walk out and kill a beef, which he sent ... to our quarters.[14]

Two of the officers escaped and were seen the next day in Anahuac with Martin and James Dunman and Elijah Franks, who took them to the Dunman house in High Island, where they all spent the night. Next morning the Dunmans and Elijah took the Mexicans eastward down an old cattle trail, crossed the Sabine River at John McGaffey's ferry, and disappeared into Louisiana.[15]

"This has been a d—— unfortunate matter for me," Hardin said. "I was upwards of twenty days in pursuit of the Mexicans and about nine days after the Dunmans. . . . I overtook the Mexicans at Calcasieu and found them so strongly guarded I was unable to arrest them." The Mexicans escaped, but Hardin captured the Dunmans and Franks and delivered them to Colonel William Logan, commander of Liberty. However, Hardin's two witnesses had disappeared and he could not remember where he had written their names.[16]

On December 2, 1836, acting Secretary of War William G. Cooke told Colonel Logan that troops at Galveston needed beef in a bad way. "I understand there are a considerable number of cattle between the Trinity and Sabine rivers, and elsewhere in the Galveston Bay country. . . . You will adopt such measure as you deem proper to procure at least 200 to be delivered at Bolivar Point immediately. . . . You will, if within your power, put a stop to any more cattle being driven from the country, and arrest all and every person . . . operating against the country in her present struggle for independence."[17]

Cooke told Logan that sufficient troops would be placed at Galveston to procure beef for the army. Logan wrote back to the secretary of war: "I ordered Capt. D. L. Kokernot to the Sabine to take charge of what men he had enrolled, and to arrest all persons who might attempt to transport stock contrary to law, and to drive such offenders' stock west to San Jacinto." For years old Bolivar families had driven their herds to Louisiana markets and felt no obligation to give or sell their animals to the desperate Texas army. In an ironic twist, David L. Kokernot, who owed his life to Burrell

Franks' family, had been ordered to work against his old Bolivar friends.[18]

Logan said he would use every effort to supply the Galveston post with beef and thought he could do so if he could get horses. "There are not public horses at this place and the people are unwilling to give up their horses to drive cattle at this time of year.... Cattle are very much scattered over the prairies and marshes.... I learned yesterday that the men ... from Galveston had arrived at Anahuac, ready to guard any ... that might be driven to Bolivar or East Bay."[19]

Once the fighting was over and Texas had achieved independence, European colonists who had heard of the free lands in Texas began to arrive. In Great Britain a severe depression had set in after the Napoleonic wars, and many fled the country to start new lives.

An Englishman named Samuel Parr sailed to Galveston in 1838 and immediately began to survey, claim, buy and sell land on Bolivar and Galveston. He later became first justice of the peace on the peninsula and proudly wore his old English "chimney-pot" hat on state occasions.

Legend has it that Parr returned to England for a visit and slept in the same bed with one of his relatives. "Tammas, you would be a long time in England before you would have the honor of sleeping with a judge," Parr remarked.

"And Samuel, you would be a darn sight longer in England before you would be a judge," Tammas replied.[20]

Parr received a visit in the early 1840s from Charles Hooton, a British traveler visiting in Galveston. Hooton, together with his neighbor, "the Major," and sundry other characters, decided to get up an expedition to Bolivar Point to stage a political rally for a Galveston lawyer, "Mr. Potter," Democratic candidate for Congress of the new Republic of Texas.[21]

When Hooton arrived at downtown Galveston, the mayor's constable, dressed in Mexican attire and riding a borrowed horse, dashed through the streets cracking a long whip, hurling clouds of sand into the air. "This appeared to be for the purpose of rousing the inhabitants ... and collecting together as large an escort as possible for Potter to Point Bolivar," said Hooton.[22]

The Major, greatly concerned over supplies for the trip, took charge of the "creature comforts," saying that without plenty to eat, drink, and smoke, no good whatever could come of their cause. "Nothing is to be had at Bolivar," he told them, "and therefore what we do not take with us we must go without." Accordingly, he ordered some ice wrapped in blankets and three boxes of cigars, as well as hams, bread, brandy and wine.[23]

A small fleet of boats carried the mayor, two horn players, a fiddler, a drummer, and other people; a Texas Navy helmsman, Mr. Wyman, who had been refreshing himself with liquor since early morning, commanded Hooton's boat. When all was arranged, the fleet set out with one cigar box opened, wine and brandy uncorked and sailed off to the tune of "Oh Come to the Bower," played by the band.[24]

On arriving at Bolivar Point the party proceeded to the first house they could find and sat around with their legs on the backs of the chairs, eating, drinking and smoking. They planned to have a ball that night for Potter, but upon discussion, they realized the need for a bigger house. After searching the neighborhood they found one large enough (presumably vacant), tore the doors off the hinges to use for tables, turned the out-house into a free cigar and drinking establishment, then purchased a neighbor's heifer to cook for dinner.[25]

During the afternoon Hooton chanced to meet Samuel Parr. "He was considered as wealthy as almost any settler in Texas, and usually had a troop of two or three hundred fine half-wild horses." Hooton said that Parr lived several miles from any other farmer with his wife and several daughters and their tutor.[26]

Toward evening the political supporters built a huge bonfire and had just begun skinning the heifer when the commodore of the Texas Navy and his officers arrived. They carved up the beef "gaucho" style, with the hide still on it, but the cooking took so long that Hooton and Parr made off with a big chunk for themselves and roasted it at a neighbor's house.

About midnight the drunken helmsman, Mr. Wyman, and a young Englishman had a violent quarrel and were about to engage in a duel when the commodore arrived and put a stop to the fight. The mayor and friends stayed all night to drink and dance, and Hooton caught a ride back to Galveston at about two in the morning.[27]

Judging from Mr. Potter's efforts to carry on a political campaign on Bolivar in 1842, it would appear that enough settlers were living there to justify the trouble.

In addition to the Parr family, the Simptons were among the peninsula's earliest settlers. George Washington Simpton, an English sea captain, sailed to Galveston with his wife Mary in 1836 and went into business as one of the first vessel pilots there.[28]

In 1838 Simpton placed an advertisement in the *Commercial Intelligencer*, the first newspaper in Galveston, announcing his pilot charges. Rates were lowest for ships drawing six feet and under, ($2.50 per foot) and for ships drawing twelve feet and under ($4.30 per foot). The channel between Galveston and Bolivar was no more than twelve feet deep, though Jean Laffite reportedly sailed through with ships drawing sixteen feet. The most experienced pilots had trouble navigating the treacherous waters, undermined with constantly shifting sand bars.[29]

George Simpton's excellent reputation won him the designation of first harbor master of Galveston. The Texas Navy hired Simpton to pilot the steam-sail ship *Zavala* in and out of the port of Galveston for $72.00, and Simpton collected his money three months later in Houston.[30]

George and Mary Simpton in 1840 moved to Bolivar, bought a hundred acres of farmland from Samuel Parr, and went into the cattle business. The same year George's brother John and his wife Jemima sailed to Galveston from England, and on the ship Jemima gave birth to their third child, Sarah. They settled in Galveston, then moved to Bolivar and had another child, George, who was the first boy born on the peninsula, as far as anyone knows.[31]

By 1850 fifteen families lived between Point Bolivar and High Island. German, Scottish, English, Cajun, and southern U. S. settlers arrived by oxcart or ship, paid for a few acres of land and built houses along the old peninsula Indian trail. Kahlas, Shaws, Hughes, Crainers, Adkins, and Guidrys brought their plowshares, violins, and children to Bolivar and stayed for a hundred years.[32]

6 / A Light on the Coast

Charles Hooton, whom we met in the last chapter, sailed to Texas from England in March 1841, and wrote his impression of the port of Galveston:

> Sprinkled with wrecks of various appearances and sizes—all alike gloomy, however, in their looks and associations—it strikes the heart of a stranger as a sort of ocean cemetery, a sea churchyard, in which broken masts and shattered timbers, half buried in quicksands, seem to remain above the surface of the treacherous waters only to remind the living, like dead camels on a level desert, of the destruction that has gone before.[1]

As previously mentioned, shipwrecks were common in the early 1800s along the Texas coast. Deep draft vessels could not get to the Port of Galveston because of shifting sandbars; as a consequence, they anchored near shore, where rowboats picked up passengers and ferried them to the dock. Lighter ships sailed into the bay but had to stay in water about two feet deep, where mule-drawn wagons hauled travelers and baggage to the pier.

The British brig *Cybelle*, arriving at Galveston in May 1844, missed the channel and ran aground on a Bolivar beach. The *Galveston Weekly News* commented:

> It is extremely unfortunate for the commercial interests of this place that so many ship masters come here who are entirely unacquainted with the coast. Ships of five and six hundred tons enter the harbor with perfect ease and safety when properly taken care of by a pilot. But brigs and schooners of two and three hundred tons and drawing but little water, frequently for want of a proper knowledge of the coast, harbor and bar, get aground and are damaged. A lighthouse is badly needed.[2]

The U. S. government, in 1848, bought a few acres of land on the western tip of Bolivar Peninsula, and four years later built a seventeen-thousand-candlepower lighthouse on the desolate, windswept site. The structure of iron-covered brick, painted red, was the first circular lighthouse on the Texas coast and had a red light seventy-six feet above sea level. In 1858 new cast iron sections were added, increasing the height to one hundred feet above sea level, with visibility of sixteen miles.[3]

As indicated by later events, though, the new lighthouse failed to prevent shipwrecks. On April 17, 1856, word came from Sabine that a brig was aground on the coast about twenty miles east of Point Bolivar; they thought it was the *Mary Hamilton* from New York, headed for Galveston. The wind had shifted to the north and increased, but no further news of the accident appeared.[4]

The cotton schooner *Louisiana*, in June 1857, ran aground, caught fire and burned six miles east of the Bolivar lighthouse. A group including Galveston's Mayor Brown and the city coroner sailed up the Bolivar coast to examine the bodies reportedly washed ashore. The mayor said his party came across East Bay, landed past the lighthouse, and traveled up the beach some eighteen miles beyond Bolivar Point, where they found five bodies partially covered with sand. Eight miles from the lighthouse they saw no sign of the wreck, but along the beach toward Sabine, the fragments increased. The searchers discovered a charred mast, an ox with part of his head burned off, broken chairs, and other debris. The coroner described the five bodies as follows:

> 1st—Nine miles from the Light House, a man five feet eight or nine inches high, sandy hair, blue twill cotton pants, torn and sewed up in a triangular shape on the thigh, cotton undershirt, plain linen bosom shirt, calf-skin shoes with brass eye-let holes, and no socks. A watch seal, gold or gold washed, was found in the pocket—nothing else. Body (as were all five) decomposing rapidly, and very offensive. This body was buried at one hundred yards from the beach, by Messrs. C. R. Patton and S. Hughes, residing nearby.
>
> 2nd—Thirteen miles up—a negro man, with check shirt and blue cotton pants, apparently a stout man.

3rd—Fourteen miles up—a woman, with plain cotton dress, much decomposed, but supposed to have been a steerage passenger—probably a German, as several were on board.

4th and 5th—About eighteen miles from Light House—two men, half a mile apart—one had in his pocket a flint and steel and tobacco, and was thought to be a German or Frenchman. The other had light hair—had on nothing but shirt and stockings, and appeared to be a man who did not labor, or as some expressed it, a man of easy professional life.

The hair of all nearly gone and portions of the skin of the head. There was no money or papers on either one. The four bodies last named were buried by Messrs. Dunman, Rivea, Hampshire and Shaw, who live from twenty to twenty-five miles beyond the Light House. . . . [5]

The coroner deputied C. R. Patton to act in his stead should there be any further necessity.

In fall 1862, the Federal fleet captured Galveston Harbor, and the Confederate commander in Texas decided to destroy the lighthouse, thinking the light would benefit the enemy. He sent a party of Confederate soldiers to the peninsula on the morning of December 29. They exploded gunpowder in the base and demolished the whole thing. An eyewitness on the U. S. man-of-war *Westfield* at anchor near Pelican Island, reported:

About two o'clock this morning we were somewhat startled by the lighthouse on Bolivar Point taking fire. It, together with the keeper's dwelling, burned brightly until daylight, and this morning a heap of ruins marks the place of this handsome and useful structure.[6]

Rebel wrecking crews completely dismantled the remains of the tower, threw away the bricks, and removed the iron plates and glass lens, assuming the parts could be used as war materials.[7]

A temporary light served from 1865 until November 19, 1872, when the second lighthouse 117 feet tall was completed. Built of brick, steel and concrete, the tower was equipped with a fifty-one-thousand candlepower revolving light and was painted with black and white bands. Two raised white cottages were built nearby for the keeper and his assistant. Each evening at dusk the keeper turned on the powerful, oil-fueled beacon and flashed a message of safety to ship captains many miles at sea.

On stormy nights ducks, geese and other birds, attracted by the light, crashed into the glass by the dozens, forcing the keeper to place wire netting over the windows.

About 1873 a hunter sailed from Galveston to the peninsula and shot a curlew near the base of the lighthouse, breaking its wing. In a few minutes nearly a thousand birds appeared, circling the tower in answer to the shrill distress cry of the wounded curlew. The hunter kept shooting until his gun barrels were hot and he had used all his shells. Finally he dragged an enormous bag of birds to his boat.[8]

The lighthouse offered shelter to many Port Bolivar people when the hurricanes of 1900 and 1915 hit. Both times huge waves swept across the land, and refugees from the east end of the peninsula huddled on the stairs inside while the storms raged.

Two years after the 1915 hurricane, America was fighting World War I, and rumors of enemy battleships off the Texas coast spread around Galveston and Bolivar. One foggy afternoon in November 1917, a large shell blasted into the lighthouse, and another landed just in front of the assistant's cottage. Then a shower of three-inch shells fell for two hours. Captain Brooks, the keeper, called the coast guard and Fort Crockett; no one knew what was happening, so Bolivar people assumed an offshore German battleship was firing at the town. Finally, word came that troops at Fort San Jacinto on the east end of Galveston had been target practicing and that heavy fog had caused an error in plotting. Instead of firing into the gulf, artillerymen were aiming shells directly at Bolivar.[9]

Years later, at the end of May 1933, Congress decided to close the lighthouse. The "relentless march of progress" had made it obsolete for navigation. By this time sea buoys and channel beacons marked the waters between Galveston and Bolivar and lights shone on the end of the south jetty in the gulf. So the familiar old beam, after serving sixty years, flashed its last signal and went into darkness.[10]

7 / Gulf and Interstate Railroad

From Port Bolivar to High Island the countryside looked like a miniature Garden of Eden in the late 1880s. Peach, orange, and grapefruit trees bloomed each spring among fields of red, white, and yellow wildflowers; green patches of watermelons, cabbages, beans, and cantaloupes filled every inch of fertile soil behind the sand dunes. The Hugheses, Bouses, Kahlas, and other Bolivar farmers harvested a cornucopia of produce but had difficulty getting it to the markets in Galveston and Beaumont. Without roads or freight trains there was only one way to go—by boat. Ice was nonexistent, and transportation had to be as rapid as possible.

A few enterprising Bolivarites built small sailing vessels and carried loads of fruits, vegetables, and wild game across the bay to the Galveston market. Bolivar men liked to hunt—they supplemented their incomes selling squirrels, rabbits, ducks, and geese, all delicacies for gourmet Galvestonians. Farmers covered the decks of their sailboats with watermelons, oranges, and sweet potatoes, then hung bunches of cleaned bird and animal carcasses from the masts. The ladies of Galveston shopped every morning from these floating grocery stores docked at Twenty-first Street.

Jefferson County, rich in cattle and wood products, faced a transportation problem as well. Cattle could be driven to market, but the lumber required a rail system that did not exist. "It must indeed seem strange . . . that we should be compelled to import so large an amount of lumber into Texas . . . having forests extensive enough to supply the whole of Texas," commented J. de Cordova, local land promoter.[1]

Schooners and steamboats plied the waters between Louisiana and Galveston, but they were loaded with cotton and had little space for other cargo. Finally, construction of the first railroad between Beaumont and Galveston began in November 1895, and ended in May 1896.

The Gulf and Interstate Railroad Company succeeded in laying the first forty miles of track from Beaumont, "working only on clear days." The company brought in an engine to assist the construction crew and to pull a passenger coach to the new townsite of Winnie, seventeen miles north of High Island.[2]

A few days later General E. K. Stimson, project engineer, arrived in Beaumont from "the front" to report that track had been laid to Mud Bayou, two miles from High Island. He said that bridging of the bayou would be completed that night with more track placed as far as High Island, twenty-seven miles from Point Bolivar. "Early in December, if there is no continued bad weather, we'll see black smoke rolling over at Bolivar, and Galvestonians may know that the Gulf and Interstate has completed its connections," Stimson predicted. The general vowed that all bridges were first-class and the railroad bed well constructed and safe.[3]

By November 27 the crew had made it to High Island, as forecast, and talk circulated about the amazing benefits that the railroad would bring to Galveston and Beaumont. Everyone was excited about prospects for the shipment of lumber from east Texas mills to Galveston and other destinations, for people to travel between Beaumont and the coast, and for rice and vegetable growers along the way to freight their produce to market.[4]

Railroad officials expected the new town of Winnie to burgeon into a major cattle-shipping center; they felt certain that High Island, a forty-five-foot hill near the Gulf of Mexico, would turn into a major summer resort, with its magical mineral waters and lovely view of the gulf.[5]

In early December 1895, the Gulf and Interstate construction crew had progressed beyond the High Island marshes and was making rapid headway. General Stimson estimated it would take no more than fifteen days to fill the gap to the end of the peninsula. Two months later, in February 1896, a shortage of materials caused delays, and the construction engine had to be sent to the Beaumont repair shop.[6]

Shortly afterward, to everyone's amazement, the G & I track had made it all the way to Point Bolivar, and trains were ready to operate. A barge would carry the train across the channel to Galveston.[7]

The *Galveston Daily News* announced that the new railroad would run between High Island and Point Bolivar on tracks near the beach. "For twenty miles the whitecaps of the Gulf can be seen on one side, and the placid waters of Galveston Bay on the other. It will be the most beautiful route in the south for that distance, and it will be a novel and pleasant sight to see the waves dashing up almost to the trains as they pass. It will be a perfectly safe route, for the track will be on the ridge, which has never yet been known to be under water."[8]

To celebrate the opening of the railroad, everyone on the peninsula gathered at Point Bolivar on March 14, 1896. The construction train of one engine, flatcar, and caboose arrived with shrieking whistle and ringing bell. When the train stopped, dignitaries emerged from the caboose and held a ceremony at the platform of the jetty construction company. Subcontractor Buffalo Jones made a long speech extolling the virtues of the new railroad, then drove in the last spike "with a ring that could be heard by the populists in Kansas," reported the Galveston paper. Jones said that while building the road "not a person was hurt and not a thing killed save time and three striped cats." A great hurrah went up and Jones took several bows. Jones went on to explain that he would be running the railroad until it was formally turned over to the Gulf and Interstate.[9]

As soon as Jones's speech appeared in the Galveston paper, Fox Winnie and L. P. Featherstone, general contractors for the G & I, filed a petition in the civil district court asking for an injunction to restrain subcontractor N. C. ("Buffalo") Jones and his partner C. J. Jones and their agents from running trains over the railway or interfering with it.[10]

At the injunction hearing, Winnie charged, "The defendants have wholly failed to complete any portion of the railroad within the time specified.... failed to furnish correct materials.... and did not turn the track over to us as per our agreement." Winnie said that the track was completely unsafe and that running engines and cars over it in its present condition would greatly damage the bridges, rails, and roadbed and would probably result in injury to the passengers and train. He further testified that the subcontractors had refused to do any further work and were running it themselves for their own profit.[11]

A witness for the defense, one of the railroad employees, said that the G & I had had numerous delays in train schedules due, he thought, to incompetency. He went on to single out the carelessness of Conductor Henry Jones, but was guarded when answering questions.

"Did a little game of Mr. Jones' ever cause any delay?" the defense attorney asked.

"I don't know.... just what you mean," the witness replied.

"Well, a little game of poker. Did you ever see it delay the train any?"

"I don't like to answer that question." Then, after some rambling, evasive remarks, "I have seen Mr. Jones playing cards when I thought he might have been doing something else."

Afterward, on cross-examination, the witness went into the poker-playing question and described the proneness of the conductor to play cards while on trips. The witness sometimes played, too, depending on how much money he had. The witness never reported the poker games to Buffalo Jones, but he was aware his boss knew about them because Jones had docked the conductor half a day's pay for playing cards.[12]

On April 14, 1896, Fox Winnie was called again to the witness stand to refute statements made by C. J. and N. C. Jones. He did it with such spirit and energy that he stood up several times and shook his pointed finger at the Joneses and their attorney, Charles Stubbs, who seemed to be enjoying the whole thing and made no objection.[13]

By the end of May, Featherstone had gained control of the railroad; he informed the newspaper that he hoped to have trains running by June 15 and said that everything was getting along nicely.[14]

On June 12, W. C. Patton of Patton's Grove shipped out the state's first carload of watermelons with the announcement, "We have the greatest melon land in the United States and have only been hampered by the lack of transportation facilities. The Gulf and Interstate has given us an outlet to the world. . . ."[15]

Featherstone left a boxcar on the main track near Patton's melon patch, where the farmer loaded 1,720 watermelons. Featherstone then ordered his crew to put in a switch at Patton's farm and made arrangements for a ventilated fruit car with a capacity of 2,300 melons to be sent to Bolivar. Patton predicted that the new Gulf and Interstate Railroad would cause land values on the peninsula to increase fifty to two hundred per cent.[16]

At the end of July construction was progressing on the north jetty at Port Bolivar, part of a large deep harbor project for Galveston. The Army Corps of Engineers had at first sunk large sand-filled wicker cylinders—that failed. Then they used pine brush and cane mattresses weighted with stones. Both efforts were disasters. After spending $1,578,000, Galveston politicians instructed the corps to use stone, and the first ten-ton chunks of pink granite and five-ton pieces of sandstone arrived at Port Bolivar on the new Gulf and Interstate by flatcar. Finally the jetty was completed.[17]

On July 26, 1896, the first excursion trip for the new train took passengers to Winnie, a prospective townsite forty-four miles from Galveston. The ferry left the foot of Tremont Street at nine o'clock on Sunday morning, arrived at Bolivar Point at ten o'clock, and at Winnie about twelve o'clock. After a two-hour stay, the excursion train left for Galveston, stopping an hour at High Island Mineral Springs, and arrived back in Galveston at six or seven in the evening. This may have been the original real estate promotion trip in Texas.[18]

After Charles Taylor Cade built the Sea View Hotel at High Island in 1897, his two daughters, Kitty and Margaret, came over from New Iberia on the G & I to visit their father. The girls were accompanied by several boy cousins armed with shotguns. As they approached High Island, the young men climbed to the top of the caboose and shot doves as the train slowly moved along. The engineer stopped the train occasionally to allow the boys to run out into the fields to pick up their doves.[19]

As time went by, the Gulf and Interstate began to have financial difficulties, and late in 1898, the Weekes-McCarthy Bank in Galveston bought $550,000 worth of G & I stock, giving the bank controlling interest. Owner of the bank, Abel Borden ("Shanghai") Pierce, legendary cattle baron, had long dreamed of a railroad link between his Wharton and Matagorda County cattle empire and Galveston.[20]

Pierce tried to run the railroad efficiently, but problems persisted, and the Weekes-McCarthy Bank plunged $160,000 more into the G & I without Pierce's knowledge. When he found out about it, he liquidated the bank.[21]

In September 1900, an immense hurricane hit the Texas coast and devastated the country for hundreds of miles inland. "We have been nearly swept from the face of the earth," Shanghai said. "The Gulf and Interstate Railroad I put into the hands of a receiver a few days ago.... it is a wreck.... about 25 miles of the track gone.... over 100 cars blown from the track and 5 Engines turned bottom up."[22]

"I won't rebuild the Gulf and Interstate. If the state wants the charter they can have it back. I am done with that road and that is all there is to it. If anyone else wants to go in there and rebuild, let them do it," Shanghai said. "Everything I had in Galveston is washed away but the land and it will remain there. I do not propose to do anything with it. I never want to see it again and I never will. It can stay there, and I do not even propose to pay the taxes on it. They can have the whole thing."[23]

Mr. Averill, former general passenger agent for the Gulf and Interstate, said Shanghai's losses would amount to $500,000, and that Pierce was treating the matter very indifferently and philosophically.[24]

Two months later Shanghai Pierce died.

The storm made shambles of the railroad line—most of the track was gone, and no money was available for repairs. The citizens of Galveston and Beaumont raised twenty thousand dollars over the next several years, and the line was rebuilt. Parts of the train buried in the sand during the storm were dug up, hauled to Beaumont and put in working order. Passengers who had traveled on the last run before the storm were given free rides on the new train. It arrived at Port Bolivar September 24, 1903.[25]

8 / The 1900 Storm

C. T. Cade, land speculator and cattle rancher from New Iberia, ordered a carload of cypress from Louisiana, shipped it on the G & I Railroad to High Island, and constructed a three-story hotel in May 1897 on the hill overlooking the gulf. Cade spent sixty-five hundred dollars on material, labor, and furnishings and was well pleased with the results. The hotel had a large room for dining and dancing on the first floor, bedrooms on the second and third floors, and an observation cupola above that. The *Beaumont Enterprise* announced, "It is an ideal place if one is in search of pure air, fine surf bathing and all the other health giving attractions.... The rooms are neat and comfortable and admirably ventilated, the galleries broad and plenty of them.... The table is bountifully supplied ... and the cooking excellent."[1]

When the train stopped at the High Island station, Cade would greet his hotel guests and take them up the dusty road to his spacious inn. "Captain Cade's car," said Jessie Hughes, "was a wagon with a colored canopy over the top."

Every Saturday the Gulf and Interstate ran a "Gulf Coast Special" from Beaumont to High Island, Rollover, Patton, and Galveston for one dollar round-trip. Hotels at Rollover and Patton (Crystal Beach) were booked solid in summer and fall every year. Business was so good that Patton Hotel owner, Charles Patton, built an elaborate dance pavilion and bathhouse over the gulf with board sidewalk from the dunes to the depot. The pavilion was lighted for night swimming with street lamps, and ropes stretched into the water for bathers to hang onto. Beaumont ladies practiced their swimming and diving in peninsula waves.[2]

At High Island, C. T. Cade installed a trolley car and screened dance pavilion on the Sea View beach; hotel guests danced to the Coy Blanchette string band and ate ice cream and cake on Saturday nights. In the morning they rode a horse-drawn cart on board tracks down the hill to the beach, went swimming in fashionable woolen bathing costumes, or sat in the trolley car out of the sun.[3]

The Gulf Bay Hotel at Rollover was a favorite resort. Excursion trains brought crowds from Beaumont to eat seafood and frolic in the waves. Two Beaumont ladies, Mrs. Goodhue and Mrs. Simmons, went from Rollover to High Island on the train to see the new Sea View Hotel; they declared the place very pretty, but not as good as the Gulf Bay. C. L. Nash, Gulf Bay manager, saw several people in bathing suits around the depot one afternoon and promptly suppressed the display. "It is not respectable for bathers to parade off the beach," he said.[4]

Those were the days of Gibson girls, leg o'mutton sleeves, handlebar mustaches, and gay waltzes. At the proper time of day the ladies went sea bathing in small wooden cabins pulled into the water by mules. Bright sun, white beaches, and pleasant breezy nights made Bolivar Peninsula an enchanting place.

On Saturday night, September 8, 1900, with no warning, a lethal storm hit the Texas and Louisiana coasts and destroyed a vast area; the death toll exceeded six thousand in Galveston alone.

The morning of the hurricane, the G & I passenger train from Beaumont to Galveston arrived at Bolivar Point, but the channel water was so rough the train could not be transferred to the Galveston barge. One of thirty passengers, Max Levy, a Beaumont businessman, said they waited at the depot a short while, and a couple of cars were added to the train for the Saturday Beaumont "Hoo Hoo" excursion. Levy and the rest of the passengers left on the excursion train about twelve-thirty in the afternoon and started east toward High Island.

When they reached Patton Beach, about midway down the peninsula, the train stopped and picked up a large group of adults and children. The train then continued to Rollover, where water was so high that further progress was impossible.

The engineer backed the train a short distance to Patton, stayed there about three hours, then attempted to go back to Bolivar Point, but the water was even higher, and the train had to return to the Patton depot. Levy and the others waited in the train from late Saturday afternoon until six-thirty Sunday morning with breakers crashing against the cars, howling winds, and driving rain.

"The storm was fearful," Levy said. "Words cannot describe the terrible fury of the wind and waves. Saturday afternoon we sat in the coaches in front of Patton and watched all the houses tumble one by one into the gulf, as the water would wash under them, and they melted away as though they were so many stacks of straw."

Levy said they watched the last house in Patton go into the waves at about six o'clock. They did not see anyone getting out of their homes and assumed no lives were lost. Later they heard that everyone had left in wagons for a ridge somewhere near there.[5]

"We stayed in the car all night," Levy said. "During the fury of the storm the agony of mind suffered . . . will never be told in language of its intensity. The waves washed mountain-high over the train, completely submerging it at times."

At six-thirty the next morning Levy, the engineer, and the fireman left the train to try to get to Port Bolivar. The water had gone down off the roadbed by this time, so they walked, swam, waded, and finally reached the town at eleven o'clock Sunday morning.[6]

Levy said that the destruction of Port Bolivar was total; the lighthouse and keeper's residences were the only buildings left standing. The two nearby army forts were wrecked and eleven soldiers stationed there had drowned; all the wharves, railroad tracks, and terminals were demolished, as well as the Gulf and Interstate shops and rolling stock. Levy stayed at Port Bolivar from Sunday morning till noon Monday, when a boat hired by the G & I arrived from Galveston. Levy and about fifty others boarded the boat and headed away from Bolivar; they counted thirty-seven bodies floating in the channel and saw large ocean-going vessels sitting high and dry along the shore.[7]

One hundred twenty people near the east end of the peninsula went to the lighthouse at Bolivar Point Saturday to escape the high tides and winds. They drank all the fresh water, then tried to get more by catching rain in a bucket suspended from the top of the tower. The bucket filled quickly, but the water was impossible to drink. Saltwater spray was shooting skyward over 130 feet and falling with the rainwater into the bucket. The crowd made several tries and finally gathered enough fresh water to quench their thirst.[8]

Mrs. Irwin, manager of the Patton Hotel, said in an interview with the Beaumont newspaper that the wind kept increasing Friday night before the storm, and at daylight Saturday the waves were huge. "They came in from the sea, met each other, and the water leaped fifty feet in the air," she said.[9]

By twelve o'clock Saturday morning the tide had risen to the dance pavilion and was breaking over the first floor. Within another hour the waves were running over the top of the pavilion.

The excursion train had come from Rollover about this time, and the engineer and passengers were debating the advisability of trying to go farther. Mr. Patton told them about a low place between Patton and Rollover he knew they could not cross, but they decided to try and left. They soon found that Mr. Patton had been right: the track was completely submerged, and so the train returned and stopped in front of the depot. Shortly after the train came back, Mrs. Irwin told everybody to leave.

"We told each other good-bye. The men kissed their wives and children, and everyone resigned to their fate. I thought we all would soon be in heaven, and I . . . offered a last prayer. All . . . prayed, in fact," she went on.[10]

Mrs. Patton began to sing "Jesus, Lover of my Soul" with her husband and sister. Mrs. Irwin remembered thinking the song was beautiful but said she never wanted to hear it again.

Some suggested going to the train, while others argued that Mr. Abrason's two-story house would be safer. Abrason's house and the Gorhams' were situated on what was known as the middle ridge, highest place between the gulf and the bay, a quarter of a mile from the hotel. Mr. Patton wanted to go to the one-story Gorham house because it was less liable to catch the force of the wind, but others thought the Abrason house would offer more protection, having two stories.

Some of the men rounded up wagons, and a group of the train passengers and hotel guests rode to Abrason's. Mrs. Irwin, the two Keith children, Mr. and Mrs. Patton and his sister, went to the Gorham house.

When Mrs. Irwin's group reached the Gorham house, the Gorhams, Snoddies, Tom Smith (a hobo), and Joe Blanchette were already there. They were standing in knee-deep water, and for the next few hours the wind and waves knocked down the entire house except the dining room where they were huddled.

"The crashing and terror of that time, when we could see and hear everything being torn to pieces was fearful," said Mrs. Irwin. They decided to try to get to the Abrason house, which they could see was still standing. She took Alice Keith in her arms and, with Olga holding onto her, they started out. All had agreed to stick together as much as possible for protection.

"When we stepped from the house, the water was about waist deep. We were on the lee side and did not feel the wind, but as soon as we made our way around the corner of the house, it struck us with full force and separated the party," Mrs. Irwin said. She still held onto Alice, but Olga was blown away from her and carried about a hundred yards by the current. At that point the waves began to push her around, and she fell down, taking Alice with her. She got back to her feet and tried to walk again, but the waves were so strong she could not make much headway.

Finally, a huge swell struck Mrs. Irwin. "It seemed an age before it passed over," she said. As the water hit her she saw Alice's head fall to one side and felt her body go limp. She thought the child was dead. Mrs. Irwin could see Olga trying to stay above water, and thinking Alice was dead, decided to turn her loose and try to save Olga, but for some reason she could not let her go. "I then offered one short fervent prayer for protection, and from that time on it seemed to grow calmer."[11]

She saw that Tom Smith had saved Olga; he carried her to Mrs. Irwin, took Alice and laid her on his shoulder head down, and rolled her around. Mrs. Irwin saw the little girl's eyes open, and as the hobo turned her head to the wind, the child gasped and caught her breath. Feeling greatly relieved, they took the children back to the house.

In the dining room the water was about three feet deep, and a table still stood in the center. Tom put the two girls on it—Olga first, then Alice in front of her. Mrs. Irwin and Tom stood between the children and the breakers, coming in with terrible force. They lifted the little ones above each wave and spent the night thinking they would never get out alive.

Daylight came and the storm had spent its fury. Mrs. Irwin's clothes had been torn to shreds in her attempt to leave the house, and she and Tom were bruised by the chairs and debris thrown against them the night before.

All day Sunday they waited for help, and on Monday morning Captain Cade and a group of Beaumont men arrived in wagons and took them to the hotel at High Island.[12]

Reverend J. W. Bleeker and family were in the group that went to the Abrason house on Saturday. "We had not been in the house long before the water had risen to a depth of about six feet in the lower floor," Bleeker said. They then went up to the second floor, and there were about sixty people jammed together. "I never saw, neither do I understand the wonderful calmness ... which seemed to possess everyone. Some of the children were crying, but all the others, women and men, were perfectly calm."[13]

Between four and five o'clock that afternoon, a heavy gust of wind picked the house up and carried it about thirty feet toward the bay. It tilted slightly, but braced by a kitchen in the back, did not turn over.

"The terror of the night was awful. We fully expected to die," Bleeker said. Finally, about midnight the water began to recede, and when daylight came the refugees discovered what they thought had saved their lives. When the house was carried back, it seemed to settle into the ground, and the waves, running through the house, brought mounds of sand and packed it on the floor. The sand, plus the weight of so many people, probably held the house in place.

Bleeker's friends stayed in the house from Saturday afternoon until Monday morning. They had eaten and drunk everything and were wondering how they would survive another day when Captain Cade and his rescue team arrived with food and water.[14]

On Bolivar Peninsula there was no telephone or telegraph; all communications had been knocked out. Early Sunday morning a relief team left Beaumont on a coach with switch engine to search for the passenger train that had left Beaumont Saturday morning and turned back at Bolivar Point. The rescue train fought heavy winds and rains and about twelve o'clock reached Whites' Ranch, about seven miles north of High Island.

Rain hit the sides of the train like hailstones, and high water came across the prairie in breakers, carrying with it hundreds of cattle. The water was about fourteen inches deep, and the train was forced to back out slowly and return to Beaumont.

A second train left late Sunday afternoon and proceeded to the same point as the one earlier in the day. Here several men waded down the track and went about two miles before the water became too deep and the current too strong to go farther. Five of the men borrowed a boat and rowed to High Island to the Sea View Hotel.

One of the men, George Tuggle, had brought with him a telephone; he climbed a telephone pole, established communication with Beaumont, and reported on the situation. Tuggle said that from what Captain Cade said, all buildings along the coast had been destroyed.[15]

A few days after the storm, H. S. Spangler, general manager of the Gulf and Interstate, went on a horseback trip along the former line of the railroad from Point Bolivar to High Island. He found devastation in every direction. The railroad bed was gone for six and seven miles at a stretch and would have to be rebuilt.[16]

Spangler described the beach in the direction of Patton as "a regular charnel house," so thick were the bodies. Farther up the peninsula, thousands of dead cattle lay everywhere, their carcasses putrifying in the sun.[17]

The Sea View, a few houses, and the remainder of the G & I track to Beaumont were spared at High Island. Spangler estimated the loss of life on the peninsula at forty-one. Hundreds of bodies had floated across from Galveston and were scattered along the beaches. Many could not be buried because there was no one to do the work. People were leaving the peninsula by any transportation they could find, and some, having none, were walking out, carrying what little food they had left. "Their patches have been completely destroyed and every boat swept away, so there is nothing for them to do, nothing in sight to sustain them, and they are leaving," Spangler said.[18]

A few determined souls decided to start life on the peninsula once again. They buried the dead, picked up scraps of lumber from the beach and built homes, barns, and fences. Children helped with the grueling labor. In the woods they found a few straggling, half-dead cattle, they scratched the salty soil, planted new crops, and they prayed.

For the next fifteen years life slowly returned to normal, and the horror of the storm faded.

9 / Oil Fever

C. T. Cade stood in the rooftop cupola of the Sea View and scanned the beaches and marsh around the hotel to see if any of his cattle had survived the storm. He saw a bleak wasteland dotted with carcasses of dead animals, holes, and debris and wondered what he was going to do with his life. He walked down to his office, poured a glass of whiskey, gulped it down, and swore, "I will find oil at High Island, by God."[1]

Cade, three years before, had consulted with F. F. Myles, founder of the Myles Salt Company near New Iberia, about High Island's oil possibilities. They thought the dome formation at the east end of the peninsula was similar to Belle Isle and Anse la Butte, Louisiana, where Anthony Lucas had found salt and oil. "We are going to see what we can get out of the ground at High Island," Cade said. Myles added: "I am convinced we can strike enough natural gas to pipe it to Galveston and make the island as light as day."[2]

The two men arranged to have machinery for "boring" shipped to the peninsula by train in 1897, and by 1898 had started to drill. Close by, George Smith was digging for mineral water on his land, and as Vernon Kahla tells it, "When he got about twenty feet down, he lit his pipe and got blowed out of the well." Natural gas! Captain Cade was elated—at last his theory was verified. "I mean to keep on investigating until I find out what is under High Island," he said.[3]

A Beaumont oil prospector, L.L. Emery, had been snooping around town and talked to Captain Cade one night at the hotel.

Emery agreed to lease all Cade lands, fifteen thousand acres, for one dollar, to explore for "minerals of whatever kind, coal, mineral or artesian waters, natural gas, petroleum, or lubricating oil," for one year.[4]

Emery failed even to begin operations, and after a year, Cade persuaded salt-dome expert Anthony Lucas to consider High Island's possibilities. Lucas, who was just about to drill at Gladys City near Beaumont, agreed, and the two men signed a lease on January 9, 1901, for all Cade lands. For twenty-two thousand dollars, Lucas was to prospect for gas, oil, and minerals by sinking shafts, boring, building a railroad or tramroad, and erecting machinery, buildings, warehouses, tanks, and pipelines. Royalty to C.T. Cade would be ten percent of the gross profits, and the lease could be cancelled if Lucas failed to carry out the terms.[5]

As fate would have it, next day the largest oil gusher in history came roaring out of the ground on Lucas's leased field at Gladys City, producing seventy-five thousand barrels of oil a day and causing pandemonium in Beaumont. News of the discovery instantly spread. The *Galveston Daily News* called it a "Big Strike in Oil" and "A Record Breaking Gusher." To celebrate the event Galveston bars served the "Gusher Punch, "Madman's Treat," "Geyser Julep," "Spouting Fluid," and the "Oilerette."[6]

While all of Beaumont rushed about in a mad frenzy, Lucas—dour and unexcitable—was busy trying to dam up the lake of petroleum, build tanks for storage, and figure out a way to transport and market the stuff.

Oil fever was burning like a barn fire, and everybody was watching Anthony Lucas to see what he would do next. Lucas, meanwhile, remembered High Island. He announced that George Smith had "the brightest prospects for oil in Texas" and leased several tracts from Smith and others, then bought eleven acres. Lucas said there was oil and gas in abundance in the areas he leased and was sure the dome formation was identical to that at Spindletop: a deep, pole-shaped salt shaft with gas and oil near the top. His confidence was so strong that he announced his intention to invest a considerable sum in "prospecting" and begin work as soon as he could ship in the necessary materials.[7]

Exhilarated by Lucas's success at Gladys City, people flocked to High Island to buy up land, and values doubled in two months. Leases flew about like wild geese in winter.[8]

Fred Oppikofer, Galveston petroleum promoter, envisioned a forest of derricks and huge refineries at High Island. He imagined pipelines running into the gulf and schooners collecting crude oil offshore. "The mound is unnatural, and the earth's surface has been forced up by internal trouble arising from a gas well and oil beneath that gas," he said.[9]

Oppikofer bought thirty-two acres on the dome and formed the "Great Western High Island Oil Company." His prospectus promised an incredible bonanza: "thirty-five miles from the 'Beaumont Gushers,' in a direct line with Big Hill and Taylor's Bayou, the recognized direction of all oil veins [was] the "Greatest Oil Field in the State of Texas," with greater amounts of oil than at Beaumont and at lesser depths." Oppikofer announced that Lucas had backed up his faith in the area by leasing all the available land at High Island and purchasing a tract adjacent to his.[10]

By now, every square inch of High Island had been sold or leased, and no other syndicate could get a foothold. The excitement was electrifying. "Governor Hogg and a party were anxious to come down and see our [High Island] Hill, but I discouraged them for the time being," Cade said, "due to our Galveston Island mosquitoes drifting toward the oil region."[11]

Cade and others worried that the lack of a railroad would hamper oil development; up to that point, drilling equipment had to be transported by boat and wagon. "The rebuilding of our Road means all, and without it we are left in the outer world," Cade said. Lucas, after many delays, shipped in derricks and machinery from Galveston at the end of December 1901, almost a year after signing the lease. Cade was becoming impatient. "Captain Lucas must begin and continue by January 9 or lose his lease," Cade wrote to Charles Stubbs, his Galveston attorney.[12]

On January 10, 1902, Cade announced: "The Guffey [Lucas] people are rushing in their rigs. Our lease expired on 9th, but I said to Griffiths, who represents them, that we wouldn't be hard on them provided they showed some diligence."[13]

The following month Cade said that the drillers told him they were having trouble with mosquitoes, lack of cable, and repairs to the cable wheel. "Mosquitoes are no excuse," Cade said. "Their object beyond a doubt is playing for time."[14]

By March the drillers were beginning to make some progress, but they complained that the tools were too light and delayed work again to exchange drilling bits. "Development may come at any moment," reported Cade. Finally the first well reached 700 feet and hit sand. "I hope it will prove more of a gusher than Sour Lake," Cade went on.[15]

Three months later Lucas hit fresh water, a strong flow that would supply all of Cade's needs for cattle and irrigation. "This is equal to an oil find to me," Cade told them. The drillers went down for two more months to 2,500 feet, and found nothing. "We have oil here beyond a doubt, and they have sufficient at Spindletop and want no other field developed. I want to force them to work as hard as I know how," Cade wrote to Stubbs. Cade demanded that they pull back to fresh water, as required by the lease, but this was never done.[16]

Lucas then drilled another well to 1,680 feet, and Cade said: "It looks now as if we are in a bed of rocksalt. That, however, is not discouraging. Too much salt and oil do not mix, but salt is found with oil." When Lucas reached 1,800 feet he hit cap rock and was forced to abandon the well. Cade's confidence in Lucas collapsed; gnawing suspicions continued to bother him. "They have more oil than they want at Beaumont for the present," he told Stubbs. "We have it here for a *certainty*, but it will be kept back as long as they dilly-dally. I want to watch them closely." In October Cade demanded his land back from Lucas and had no trouble getting it.[17]

C. T. and a group of still-optimistic High Islanders signed a lease with Monroe Carroll of Beaumont in December 1902 to explore for oil. "Carroll is much enthused," Cade said. The following spring Cade reported to Stubbs that Carroll's operations had met with a setback—his foreman had been injured in a buggy accident on the way to High Island.[18]

Carroll was unable to obtain any twelve-inch pipe and had to pull some out of the Lucas well. Just as he started to work again, Carroll was called to jury duty, then confined to bed for ten days with a severe cold. Monroe Carroll's drilling effort turned out to be a total failure.[19]

Lucas, meanwhile, had gone over to George Smith's land near his mineral springs and drilled nine wells, but none produced more than twenty barrels of oil.

The future looked bleak. Cade, hounded for money by a desperate wife and the Galveston County tax assessor, began to sell some shell from his beach property and some small tracts of land. He borrowed $2,500 from his attorney, Charles Stubbs, giving as collateral the Sea View Hotel and other High Island land. C. T. drowned his troubles in whiskey and went back to raising cattle.[20]

For ten years he struggled on, making trips to Mineral Wells to cure his alcoholism. He died there, broken and disappointed, in March 1912, leaving to his wife and daughters thirteen thousand acres of marshland, seven hundred head of cattle, one hundred horses, a wagon, buggy, and $3,000.

In 1931, Michel Halbouty, young employee of Yount-Lee Oil Company of Beaumont, banking on the idea that High Island's salt dome was mushroom-shaped, brought in a four-thousand-barrel-a-day well on C. T. Cade's land below the hill. For the next sixty years, oil men produced millions of barrels of petroleum from the perimeter of the dome, not the top, where Cade and Lucas believed it to be.

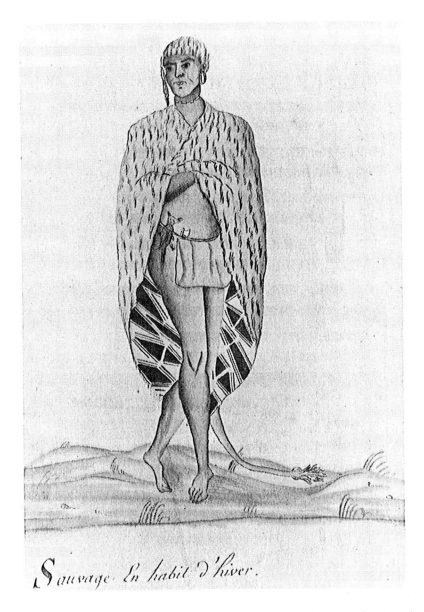

Indian warrior believed to be an Atakapa, rendered circa 1732 by Frenchman A. De Batz. He wears his winter attire, a buffalo robe. (Courtesy Peabody Museum, Harvard University)

The dashing privateer Jean Laffite, who roved the gulf waters in the early 1800s. The U. S. Government ousted Laffite from his Galveston stronghold in 1821. (Courtesy Rosenberg Library, Galveston, Texas)

Jane Long, "Mother of Texas." Mrs. Long and her filibuster husband, James Long, occupied Bolivar Point after Laffite left. (Courtesy University of Texas, Barker Texas History Center)

Customs collector Gail Borden's map of "Tory land" (Bolivar Peninsula) from Customhouse Records, June 1837. (Courtesy Rosenberg Library, Galveston, Texas)

Bolivar lighthouse and keeper's residence in 1910 with Santa Fe railroad tracks in front. This lighthouse was constructed in 1852. (Courtesy Rosenberg Library, Galveston, Texas)

Santa Fe train at Patton (now Crystal Beach) between 1914 and 1920. Steam engine with coal car and freight cars. (Courtesy Ora Fredericksen)

Sea View Hotel on the hill at High Island, built in 1897 by Charles Taylor Cade of Louisiana. The Sea View was one of the most popular hotels on the peninsula and survived both the 1900 and the 1915 storms. (Courtesy John Middleton)

C. T. Cade's daughters Kitty and Margaret with friends swimming in front of the Sea View Hotel around 1898. (Courtesy Cade Family Collection)

Postcard of the Crockett store in 1911, later Bouse's Store and Post Office in 1917. (Courtesy Ora Kahla)

Gulf View Hotel and Bouse's first store, with railroad track in front. The hotel, store, and railroad depot constituted the town of Caplen in 1914. (Courtesy Ruth McLean Bowers)

Gulf View Hotel, built by Marrs McLean at Caplen and destroyed in the 1915 hurricane. (Courtesy Ruth McLean Bowers)

Gordon and McLean family members with friends, enjoying peninsula waters at Caplen circa 1907–1909. (Courtesy Ruth McLean Bowers)

Port Bolivar iron ore dock in 1914. The dock, used to transfer iron ore from railway cars onto ships, was severely damaged by the 1915 storm. (Courtesy Harry Brown)

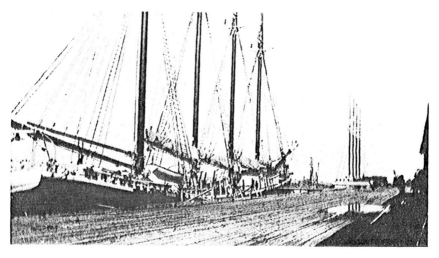

Schooners at Port Bolivar wharves before 1915 hurricane. Port Bolivar almost succeeded in becoming a major port. (Courtesy Harry Brown)

10 / Visions of Grandeur

L. P. Featherstone's large moustache, receding hairline, and steel-rimmed spectacles made him look more like a professor of English than a Texas entrepreneur. He took over the G & I railroad after Shanghai Pierce died in December 1900, intending to bring the railroad back to life and make Port Bolivar a "future Brooklyn." Galveston had been a major deep-water port since 1896 and rivaled New York in growth—some called it "the Octopus of the Gulf."[1]

Featherstone formed the "Port Bolivar City Company" in 1905 and bought twenty-five hundred acres at Point Bolivar for $100,000. The purchase included a townsite of fifteen hundred acres; the rest was for industrial use. The company issued a prospectus detailing plans for an important harbor, a "subport" to Galveston and promised that within two years Bolivar would have deep water. The plat showed "Bayview Avenue" and "Broadway" running through the center of town. Picturesque postcards were printed showing the local schoolhouse, Crockett store, and other sights. At the edge of the bay the townfolk erected a dance pavilion. Things were looking up.[2]

Featherstone put pressure on Congress in 1907 and succeeded in getting a $50,000 allocation in the Rivers and Harbors bill for dredging a twenty-five-foot deep channel from Bolivar Roads (shipping lane between Galveston and the peninsula) to the proposed wharf front at Port Bolivar. This would make possible the berthing of large vessels.[3]

Featherstone's prospectus hinted that the next Congress would appropriate funds for a seawall and filling at Fort Travis, on the gulf side. Together with the north jetty, this construction would serve to protect the town partially from storms.[4]

The Santa Fe Railroad bought out the Gulf and Interstate in early 1908 and began to refurbish tracks along the peninsula and to build a large terminal, "to compare favorably with any in the South," the *Galveston Daily News* said. "Cars brought to Galveston loaded with cotton and grain can be ferried across and sent into East Texas to load with lumber and other commodities for the Northern markets."

In 1908 the town had several hundred inhabitants. "No boom is on, but it is expected that with the completion of the terminal and waterfront property. . . . growth of the little village will be more rapid," said developers. "The land for the most part is higher than Galveston was before the filling, and parts of the Peninsula where the townsite lies were not covered with water in the 1900 storm."[5]

Port Bolivar had a boat and barge-building shipyard, and a planing mill was under consideration. The shipyard was completing a huge ferry barge 240 feet long and forty feet wide to take eighteen Santa Fe cars across Bolivar Roads to Galveston. Name of the barge: the "L. P. Featherstone."[6]

The Santa Fe spent $300,000 erecting a pier large enough to berth three ships, then built a second one with rail lines connecting their nearby terminal. The government dredge boat was busily working on a twenty-five-foot deep channel to the wharves.[7]

A momentous event in peninsula history took place June 15, 1909, when the first cargo ship sailed in to Port Bolivar and docked at 11:30 A.M. A big crowd cheered as the three-masted schooner *Margaret M. Ford* from Bath, Maine, eased up to the wharf, carrying a thousand tons of New England granite for the new federal building in Houston. Featherstone and Santa Fe officials declared the wharf officially "christened."[8]

The north jetty suddenly became "The World's Longest Fishing Pier," six miles long, where fishermen could catch tarpon, Spanish mackerel and redfish from the rocks. The Beach Hotel, in June 1909, was nearing completion at the base of the jetty, with breezy sleeping apartments downstairs and a dance hall upstairs. The Gulf and Interstate train planned to stop a short distance away for guests, who would be driven to the hotel in horse-drawn hacks.[9]

Featherstone announced in October 1910 that he had signed a contract with Charles M. Schwab, owner of Bethlehem Steel, to ship east Texas iron ore from Port Bolivar to Schwab's mill in Philadelphia. Featherstone and Schwab, together with Galveston and eastern investors, had formed a syndicate and bought thousands of acres of surface and mineral rights around Longview. Vast iron ore deposits there were so pure and of such a high grade that samples showed fifty percent metal. The syndicate forecast the area would produce 200 million tons of ore, and Featherstone, backed by the Santa Fe, started construction of a railroad from syndicate holdings at "Ore City" to Longview and named it the "Port Bolivar Iron Ore Railway."[10]

The *Manufacturers Record* said Featherstone's project was a "sensational development in the iron ore business." The Santa Fe offered to give one dollar per ton freight rate from the iron ore mines to the port and said they planned to construct immense ore bins and contract a line of vessels to transport the ore from Bolivar to Philadelphia.

"I am convinced that I can build an iron industry as well as exporting ore," Featherstone said. He planned to have vessels return from Pennsylvania with coal for a coke plant and iron furnace. Half the ore mined at Longview could be retained in Port Bolivar for conversion into pig iron and exported to steel manufacturers or made into steel at future Bolivar plants. "I am confident that within a few months Port Bolivar will outdo Birmingham [Alabama] in making and exporting iron," Featherstone said.[11]

The government, in October 1910, was building a seventeen-foot seawall around Fort Travis, a fortification on the gulf side of the western tip of the peninsula. Engineers had started dredge operations to deepen the channel into Port Bolivar to thirty feet.[12]

In January 1912, the Santa Fe put the finishing touches on a huge $40,000 temporary iron ore dock 325 feet long and 58 feet high, with plans for a $200,000 permanent dock. The first shipment of iron ore was expected to arrive at the end of the month from Ore City. Complete plans for ore handling now included construction of a blast furnace and steel plant; eastern investors had selected and purchased the site.[13]

In 1913 the secretary of war recommended that the government build an armor plate factory, and Featherstone offered Congress a free location at Port Bolivar, but Congress never responded.[14]

That year in "the future Brooklyn," 104 ships took on cargo—cottonseed cake, steel rails, cotton, fruit and vegetables, livestock, salt, and 5,550 tons of iron ore.[15]

The bay community gained some recognition as a lumber port. The Santa Fe Railroad had two storage sheds eight hundred feet long with a capacity of six million feet of lumber, served by three tracks and a long skidway for unloading the lumber into the water. East Texas lumber companies, at peak production, generated millions of feet of long-leaf yellow pine a year, and in 1913 forty-six million feet of lumber were shipped out of Port Bolivar, six times more than New York.[16]

After two or three shiploads of ore left Port Bolivar, World War I loomed like a black cloud on the horizon. In 1914, at the beginning of the war, Germany began to use submarines, a new and potent maritime threat. In addition, the Germans secretly armed five merchant ships and were raiding Allied commercial vessels in the Atlantic. Although British squadrons were patrolling the shipping lanes between Europe and the U. S., German raiders were capturing many American merchant ships; one of the attack vessels, *Kronprinz Wilhelm* was based in New York. The United States was not yet involved in the war, but investors feared for the safety of U. S. shipping, and Featherstone could not raise the capital to continue his scheme. The great ore dock sat idle.[17]

R. C. Bouse, Jr., of Port Bolivar remembered how the town looked between 1900 and 1915:

There was a big shipyard here where they built barges, and there were longshoremen that worked on the docks. The Santa Fe barge landing was right about where the ferry landing is now. They used to load ships down here—had an iron ore dock, too. It was a big thing pretty near as big as that lighthouse, and they'd pull them freight cars up on it. There was a trap door and a chute goin' into the ships. Ships come in here. They had a big outfit with a cable and they'd pull the cars up there with that cable. Then they'd let it back down and bring up another one up.[18]

Featherstone's plans for the "future Brooklyn" looked uncertain as 1915 rolled around, a year that proved to be the deciding factor in Port Bolivar's fate.

11 / The 1915 Storm

On Sunday, August 15, 1915, Galvestonians had a choice of two movies—*Rags* starring Mary Pickford at the Palace Theater and *The Bank* with Charlie Chaplin. The *Galveston Daily News* announced that Japan had a new paper lifeboat, warned people to brush their teeth five times a day, and advertised twenty-nine-cent hats at Fellman's. The war in Europe was mentioned briefly. "Foster's Weather Bulletin" from Washington warned of a "disturbance" crossing the continent that was expected to cause dangerous storms off the southern and eastern coasts; the worst period would be around August 17.

Next day the Galveston weather bureau began to fire rockets at half-hour intervals to warn boats in Galveston Bay. An unusually high tide and surf indicated possible trouble; ships at sea sent wireless messages that a gale of seventy-four miles per hour was blowing in the gulf. Hundreds of swimmers, undaunted by the "mountainous breakers," cavorted in turbulent water pounding the beaches and seawall.[1]

Dixie Shaw was living in Caplen at the time and remembers events well. "Just before the storm they sent a passenger train from Beaumont. It came down the peninsula and turned around at Port Bolivar on a turntable. The train men told everyone along the way, 'Get ready, because a hurricane is coming, and we'll pick you up on the way back.'" She said there was just enough time for everyone to collect a few possessions. "My mother said she didn't have anything except what she was wearing. She took some clothes for the kids, and later on somebody loaned her a dress to wear while she washed the one she had on."

"The train turned around and started back, picking up people along the way," Dixie continued. "My dad and mother had just married, and Dad put his five older children on the train—they went to Fannett where my grandparents lived. Some people went to Beaumont and some got off at High Island—wherever they felt they would be safe. Some of the people stayed at the lighthouse. This was the afternoon before the storm."

On Monday, August 16, every hotel in Beaumont was filled with refugees from Port Arthur, Sabine Pass, and Bolivar Peninsula. At seven o'clock there were no more rooms, but great crowds of people streamed in, and many spent the night in the hotel lobbies on the floor.[2]

Train passengers arriving from Rollover said the water there was two feet over the tracks, but railroad officials denied the fact. All wire communications were down from High Island to Port Bolivar, but there was no alarm in Beaumont, since storm warnings had been issued for two days, giving everyone time to get to safety.

George Carpenter, manager of the Rollover Hotel at Rollover did not feel the situation was dangerous; however, he brought all his guests to Beaumont Monday morning because a few of the women were worried. "The water was a little rough," said Carpenter, "but no worse than I have seen it a number of times in the winter." P. E. Parminter, owner of another hotel in Rollover and his caretaker Oscar Scanlan decided to stay put; they were worried about vandalism and felt sure the substantial concrete structure would make it through any hurricane.[3]

Mrs. E. W. Corder, wife of the Sea View Hotel manager at High Island, told a Beaumont reporter at the depot that everything was all right at High Island. She said people in the town had nothing to fear from high water and that it would take a "mighty strong wind" to do any damage there. "I think the storm reports have been greatly exaggerated, and I believe warnings ought to be given, but there is no cause for undue excitement or alarm," Mrs. Corder stated.[4]

In Beaumont Monday morning, Boy Scout troop number two, in spite of high tides and storm warnings, set out on a hike from Beaumont to Rollover. The nine boys and their leader, Tom Holland, said they were confident the storm would be over by the time they reached the coast, and they planned to camp at Rollover.

A few days later the *Galveston Daily News* reported that Bolivar was a "water-covered waste" swept bare of all houses, fences, and barns, and destitute of all livestock and crops.[5]

Hugh Jackson, a wealthy Beaumont businessman, had built his ranch house near High Island with a heavy wood floor attached to a foundation of concrete piers. The house survived the 1900 storm undamaged, but Monday night it completely disappeared. The piers alone remained.[6]

Mr. and Mrs. Frank Kirkland ran with their niece to the Jackson's house when the water and wind began to rise Monday afternoon. Early that evening waves began to break up the house, pushed it off the foundations, then smashed it in. The Jacksons and Kirklands were thrown into the water in all directions, and Mrs. Kirkland found herself in the branches of a tall tree. Hugh Jackson, his grandson Claude Roberts, Jr., and the others disappeared.

Mrs. Kirkland clung to the tree all night while the wind roared and waves struck her, stripping off all her clothing. In the morning she saw at the foot of the tree, floating face upward in the underbrush, the bodies of her husband and her niece.

All day Mrs. Kirkland stayed in the treetop, sometimes in a stupor, sometimes awake to her terrifying situation. During the day torrents of rain fell, driven by blasts of wind. Water covered everything in all directions, with no sign of human life. She cooled her dry lips and tongue with rainwater from her hair. Darkness fell and she spent another night clinging to the tree, then morning came, and she could still see the two bodies below.[7]

At noon that day Claude Roberts of Beaumont and Henry Sullivan of High Island, in a boat searching for Roberts' son, found Mrs. Kirkland barely alive and unable to talk. Later, ten miles away at Double Bayou, they found the bodies of Hugh Jackson and Roberts' son Claude.[8]

The White family, who lived a few miles north of High Island, left their house early Tuesday morning when the water was about four feet deep and went to the top of their barn. When the water receded, they went back to the remains of their house, pushed about fifty feet by the storm. When they went inside, they saw their dog lying peacefully on the dining room table. A rocking chair had floated up on top of the kitchen stove, and in the chair lay a small pig.[9]

At High Island the day of the storm, Marrs McLean and friends Monroe Carroll and A. E. Borsum (all from Beaumont) were working on an oil lease. McLean decided he wanted a better view of the storm and convinced the others to watch it from W. D. Gordon's home, "the Breakers," a half-mile from the beach at Caplen. He thought "the blow" would be over in a few hours at most, so the three men drove to the nearby resort.

Monroe wanted to save one of his favorite cows, pastured at Caplen, from high water before they went to the house. He put the animal on a freight train at Caplen station and told the others he had decided to go on back to Beaumont. The passenger train, scheduled to come by soon, never arrived. After several hours the gulf had come far inland, so the three men left the depot and waded through deep water to the Breakers.[10]

Late that afternoon the men watched huge waves pick up neighboring cottages and float them away. The Gordon home shook badly as the force of the tide and wind battered it, but the old cypress structure held on.

A little after dark the beach side of the first floor caved in, letting in a flood of seawater. McLean, Carroll and Borsum dashed to the stairway, ran up to the second story and spent the night there. Several times they felt a terrific jolt as something hit the house, but they could not tell what it was. Wednesday morning the three men swam and waded to High Island and caught the relief train to Beaumont.[11]

After the storm, the Breakers was the only house left in Caplen, where three feet of water still surrounded it. The hotel and every business and home in Caplen and Rollover were swept away without a trace. The railroad track had disappeared for miles, and only one telegraph pole remained.

The three men told Beaumont reporters they thought that "Old Man" Parminter, who stayed at his Rollover Hotel, had drowned, unless he had boarded one of the fishermen's boats that had come by the hotel after the water began to rise.[12]

Sixty-one Port Bolivar people, who had decided against evacuation, fled Monday through high water to the lighthouse. Later that afternoon huge waves washed across the peninsula and pounded the tower. As floodwaters rose, everyone on the lighthouse stairs climbed higher; the tower was swaying so badly they could hardly stand up. Some of them looked out the tiny windows and saw their homes being battered to pieces, disappearing into the water.[13]

J. T. Rohacek, from Caplen, said friends told him the lighthouse was shaking like a tree. He remembered the water in Port Bolivar being one foot deep in the 1900 storm, compared with over seven feet on Tuesday. "It is the worst storm that ever visited this coast," Rohacek said.[14]

Monday evening Rohacek and three other men made their way to a ridge about a mile north of Patton, climbed into oak trees and spent the night. Tuesday morning they climbed down into five feet of water, waded and swam eleven miles to Port Bolivar and boarded a boat to Galveston.[15]

After the floodwaters receded, Port Bolivar residents found huge holes and piles of lumber where their homes had been, many dead animals and hundreds of snakes. The town was a complete wreck; the wharf depot was blown away, freight cars turned over and damaged, all docks smashed, and nearly every house in town demolished.

Monday afternoon fourteen people rushed onto the Austrian steamer *Morawitz*, detained at Port Bolivar when World War I began the year before. The ship attempted to escape the storm, lost steam, drifted up the bay, and went aground on Redfish Reef. Everyone on board was rescued and taken to Galveston.[16]

The railroad track along the peninsula was washed 150 feet from the right-of-way, and sections 30 feet long were standing upright. There were no telegraph poles for ten miles from Port Bolivar. Hundreds of dead cows and horses were floating in the bay, and at Flake, a little settlement eight miles from Port Bolivar, a three-masted schooner was sitting in someone's front yard.[17]

L. E. Featherstone and B. E. Quinn, after visiting Bolivar on Saturday, caught a boat to Texas City. As they were leaving they noticed a large steamer near the north jetties. The captain of their boat told them the steamer was sinking; through a spy glass they could see the vessel slowly going down. Later, in Galveston, they learned that the ship had been calling for help, and several small boats had tried to get to her without success. The ship was lying so near the jetties, the crew could not have escaped; they would have been beaten to death on the rocks. The ship was a Morgan line freight steamer, and further news of her fate was not reported.[18]

Oscar Flake, a long-time peninsula resident, estimated that livestock losses were two thousand head of cattle, fifteen hundred sheep, five hundred hogs, and nine hundred horses, in addition to all the crops, farmhouses, equipment, and buildings. The State Health Department received information that five thousand carcasses of dead animals were floating in high water around Anahuac.[19]

W. H. Marmion, Beaumont grocery store owner, and others went on a relief train from Beaumont to Winnie on Thursday, and from there took a boat to High Island, seventeen miles south. At High Island they distributed food and water to several hundred people stranded at the Sea View Hotel and letters to the Boy Scout troop. The hotel was damaged but still standing.[20]

Galveston County Commissioner J. A. Boddeker, with Charlie Holt, George Smith, R. J. Madden, and Charles Payton, left Galveston on a boat Saturday morning after the storm with medical supplies and food. They headed across East Bay and saw devastation everywhere. The entire peninsula was under water. They distributed everything they had at High Island and tried to get information about missing persons. Thirty-eight were known dead and four unaccounted for. Twenty-seven unidentified bodies had been buried in the vicinity of Port Bolivar, and these, they thought, had washed up from other places. Bodies of P. E. Parminter, owner of a hotel at Rollover, and an unidentified fisherman were found later.[21]

Tom Holland, scout master, took his boys down to the beach near High Island a few days after the storm. "No words can express the horrible situation. Nothing of the sort has ever been known before," he commented.[22]

Holland and the scouts saw many carcasses, trunks, beds, clothes of all kinds, bales of cotton, and army articles belonging to soldiers at Texas City. Two of the boys discovered the head of a forty- or fifty-year-old woman, with thick hair, good teeth, blue eyes, and high forehead. Holland buried it on the beach where the boys found it, about a half-mile west of the Sea View Hotel.[23]

The Henshaw home at Rollover was washed away, but the family had rented the place to someone else that weekend and were staying at the Sea View Hotel in High Island. Tolley Davis said that her grandfather and the Henshaws found in the floodwaters a few potatoes and some live sheep. Her grandfather, accustomed to butchering sheep on his plantation in Louisiana, killed one of the animals for them to eat. After the water went down, the men left the hotel to check on the Henshaw house, and all they found were two brass andirons.[24]

Two weeks after the storm, W. D. Gordon of Beaumont made a trip down the peninsula to see how his house at Caplen, the Breakers, and his orange grove had fared.[25]

Gordon and a friend took the train to High Island, then borrowed a motorboat and went into East Bay, passing the foundations of the Hugh Jackson house. They landed on the bay side between Rollover and Caplen, waded to shore and walked by the wreck of Jim Keith's cottage, the only remnant of a house left in that area. The gulf had cut a channel half through Rollover, giving Gordon the idea that another such storm would make Bolivar an island.[26]

The row of cedars formerly running along the railroad track toward Caplen had been washed away, and the beach, now much wider, covered the old shell road.

Cavernous holes were the only signs of several summer cottages. All that remained of the McFaddin cottage was a pile of debris banked up against some salt cedars. In this mess, lying bottom up, apparently uninjured, was the McFaddin automobile. Gordon saw Asa Hamshire's car tilted on its side nearby.

When they reached Caplen, nothing looked familiar. Bouse's concrete store was gone except for scattered pieces. A big hole at the edge of the beach indicated the former site of the Gulf View Hotel, and a pipe sticking out of the ground was the only evidence of the hotel water well.

"There is not a vestige of the depot, the station house, the Will Gage cottage or any of the other houses in that vicinity to be found; no sign that any building ever stood there," Gordon commented. He said the railroad track was undoubtedly the weapon used by the elements to demolish all the buildings. The wind and waves picked up the track, broke it, and hurled it hundreds of feet in sections toward the bay, carrying all the buildings in its path.[27]

When Gordon and friend made it to the Breakers, they were relieved to see that the house had only minor damage. A hundred-foot-long section of railroad track had hit the cement steps, broken in half, pushed the building off its blocks, and crushed the porch in, leaving the main structure intact.

The Bluch Kahla, Frank Kahla, and Otto Harrington homes, near the Indian graveyard, six or seven hundred feet from the beach, escaped with slight damage. Behind them, in his orange grove, Gordon's small cabin was still standing.

The shell road from Rollover to Port Bolivar was entirely gone except in one place. Gordon had soaked a small stretch of road in front of the Breakers with crude oil because of the dust, and the oiling of this section protected it from the elements. The water seemed to have made no impression on that part of the road. Gordon was so excited about the phenomenon that he took several snapshots to show his friends.

Gordon said he found his orange crop ruined, but the trees appeared to be alive, and he thought the orchard would survive. He was planning to start repairs on his house and hoped to enjoy his next summer vacation there. "The beach is very expansive and more beautiful than ever before," he said.[28]

Wrecked Santa Fe train at Port Bolivar dock after 1915 storm. Iron ore dock in background. (Courtesy Harry Brown)

Will Crenshaw house after 1915 storm. This is one of several houses that was left on the peninsula after the most devastating hurricane in Bolivar history. (Courtesy Agnes Stephenson)

First ferry landing, 1930. A long wooden ramp came down from a Fort Travis bunker and extended far into the water. Ticket booth and attendant selling tickets at left. (Courtesy Odessa Mouton)

Downtown High Island in the 1930s, oil boom days. Tall building on left is the High Island Hotel. (Courtesy Joel Kirkpatrick)

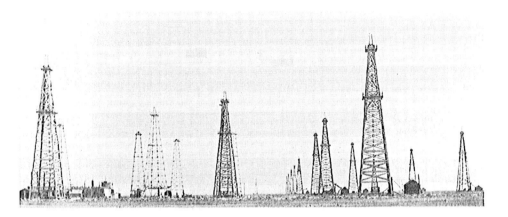

Oil derricks surrounding High Island in 1939. C. T. Cade attempted to find oil on top of the salt dome and failed. (Courtesy Joel Kirkpatrick)

Tommy Daniels, overseer, standing in wreckage of Frenchtown shrimp and oyster cannery after 1932 storm. (Courtesy Stella Suhler)

Cannery workers in Frenchtown just after the 1932 hurricane. This storm destroyed the cannery and left many without jobs. (Courtesy Stella Suhler)

Port Bolivar goat ropers lassoing wild goats on Goat Island, June 1986. The goat roundup provides annual entertainment and meat for the Fourth of July barbecue. (Collection of the author)

Two young goat ropers tackle a stubborn billy to get him loaded onto the goat barge. Little boys are never helped by their fathers and must do the job alone. (Collection of the author)

12 / A Later Look

In 1936, High Island oil production ranked among the highest on the Gulf Coast. Clusters of wooden derricks pumped steadily, and gas flares blazed around the base of the hill. Beaumont oilmen had overcome one of High Island's major drawbacks—lack of electricity to operate the rigs. In 1930 they had run a power line from Beaumont to High Island, and the boom started.[1]

The town on the salt dome boasted the High Island Hotel, one cafe with the only telephone, a drugstore, dance hall, two bars, and three poolhalls. Marrs MacLean, Beaumont oilman, owned the Sea View Hotel, favorite haunt of wildcatters, deal-makers, roughnecks, and other characters.

Tourism was unheard of in High Island; the town looked like a tough frontier settlement with a rugged bunch of natives. They were a friendly lot but had well-established ideas about justice—claimed they didn't need police and courts to settle their problems. "There wasn't no law then but old John Payton," said Pike Kahla. "He was Sheriff of [Port] Bolivar and High Island. He couldn't arrest nobody 'cause he didn't have no car or horse, so he couldn't take 'em to town. If somebody killed somebody, by the time he got there, all the evidence would be gone."

Much drinking and dancing went on at the Sea View Hotel every Saturday night, and the evening invariably ended with brawls between groups from Beaumont, Port Bolivar, High Island, and Port Arthur. The manager of the Sea View, Henry Sullivan, was a huge man respected by everyone, and "nobody wouldn't fight him, 'cause he would pick 'em up by the collar and throw 'em out the damn door," Pike said.

The fights got so bad that finally some of the High Island citizens built a jail. "That was a heck of a jail," Pike went on. "It had a whole bunch of bars they got out of the oil field, and they made a cement floor, then put a top on it. They'd catch somebody and put him in there, and the mosquitoes like to kill the poor devil, they would. They'd box him up a couple of days, feed him, then turn him loose, like an animal." Finally, Pike said the drinkers got so tired of the jail that "they got ahold of some dynamite and blowed that son-of-a-gun jailhouse up." Such was the first and last prison on Bolivar Peninsula.[2]

In 1934 construction began on the Intracoastal Canal, running from Point Bolivar past High Island. Everyone on Bolivar was horrified. Most of the oyster beds along East Bay were dredged up and the entire ecology of the marshes changed. Cattle could no longer walk to the rich salt grass across the canal, and land owners lost access to their property.

Charlie Holt worked with the Army Corps of Engineers as they surveyed canal lines within Cade lands to make sure they took no extra inches or went the wrong way. Pike Kahla said the two of them spent a whole year surveying from Caplen to High Island, where Pike, worn out with tromping through the marshes, refused to go any farther, and Charlie had to find another assistant.

When work began on the canal, one of the Tellepsen Company construction workers, while preparing foundations for a railway bridge, found three huge bones thought to be those of a prehistoric "hairy elephant." The discovery attracted a lot of attention, but nobody knew what to do with the bones, so they were turned over to Sheriff Payton.[3]

At Gilchrist (formerly Rollover) a few weather-beaten shanties stood along the bay. When the tide rose during storms, waves from the gulf rolled over the narrow strip of land. Along Caplen's beaches in the 1930s prominent Beaumont citizens built a colony of summer cottages that stretched for several miles. Staunch old survivor of many hurricanes, the Breakers, built in 1884, stood erect like an old patriarch who refused to die. Patton and Flake were tiny hamlets, and Port Bolivar, with a character all its own, claimed one general store, Bouse's. The ferry landing nearby, built in 1930 of rickety wooden struts, extended from the top of the bunker at the fort out into the harbor; a ticket booth sat on one side of the ramp about halfway out. At the same time the ferry landing was put in place, construction began on the first road on Bolivar. Before 1930, travelers used the beach to get from one end of the peninsula to the other.[4]

Part of Port Bolivar was known as "Frenchtown," a community whose inhabitants came by train from Louisiana and Mississippi in 1928 to work in the local shrimp cannery. They brought with them Cajun language, songs, customs and legends. Storytelling and music were comforting in those days of hardship and struggle. On Saturday nights the foot-stomping rhythms of violins and mouth harps drifted through the air—some folks danced and others sat on the porch telling the children old Louisiana tales in half-French, half-English dialect.[5]

One story said a big white wolf, *le loup blanc*, roamed at night in the tall salt grass. No man could kill it, and no bullet could harm its charmed body. When a cow was lost, everybody knew why—the white wolf had been around. Some of the old men swore they had tried to shoot *le loup blanc*; bullets spattered the mud all around him and apparently passed through his body, but the wolf moved away untouched.[6]

They talked about *le loup garou*, the werewolf, too. He was the special servant of the Evil One, and some said, the Devil himself. Hearing his eerie cry at night or catching a glimpse of him slinking through the morning mist was considered a bad omen. His shadow had been seen the night before a terrible freeze that destroyed all the cattle around Frenchtown.[7]

Legends of Jean Laffite's buried gold and jewels passed through many generations, but during the 1920s folks considered it dangerous to get serious about digging. Frenchtowners said an evil and vengeful spirit guarded the treasure and would drive away anyone who found it. One person, they say, actually dug up an old Laffite chest but ran away terror-stricken and died the next day.[8]

"My grandfather and them knowed Laffite," Pike Kahla said. "I used to work out in the garden with Grandpa, and he'd tell me how Laffite used to do." Grandpa Kahla told Pike that the buccaneer used to sail schooners across the bay up into bayous behind Elm Grove, a place thick with palmettos and elm trees. The ships had high masts, and the pirates climbed to the top of them and watched out over the gulf. "They'd see somethin' comin', and they'd sail around and cut 'em off and take all their stuff—knock 'em in the head and take what they wanted," Grandpa told him. "Then they'd bury the loot."

Pike claims his family had obtained a "blueprint" detailing a buried treasure at Fannett, near Beaumont, but by the time they got there, someone had just removed it, and all they found was a big hole with rust marks in the dirt.

Pike remembers as a young boy seeing a gold or brass spike in a tree, like a pointer, at Elm Grove. He told his father about it, and the two discussed searching for treasure, but they never made the trip. Then a storm knocked the tree down, and nobody could remember where it stood. Joe Bill Kahla, Pike's cousin, started excavations in the grove, but as fast as he dug, water filled the hole.

Bolivar forgot about pirate treasure when World War II started. No fires were allowed on the beaches, and blackout shades covered the windows at night. Even car headlights were forbidden. German submarines patrolled the Gulf of Mexico, and a huge antisubmarine net was laid between the north and south jetties. The coast guard took over the old Sea View Hotel as headquarters for beach surveillance.

After the war, on March 13, 1947, the abandoned Sea View, a landmark for decades, burst into flames. Fierce winds whipped the fire so violently that local oil company fire fighters gave up trying to save the old frame building. A small group of High Islanders stood around watching the crackling funeral pyre and thought of "the good old days." They imagined a grand and beautiful era going up in smoke. After forty-five minutes the fire burned itself out and nothing was left but three scorched mattresses and an ancient rocking chair. "At least," one old-timer remarked, "she went out in a blaze of glory."[9]

The next year electricity arrived at Port Bolivar. Two hundred locals and visitors jammed into the schoolhouse to witness the ceremonies. When Gulf States Utilities officials threw the switch at 9:00 A.M. on July 21, a loud cheer went up from the crowd. Judge Andrew Johnson, Jr., congratulated R. C. Bouse, Jr., who had struggled for twelve years to get power to the town. Excited residents drew numbers to win irons, mixers, washing machines, and other electrical appliances. There was hope of getting telephones, too, and negotiations were under way to purchase an old fire truck from the Galveston Fire Department. For better or worse, Bolivar was linked to the world at last.[10]

13 / Crystal Beach and the Cowboys

Today's visitor to Bolivar may experience something of a time warp—things look pretty much as they did in the 1930s and 1940s. To get there from Galveston one still rides across on the ferry and enjoys a pleasant twenty-minute trip observing shrimpboats, Russian grain ships, jack-up rigs, and other assorted vessels plying the waters of the gulf and bay. Upon landing, he or she sees the old lighthouse, black and rusting with age, guarded by its two white keepers' cottages that seem to be waiting for someone to come back and turn on the beacon.

The sleepy town of Port Bolivar sits on the bay side of the peninsula, going about its business of shrimping and cattle raising. Nothing remains of the Cajun settlement called "Frenchtown" or the canning factory, both destroyed by hurricanes. Fort Travis, a grassy park surrounded by an old seawall, still has a few bunkers and a brick road winding along the west end. A flock of brown pelicans sit on pilings near the seawall looking out to sea.

From the western tip of the peninsula to the eastern end, a distance of twenty-seven miles, the beach is thickly populated with summer homes on stilts; to the left of the road are fields and marshes with grazing cattle and tugboats in the Intracoastal Canal that appear from a distance to be gliding over dry land.

At High Island, Highway 87 to Sabine Pass ends abruptly, torn up by successive storms. Nearby, a few oilwell pumps are still pumping up and down, and the old main street to the town has been bypassed by Highway 124. No trace of the Sea View Hotel can be found—the place where it stood has a thick woods growing on it. High Island's only motel, the Gulfway, welcomes bird watchers from all over the world each spring. They come to get glimpses of colorful migratory finches and vireos on the hill and thousands of wading birds that wander around the oilfield ponds.

High Island has recently become one of the nation's hot spots for birding. When the announcement came in May 1984 that a single Yucatan Vireo had landed in the oak trees at the Indian graveyard, people came from Chicago, New York, and beyond to catch a glimpse of the shy gray-brown creature that had never before been seen in the United States. Groups of watchers rolled up in their campers, vans, and automobiles and parked fifty feet away from the bird's resting spot. They swarmed through the grass armed with lawn chairs, binoculars, Diet Cokes, bird books and long-lensed cameras. Just as everybody caught a glimpse of him and focused quickly, someone shouted, "There he is!" and he disappeared into the leaves. One or two lucky ones did get photographs, and Bill's Restaurant put out a portable sign that announced, "Welcome Yucatan Vireo."

Not too far from the Indian graveyard, between the old towns of High Island and Port Bolivar, a newer community has sprung up where the Patton railroad station used to be. A great majority of the residents are weekenders, who live somewhere else and come to Bolivar for a rest. There for a while, Crystal Beach, as it's called, was anything but restful.

In 1971 the town residents voted to incorporate—they wanted to take advantage of oil production in the gulf and boost the town's revenues, so they extended the city limits five miles into the Gulf of Mexico, where offshore wells could be taxed. Two oil companies and the state of Texas thought little of this scheme and sued Crystal Beach to invalidate the incorporation. A compromise was reached, and the state passed a law restricting coastal towns from annexing more than a mile seaward.[1]

Things settled down and went along peacefully until April 1987, when a band of dissatisfied citizens who hated paying city taxes and swore that their officials were misusing the money, instigated a move to disincorporate their city of 2,400. When the votes were counted, they had won, and a month's time was allowed for the transition to Galveston County. Mayor Bill Stirling decried this action, saying, "This disincorporation vote is one of the most foolish votes I've ever seen in my life."[2]

Nevertheless, Crystal Beach lost its mayor and police force as well as the city limit signs. Streetlights were turned off, and the city stopped garbage collections and picked up its portable toilets from the beaches. "It's like a zoo over here," said Stirling.[3] Fears spread that lawlessness and violence would break out, although the city police were still patrolling.

At the same time the vote was taken for disincorporation, the mayor's race was decided, and Bill Stirling lost to Bill Kelsey. Local media dubbed him "Mayor for a Minute," because he had no city to govern. George Vratis put up a sign in front of his Gaslight restaurant that read "Onward Through the Fog."[4]

The dust had scarcely settled when Bill Kelsey announced that the election had been fraudulent, that voters had been intimidated, absentee ballots were questionable, and that there had been improper electioneering at the polls. Kelsey organized a group called "The Crystal Beach Save the City Committee," called for a recount, and said there would be another election.

Time magazine quoted exultant A. B. Charpiot, leader of the antigovernment uprising: "Crystal Beach is history. We have thrown out the city."[5]

Kelsey's committee filed a lawsuit in Galveston in May 1987, contending the elections never should have been allowed and seeking to nullify the results. A. B. Charpiot declared the lawsuit "laughable."[6] Meanwhile County Commissioner Eddie Barr stated that he was maintaining emergency services for people on the peninsula.

The judge ruled that the election was void and that the city once again existed. On August 25, Bill Kelsey was again duly sworn in as mayor, and A. B. Charpiot appealed the ruling. Meanwhile, the

"Citizens for the City of Crystal Beach" and their opponents, the "Citizens for Good Government," circulated petitions for both sides.

Two years later voters decided *again* to disincorporate. Two months before, Mayor Bill Kelsey had been impeached on allegations of official misconduct and Monte Potter named acting mayor. Potter, who opposed disincorporation, announced that there would be an orderly transition of the city's assets to Galveston County.[7] "I think truthfully we will all be so much better off," said Charpiot's wife, Pat. "There won't be all that fighting and bickering now."[8]

She was right. Fighting and bickering, strong local traditions, have practically disappeared. Things are tranquil except for minor feuds between the mud minnow catchers and the cattlemen. Occasional tourists see nothing of these things—they are busy clicking photos of oil wells at High Island or of cattlemen working in the fields.

On a November day in 1989, a crew of New York advertising executives spied Bolivar Peninsula from a helicopter and decided to make an ad for Subaru cars there. They liked the wide-open spaces, the beach, and the herds of cattle scattered throughout the marshes. This scene was perfect for their idea to depict a Subaru speeding down Highway 87 with gulf waves crashing in the background and a herd of Texas cows thundering along in the foreground.

They arrived along with a Los Angeles film crew in vans, equipment trucks, catering vehicles, cars, and other equipment and parked everything out in the middle of the cow pasture. One or two had purchased cowboy boots and were wearing them, while the rest wished they had, because their tennis shoes did not protect against fire ants and mounds of cow dung.

Principal actors in the film had been chosen—head cattleman Louis Dailey, Jr., and two of his cowboy friends—who were to herd all the cattle down the fenceline in a big rush just as the car drove by on the highway. This was late in the afternoon, and time was short. Out on Highway 87 a sheriff's deputy had stopped traffic in readiness for the shoot, but the cattlemen could not get their herd to cooperate—they kept milling around off at a distance. The New York ad men decided that all the trucks and cars might be distracting, so they drove the vehicles out of sight. This strategy worked, and the cameraman was able to get an excellent shot of the car, the rushing cattle, and the cowhands, all performing well.

The director then yelled at Mr. Dailey to herd the cattle by once again, to which Dailey replied, "The cows won't do it." The director insisted, and the cowboys made efforts to duplicate the action, but without success. As the sun was low on the horizon, the ad man said, "Let's forget the cattle and just use the cowboys."

The next shot had the three cattlemen galloping along full speed on their horses, then the Subaru appeared behind them, but the car never did catch up with the horsemen, which looked bad for the car. At this point the film crew gave up and moved their scaffolding, tripods, catering truck, equipment truck, vans and cars down to High Island for another "take." This time they portrayed the Subaru racing along the road framed by an oilwell pump just as the sun was disappearing in the west. Perfection.

The New York ad man and his film crew went away happy, probably never to return. They said they had once trained some steers to come up over a hill all in a line, but they just couldn't deal with the Bolivar cattle. This is understandable, because the marshlands had never before been the scene of a movie, and the old cows weren't used to catering vans being parked in their territory.

Cattle had ruled Bolivar starting in the late 1800s—they were always a big part of life for peninsula residents, who worked long and hard rounding them up, branding them, and doing many other bovine chores. In the early 1920s rodeos were a big thing, and local cowboys showed their stuff on weekends at home-built rodeo pens in Port Bolivar and High Island. In the late 1920s there were so many cattle that no one had land to graze horses, and so the cowboys began to lasso and wrestle goats instead.

Two Port Bolivar residents, Monroe Kahla, Sr. ("Pike"), and

cousin Joe Bill Kahla, built up big herds of goats and kept them on islands separating the Intracoastal Canal from Galveston Bay. The goats thrived on the grassy land, and once a year the owners had to drive them into pens to cull a few. This turned into an annual tradition that involved swimming horses across the seven-hundred-foot canal, rounding up the goats, roping contests, taking the goats by barge back across the canal, and finally a big barbecue on the Fourth of July.

As years went by, the goat owners began to have problems with thieves and predators, but they never could find a solution. Finally, Joe Bill Kahla announced he would have no more goat roundups because he had so few left. All kinds of animals had been attacking and killing them—wild dogs, wolves, coyotes, and a big red fox. He said the wild dogs were the worst, because the men couldn't catch them. There was no way to guard the place night and day.

"One time we saw a big black Lab with a white spot on his throat and another dog swim across the canal and run up on Goat Island," Joe Bill said. "We were in a skiff and had rifles, but the dogs took off through the bushes, and we couldn't get a shot at 'em."

Joe Bill had remembered seeing the big black one in a subdivision near his house, so he and Sid Bouse went over there and looked around. There was the Lab with the other dog in someone's yard. Joe Bill knocked on the door, and a lady answered. "I'd like to buy those two dogs from you, lady," he told her.

She looked surprised. "Whatever for?"

"We caught 'em over on Goat Island killin' our goats, and I was going to shoot 'em, but instead I'll buy 'em from you."

She said no, she wouldn't sell them, that they belonged to her husband.

Joe Bill went back several times and finally talked to the husband. He said, "Just do whatever you want to." So a few days later Joe Bill waited until the wife had driven off in her car and went to the back of their house, took a pistol out of his pocket and went POW POW. "I shot both dogs right there, threw 'em in the truck and left."

The other herd of goats still survives, although its owner, Pike Kahla, has a difficult time catching predators. His son Monroe, Jr., spotted a large gray wolf among the goats one day and took a band of fifteen men over to the island to look for him. They carried rifles and marched in a line ten feet apart all the way down the island—and never saw the animal. During the next goat roundup Rodney Kahla swore he saw a coyote in the fields, but none of the men had guns, and they were unable to give chase.

In spite of all the hardships, Uncle Pike, as everyone calls him, carries on his roundups. Each year could be the last. The eighty-four-year old cattleman has a hard time recruiting enough experienced cowboys, and some of those are afraid to swim their expensive horses across the ever-widening canal. In 1985 when the men were pulling their animals through the water behind boats, two of the horses became tangled in the lead ropes, and one drowned.

So the problems get tougher, but Uncle Pike goes on, undaunted. In his battered straw hat and overalls he stands firm at his command post in a field full of swirling goats or steers, shouting curses and waving his cane at the cowboys, who are his sons, grandsons, and nephews.

In the summer of 1989 this patriarch of the peninsula insisted on staging the goat roundup even though a raging storm had set in, and the bedraggled participants, clad in plastic garbage sacks, rounded up a few wet goats. Luckily no one was struck by lightning. A TV man from Houston had promised to come out and film the whole event but failed to show up because of the weather. Uncle Pike, sorely disappointed, said, "We'll just have to do the gol-darned thing again next year."

THE PEOPLE

Introduction

One would think that in a simple place like Bolivar Peninsula, the local citizenry would be at home much of the time doing chores or relaxing. Not so. They're an elusive lot, engaged in so many activities that I had to use long-range strategy and cunning to get them into interviews. I'd have to telephone several times to catch them at home and set an immediate appointment before they could escape, then rush to their house with tape recorder, hoping the batteries were still good.

Without exception they welcomed me cordially and said they would be glad to tell me what they remembered about the old days. At first I was puzzled about this gracious reception until I found out that they all knew about the goat roundup where Bernard Guidry had thrown me into the Intracoastal Canal thinking I was a newspaper reporter. Also, the fact that I had ridden Charlie Bouse's frisky horse up to Elm Grove without falling off had helped my reputation.

At any rate, we would gather in the living room, and the wife would accompany us to correct her spouse or listen in. I noticed right away that each house had open windows and a huge roaring fan close by the principal speaker. The first interviews sounded as though they were taken in a wind tunnel, so I had to find a special microphone to solve the problem. On occasion the wife told better tales than the husband when I was interviewing him. Or the relatives came.

For instance, I had chosen a quiet Sunday afternoon to visit Uncle Pike Kahla, and we had been chatting in the living room for about half an hour when in burst about seven or eight kinfolks. They banged open the front door, stomped in and yelled, "Hey, Grandaddy, how you doin'? What's for lunch?"

At that, Uncle Pike got up, went into the kitchen, and helped his wife Elaine serve up a gigantic meal of veal stew, cornbread, mustard greens, tomatoes, blackeyed peas, rice, iced tea, and peach cobbler. We all ate together, and as the food disappeared I wondered when they would leave. No problem there. As soon as they had piled the plates in the sink and finished off a cup of coffee, everyone filed out and banged the door again, but not before kissing and hugging Pike and Elaine.

Our interview continued out on the front porch with no interruptions except the gobbling of turkeys and crowing of roosters. I was pondering in the back of my mind about how to get Uncle Pike into a quiet atmosphere, but there was no way. We continued our talks either on the front porch or in the kitchen with relatives and barnyard accompaniment.

Another problem was catching Vernon Kahla. I had heard raves about his prowess as a storyteller and was determined to find him, but this was not an easy thing. Vernon lived in a trailer house somewhere around Winnie, seventeen miles north of High Island and had no telephone. I enlisted the aid of his son Claud, who was my only hope. Even Claud said it was going to be hard.

For one whole year, Vernon eluded us and at last agreed to meet me at Claud's office. I was so elated over the forthcoming interview that I decided to plug my recorder into the wall outlet instead of using batteries, a precaution against disaster. The interview went well, except Vernon seemed tamer than I had been led to expect. When I went home and listened to the tape, I was horrified to hear an intermittent loud buzzing noise that cut into the conversation and drowned out half of it.

After salvaging what I could of the words, I was just able to put together a short chapter, thinking I would never see Vernon again. I asked Claud if he could possibly snare his father a second time, and he succeeded, but this time we had to meet at the Dairy Queen in Winnie. I made sure to use batteries in the recorder, but I had to keep it in my lap because Vernon kept pounding on the table to accentuate his stories.

This series of talks with the Bolivar folks had started out to be a way for me to learn about the peninsula's history, but after I listened to each one telling his memories in such inimitable fashion, I was so charmed that I instead left their narrations intact so the reader could enjoy them.

One other thing. As all this talk was going on, I never could figure out how all these families were interrelated, and after they had explained it fifty times or more, it still didn't make sense. Just be aware that you can't talk about anybody on Bolivar Peninsula, because it *will* be someone's cousin.

The Portraits

When Rice editor Susan Bielstein finished reading everyone's tales, she said, "We really need to see what these people look like—let's take pictures of them." This sounded like an excellent but difficult idea, and I agreed, thinking what a chore it was going to be just *finding* all of them again. Susan already had a plan in mind. "The ideal person, if we can get him, is Keith Carter. We just published his book of photographs last year, *The Blue Man*, and he has great talent." So we sent the Bolivar stories to Keith, who read them and accepted our assignment. He and I started "shooting" in High Island.

We met on a sunny January morning at the Gulfway Cafe to plan our strategy. Keith said he wanted us to visit with the subject for a few minutes to get him relaxed; meanwhile, he would cast an eye about the house for a portrait location. After Keith set up his tripod I was to be quiet while he worked with the camera.

Our first assignment involved two people at Herman Johnson's house. Herman had captured Vernon Kahla, who lived in Winnie with no telephone, and had brought him to High Island for the portrait making. We knocked on Herman's door and were greeted by Vernon dressed in a light gray suit, vest, blue tie, and black baseball cap. Keith had told me to advise everyone to wear their everyday clothes and NOT to dress up, but Herman had told Vernon nothing of this plan.

Vernon started talking at once. "Did you know why my grandmother moved my grandfather to High Island? I bet you don't," Vernon asked Keith. Keith, who had read Vernon's story, knew the answer but was afraid to say so. He answered: "Will you be pissed off if I guess right?"

Still sure of himself, Vernon replied, "Just guess."

"Alcohol," said Keith.

"That's it!" Vernon said. Without losing a second he continued to explain about Grandpa Smith's fondness for booze.

While Vernon yakked and Herman tried to get in a word edgewise, Keith casually moved about the house eyeing things. After about twenty minutes he walked over to the wall, lifted a large painting of ducks from its hook and reinstalled it by the back window, then moved a footstool up in front of it and asked Herman to sit down. The painting made a striking backdrop to Herman's rugged face and brown plaid flannel shirt. Then Keith noticed a fuzzy black cat wandering by, picked it up and asked Herman to hold it. Obviously the cat was used to being in Herman's arms and posed there calmly looking toward the camera with large green eyes. The shutter clicked several more times, and a masterpiece was created.

Next came Vernon dressed in his Sunday best. With infinite delicacy Keith persuaded Vernon to get rid of his hat and remove his necktie, which Vernon didn't want to do because his underwear would show. "I like the underwear," said Keith. Vernon was sitting in front of the duck picture, too, but somehow the ducks looked different with Vernon there.

After a few shots of Vernon's craggy face, Keith persuaded his subject to unbutton his shirt and let it hang open. Finally Vernon looked like himself and posed without moving an eyelid until Keith finished shooting.

The session was over, and Vernon had lost his hat. We made our farewells while he searched for it under the sofa.

The time had come to photograph Uncle Pike Kahla, and I had warned Pike that the fewer people at his house the better, because Keith wanted to work with him one-on-one. "Okay, that's fine," Uncle Pike had told me. "You don't have to worry about a thing."

When we arrived at the modest green house there were two cars parked in front, and we suspected some of the relatives had come to witness the event. As we walked across the front yard, Uncle Pike's son Leslie arrived, and inside we were greeted by a delegation of sons, wives, and grandchildren. Keith, after introducing himself, began to act like a hound dog hot on the trail, snooping around the living room and front porch, then sleuthing into the kitchen, where Uncle Pike's wife Elaine was frying tons of chicken.

After a quick hello, Keith jumped up on a chair and started photographing Elaine stirring the sizzling meat. "I thought you was supposed to be taking Pike's picture," she said.

"Yes, but this is for me," Keith told her.

She smiled a huge smile and kept stirring.

Keith then drew the chair closer and began taking photos of the skillet of chicken. "What on earth are you doing now?" Elaine asked, laughing.

"I want to take pictures of this kind of food. It's a dying tradition, and you don't see this very often."

"That's right. Everybody goes to Kentucky Fried Chicken now," she said.

By this time the frying was done, and Keith walked Uncle Pike out into the side yard followed by his two sons, grandson, and one or two others. The plan was to show Uncle Pike feeding his big burly calves. Pike dutifully placed feed in the trough, but the calves, unnerved by the tripod and audience, ran and bucked around the trough and didn't come near Uncle Pike.

The next idea worked better—Uncle Pike feeding the chickens and guineas in the back yard. The chickens, more faithful than the calves, hovered and clucked around Pike's feet as he threw handfuls of feed from a bucket. For his portrait Pike was wearing a fresh cotton shirt and semi-new felt hat instead of his usual old work shirt and prehistoric straw topper.

Keith liked the look of the front of the house and asked Pike to pose on the steps with a large hound dog that had wandered up. "This ole dog helps cull fish on Butch Kahla's shrimpboat, and even knows how to throw the crabs overboard," Pike said. So the amazing dog and the fabulous old man sat together in silent admiration of each other, and Keith captured another poignant image.

At this juncture Elaine was getting upset because lunch, set out on the table, was growing cold. "Come on, y'all, get in here and eat," yelled Pike. No further urging was needed, and the crowd of relatives, which had grown larger during our absence in the yard, filed into the kitchen.

Just as Elaine removed the plates she had placed on top of all the dishes to keep them warm, Keith jumped up on a chair and said, "Wait just a second." Several clicks later he asked Uncle Pike to sit down and place his hands on the table holding a knife and fork. Pike obliged, and Keith made several more photographs of the cooled-off food. Then in wandered one-year-old T. J., Pike's great-great-grandson, and Keith caught a fleeting second of the tiny tow-haired boy looking up at the patriarch.

The crowd would wait no longer—they surged into the room, sat at the table and dove in. Dishes of white beans, cornbread, gravy, coleslaw, fried chicken, potato salad, and dewberry cobbler made it look like Thanksgiving, and everybody ate with gusto.

The photography session was over, and we gathered our equipment to leave the Kahla home. As we waved goodbye, Pike and Elaine, standing on the porch, gave us one last comment:

"Do you know how we met?" Elaine asked. "He had some grapes in a can and asked me to come over and show him how to make grape jelly, so I did. Then, before I could leave, his son wanted to know how to make crab cakes, so I did that. I never did leave."

"Yeah," said Uncle Pike. "I got her."

14 / Louis George Hughes

Louis was born October 27, 1888, at Caplen, and died in Phoenix, Arizona, on May 8, 1987, at age ninety-eight. He managed to capture much of the history of the peninsula while working on his family genealogy. The following material is taken from his diary, which includes, among other things, his recollections of being a youngster on Bolivar. He said that his schooling had been limited to three months a year and that he had learned to spell "biscuit" before he went to first grade from the Uneeda Biscuit box. He loved to walk the beaches at daybreak to see what the tides had left, and one day his dream came true when he discovered a two-foot-long toy sailboat with three masts and full-rigged sails.

(Louis's material is presented in his own words, but sections have been condensed and punctuation corrected for clarity.)

My grandfather, Samuel F. Hughes, was born September 12, 1819, in the Parish of Stone in Worcester County, England. His father's home stood on an old stone road with large trees along the fenceway. It was the abundance of natural stone in this Parish that gave it the name, and the house, barn and fences were made of it.

When grandfather was a young man, the social order in England was divided into two classes; those who labored for their livelyhood and those who had incomes from businesses or other sources. The laborer was the commoner and the businessman the aristocrat. Grandfather fell in love with an aristocratic girl, and the association was intolerable to her folks; they warned her that she would be disowned unless she gave him up. She told them that her love was greater than social custom and that she would marry him, and she did, on January 2, 1844.

A few months later the British Navy called him into service on a sailing cruiser. He had but a few days to get ready.

When new recruits sailed it was usually for a short practice cruise, and grandfather figured that would be it, but when the ship was a good way out, the captain read what was known as "Sealed Orders." This called for three years cruising along the west coast of Africa to apprehend slave trading vessels. Thus grandfather, a bridegroom of a few months, found himself at sea without a chance of return.

The cruiser was powered entirely by sails, and in those days the loading and unloading of the ships was done by manual labor to the rhythm of music and vocal sing-song of "Heave to." Grandfather played the violin and coronet and was fortunately assigned to a small band that furnished the musical timing for lifting.

During this period many ships were engaged in slave traffic, and the Dutch were the most aggressive offenders. It was the captain's duty to stop the ships for search, and if found guilty to take the vessel captive. The British would do their scouting at night with all lights darkened and wait for daybreak. They would rush alongside the Dutch ship before their men were awake and take over.

Sometimes, though, the British had to chase them, and final capture depended on a little five-pounder and the gunner's marksmanship. Grandfather said it was very difficult to shoot from a certain kind of vessel when both boats were under sail running full speed and rolling with the swells of the sea. At first they would fire a warning shot across the bow, then the second shot aimed to cut away a main jib, and more shots to bring down sails until the Dutch were forced to surrender. Even then their opponents would try many tricks. The Dutch were a cunning lot.

The British sailors had many opportunities to talk with their

Louis Hughes, Caplen Beach, 1912. (Courtesy Benny Hughes)

Dutch captives about the United States, and they heard many fantastic stories about the new country, and especially the freedom to settle new land, and to hunt and fish, with but little taxes. Many of the men made up their minds to go there, and Grandfather was one of them.

He returned to England and told Grandma of his intentions. She agreed, and it required a year for them to dispose of their possessions and raise sufficient funds for passage. In those days so few boats were sailing to America that it took many months to get passage. They set sail from England in 1848 for the Southern United States. At that time Abraham Lincoln was a thirty-nine-year-old practicing attorney at law.

The full-rigged ship took a little more than three months to make the trip. After Grandfather's three years of sailing in the British Navy, he felt he was a regular "old salt," but it was a long, rough voyage for Grandma and their three-year-old son.

They finally sailed through the Gulf of Mexico and landed at Sabine, Texas. From there they went to Orange and settled in their first home in the new world. After their child Ellen Agnes was born they moved to Dickinson and had three more children—Eliza, Harry, and Edwin, my father.

When the Civil War came along, grandfather was forty-two years old, and because of his age and the size of his family he was assigned to non-combat duty to transport beef cattle to Galveston Island to feed the soldiers. While transporting cattle he had an opportunity to see the surrounding countryside and decided to move to Bolivar Peninsula, where he could live at the water's edge.

Shortly after the end of the war, in May 1865, he moved his family to Bolivar and homesteaded one hundred sixty acres from the State of Texas, twenty miles eastward from Galveston. Grandfather built his house about a hundred yards from the Gulf, with the sand dunes in between. From the top of the dunes they had a splendid view over the Gulf, and the passing of all types of ships from over the world. It was this picture of the great expanse of water and ships that enchanted grandfather.

They were at this location only a short time when they realized it was a half-way point for stagecoach travellers between Galveston and Sabine. Many stopped there, especially to get drinking water. The only road was the smooth sand of the beach. Later they converted their house into a regular half-way stop for the coach and established a luncheon inn and livery service. Grandfather took care of the horses and had them fed, groomed, and harnessed; he exchanged the animals while the passengers had refreshments of tea and tidbits.

Grandfather became the official land surveyor and did most of the surveying on the peninsula.

He had a boat with one large mainsail, commonly known as a cat-rig. This he used to make trips to Galveston for supples. I visited the boat landing many times. He used the bay side of the peninsula for his anchorage at a place called Yates Bayou. In fact, three boats were kept there—grandfather's, father's, and Uncle John Heiman's.

Grandfather had a beautiful yellow stallion named "Yellow horse." He was a powerful animal, very tame and dependable. Grandfather also had an old-time one-horse cart which he used to haul freight from the boat. Some of my earliest memories go back to trips made with grandfather through the marshes in the old cart with "Yellow horse." There weren't any roads; we simply followed our old trail, and most of the two miles was muddy marsh. The memory of decaying vegetation still lingers in my nostrils.

The marsh lands were a separate area unto themselves. The wildlife was different from the dry land—the home of raccoon, mink, water-rats, and snakes. The birds were also specific to the marsh grasses, and there were many small ones of beautiful bright colors.

Grandma's house was always a special place to me. Even in the 1890s everything in the old home bespoke of yesteryear. It was a simple house of four rooms with the traditional southern porch all the way across the front. The chimney was adobe of native clay and rush fiber from the marshes. There was a cistern to catch rain water, a barn and several outhouses including corn crib, tool shed and smoke house. At the back of the house were about eight orange trees thirty feet high. They had some salt cedars or Australian pine, century plants and other cacti.

In this locality each home was a complete, self-sufficient unit. Grandfather had a vegetable garden, chickens, milk cows, fruit trees and a small farm. From this he was able to provide all their food except coffee, tea, salt and spices.

My deepest memory of Grandma's house was the absolute quietness in the evening after darkness had closed in around us. Grandma and Grandpa would each be sitting in their favorite chairs with their books, and the dog curled up asleep before the fireplace. As we sat around the little table with the kerosene lamp, all would become a hushed stillness. I did my best not to move or make a sound, so I could hear the sounds that came from outside. The only noise in the room was the endless tick-tock of the old mantle clock, but outside I could hear the chirps of crickets and croaking of frogs.

My father was the last of his family to marry. My aunts, uncles, and parents built their houses in the vicinity of my grandparents. Ours was about half a mile to the north on what was called the back ridge. These four houses made up the entire neighborhood. There were no stores, doctors, dentists or neighbors. To the north were marshes all the way to the bay; east and west were open prairie, and to the south was the beach and endless Gulf. Our only source of supplies was by boat to Galveston.

When we made the boat trip to Galveston, one of the most interesting experiences was looking at the vast number of different types of sailboats tied at the wharves. There were at least twenty separate anchorages known as slips. The one for small boats was Pier 20, and sometimes the boats were so numerous there would be four boats deep from the wharf. These were made up of every type of small sailing craft, from cat-rigs to three-masted schooners. They brought to market everything that could be produced on the farm.

I loved to wander from pier to pier and especially where the foreign ships were tied up. These were the largest and finest of the ocean-going vessels. Most of the largest nations were represented, and the men aboard were speaking in their native tongues, with their national flag flying from the mast.

The entire Gulf Coast was subject to severe storms ranging from thunder squalls and water spouts to tropical hurricanes. Once when one of these hurricanes was blowing itself to a finish, Ernest Heiman and I went over to Grandma's to see if she was all right. It was fortunate we went there, as we found her alone and in a state of hysteria from worrying about grandfather and some of the others, who should have been on their way home from Galveston in the sailboat. If the boat had been caught out in the bay they could hardly have survived. It took some time before Ernest and I could quiet her. However, they made anchor and weathered the storm.

I visited Uncle John Heiman's home time without number and stayed overnight often when I was small. Uncle John was quite humorous and very kind, although he was a man of very few words. One night there was a heavy storm of rain, wind, thunder and lightning. All of the family gathered around the dining room table paying no attention to the weather and played a game of cards known as "Spades." Ernest, who was really the clown of the family, began doing some calisthenics over our heads on the rafters, hanging by his feet and doing various flips.

Father's land was about one-half mile inland from the beach. He grew vegetables and did general farming on additional land. Father was a carpenter and an accomplished musician on the violin and flute. He was fond of the opera and played some of the arias from them; he also had an endless repertoire of folk music.

In 1900 he began to teach me the guitar, and after several years I accompanied him wherever he played. Between 1904 and 1911, father, my first cousin Henry Hughes and I made a string trio; my cousin played the lead violin, father the second violin, and I the guitar. We played for picnics, weddings, amateur plays, parties and dances within a distance of twenty miles, and we usually went on horseback carrying the instruments with us. Father was able to play through the night to the break of day and never played the same piece twice.

In the early days when we lived on the back ridge, the wild ducks, geese and brant [a type of wild goose] would come in flocks of thousands, and father hunted them for the market. He had a pony trained so that he could fire a gun near him or shoot from the saddle. At the same time grandfather had a retrieving dog that loved to go hunting, and he was as smart as they come.

Duck hunting was at its best when a cold, rainy wind was blowing from the northwest. These weather changes were known as Northers, and father would wait for them to come to go hunting. Each time a Norther would blow in, the dog would come over to our house and announce himself by scratching on the front door, always precisely at four o'clock A.M. Father would know by the weather that the dog would be there, and he was always ready to go. Father would take the dog in, pet and feed him, then they would be off.

Father was an experienced gunman and a splendid marksman in shooting fowl on the wing. As the ducks would fly over he would wait for two ducks to be in line and get both of them with the first shot, then pick another one with the second shot. He used a thirty-two inch double barrel, ten gauge L.C. Smith.

When hunting in the marshes, it was never a problem to kill enough ducks; it was to keep count of them because forty mallards was all the load the pony could carry through the mud.

From the earliest periods up to the 1890s farm homes had to be self-sufficient, self-sustaining units. They produced all their main food and most of their clothing, and also their bedding. Of course, this meant endless work for everyone—father, mother, and each child. It meant being up at daybreak, and after a full day's work they continued in the evening while they were resting—knitting, carding wool, shelling peas, cleaning the guns and loading ammunition.

The woman took care of the cooking, put up a year's supply of canned goods, made all the children's clothing, most of her own and her husband's work clothes. She did the mending, washing and ironing, and extra work on special days of making syrup and butchering. They made sausage, bacon, ham, Tasso, salted meats and rendered grease to make soap.

During the harvest the wife helped in the field gathering the little whippoorwill peas. Each of us had a long sack strapped to us that we dragged along, and we filled it with the peas. Then the peas dried in the sun, and it was the job of us children to walk in circles over the sacks to shell them. Then they were poured from a higher elevation, and the wind blew the shells away. We stored bushels of them for a year's supply.

When father harvested cabbage he would get an extra wagon, and mother drove one of them. One day a horse she was driving became frightened and ran out of control. Mother was thrown from the wagon and broke her leg. There were no doctors nearer than Galveston, so a handy man, Mike Shrier, set the bone. Fortunately he did a good job and she recovered quickly.

In addition to father's activities he became very adept at hand knitting fishing seines and cast nets. He made many of them for neighbors far and near, and he also hand-sewed all the sails for his boat.

Our houses were not built for cold weather, and they were difficult to heat with a wood burning cook stove. In the winter of 1894 we had the first snowstorm in some twenty years, and it was below freezing. Florence was six months old, and we were all huddled around the old stove. Father was sitting near the stove holding the baby wrapped in a blanket. I can still hear him say, "We'll keep the baby warm if nothing else."

With the farm located on the back ridge, it was the first place to be visited by small animals prowling from the marshes. In fact, all of them seemed to visit our place. There were numerous rabbits, raccoons, wild hogs, skunks, minks, and occasionally a coyote or wildcat.

My brother Sidney and I took care of the rabbits with a series of wooden box traps. We kept the rabbits until father sailed to Galveston, where he sold them on the open market at twenty cents a pair. We also trapped raccoons with steel traps and sold the furs, which gave us some pin money.

The wild hogs were a real problem. When they got into a field of watermelons they would really make pigs of themselves. They came to forage about once a week, and when they were active father would hide in the treetops on moonlit nights and shoot them as they trotted along their regular pathway.

To kill them was a dark secret. We children were cautioned not to tell a soul, and I do believe the subject was never mentioned. The hogs were supposed to belong to someone, but no one knew who. However, to shoot them was the only way to stop their destruction. When father shot one we were sent directly to Aunt Eliza to whisper to her to send someone over for meat. We usually ran all the way there and back.

One lazy Sunday afternoon in spring we were sitting on our front porch when the dog suddenly began to whimper and hide behind our chairs. Father knew immediately what it was and whispered, "A wolf. Don't anyone move or say a word." He slipped into the house to get a gun, and the moment he returned the wolf stopped sneaking through the tall grass, turned away and loped away over the grass tops. We had some little pigs, only a day old, and father said the wolf was likely looking for his dinner, but the whimper of the dog saved them.

On September 5th, 1900, a gale began blowing from the Gulf, but this was a common occurrence and attracted but little attention, although we had the usual storm warning. Each year during August and September we would have several hurricane-type storms, but none had ever done any noticeable damage. Therefore, they were accepted as a regular feat of the weather. Homes had been made to withstand these annual blows, and they had stood up to everything in the past.

However, the next day the wind was following the usual behavior, but much stronger. The old-timers satisfied themselves by shrugging their shoulders and saying, "Well, I guess we are going to get it again." They had experienced these blows all their lives without any harm, but on the third day [September 9], which is usually the last day of a tropical storm, it came on us with a terrific gale and rain.

Father became quite worried, and by mid-morning he was badly worried. He hurried us down to the boat landing to tie down all the rigging and to put out the two heavy storm anchors for his boat. By four o'clock in the afternoon father became so alarmed he told us to get ready to leave at once. He feared for the very worst and wanted us to get to higher land.

Our house was in the lowest part of the peninsula, and father decided that our best safety was to go westward toward the center of the peninsula. Grandfather was visiting us at the time, and father told him to get ready quickly and go with us. He replied, "No, you go along with you. I have never left a sinking ship, and I shan't do it now." There was little time to argue. Father pleaded with him, but grandfather answered only a determined "No." Father had no choice but to go without him. Grandfather was then eighty-one years old.

There was no time to get the horses and wagon, so we began to walk on the railroad track. There were father, age forty, mother, thirty-two, I was twelve, Sidney ten, Florence six, Charles four, and Felton one-and-a-half. Father was carrying him. It was fortunate that the wind was on our backs. At that time it was estimated at one hundred miles an hour, and it was a challenge to stand up in it.

Father's older brother, Charles, lived about a half mile westward. When we came near his place we saw most of the neighborhood already there. When we got to the house we found a group of very frightened and excited people. Just then mother thought about food, and sent Sidney and me to run back home. This was against the wind, and we bent halfway forward trying to run, but we were going no faster than a walk. We soon returned with the supplies.

About five o'clock a passenger train stopped in front of the house only long enough to shout that they were going to see if they could make it to the mainland. In a few minutes they returned saying we were completely cut off from the mainland. The waves were washing logs onto the railroad, and the workmen were busy clearing the tracks. Just as the train pulled away, a great wave broke over the sandhills and pandemonium broke loose. It was what to do and where to go, with every second counting like an hour.

There was a good size flat-bottom freight boat alongside the house. The men brought it to leeside, and all women and children were told to get in. The load was too great for the boat, so the order came for all able-bodied women and larger children to get out and walk.

The boat was nearly empty when we left, but it never did float. There were only five able-bodied men in the crowd. Father left with them carrying baby Felton and one other child. Sidney took mother's left arm and I the right, and we began to move with the crowd toward Uncle Harry's home, about a half-mile distant. All the while the force of the wind was increasing, and the water was knee-deep and running cross-wise to us. The rain struck our faces like buckshot, and the women folk were badly handicapped because of their long skirts wrapping around their legs.

We seemed to manage very well with mother, but the women walking without help were falling all around us; however, they managed to get up and kept going. Mary Esder was walking on our right, carrying her baby. She was crying and had fallen several times. Just then the men returned from the first trip, and father came over to help us. He saw that Mary was nearly exhausted, and when she begged him to take her baby he couldn't refuse. He carried hers and another child to the house, and the other men worked as hard and fast as they could carrying the smaller children.

The wind was now so terrific it bent the treetops low enough to touch the water. When we came to a stile, we were lifting our feet to go over the top step and some of the party were blown off. We

Harry S. Hughes home between Caplen and Rollover. The house survived the 1900 storm, but it was demolished by the 1915 storm. Kate Hughes's husband, Buddy, is shown at right in front row. (Courtesy Kate Hughes)

were now on Uncle Harry's high land, and the worst of our ordeal was over.

Some of the men met us halfway up the lane to the house and told us that several of the party had been left behind—my sister Florence was one of them. They said they had to get back to them at all costs, and returned later sick with worry. They found the lane we had crossed minutes before a raging torrent, and it was impossible to cross.

When we got to the house we were surprised to find no one at home except the children in our party. We found out later that Uncle Harry's folks had gone westward to Uncle John's.

We immediately took a count of our group and found we were thirty-five, with six left behind in the boat—these being Uncle Charles, Mrs. Stowe, her daughter, two grand-daughters and Florence.

We were all soaked to the skin, but we had to make the best of it since dry clothes were impossible. We felt the house was our safest place and decided to remain there. The greatest anxiety was for those in the boat, and the men were badly downcast. They seemed to take personal blame for the ones left there. One of the men said, "We must not hold out too much hope. Uncle Charles is fifty-five and infirm, Mrs. Stowe is elderly and fat, and the only able-bodied one is Mrs. Stowe's daughter."

It was now about eight P.M., and the rage of the storm was heavier than ever. It was now a terrific roar. We were pleased to remember that we were in a house with walls loaded with clamshells when it was built. The men felt confident that it could neither be floated or washed away.

Some of the men were busy watching the constant increase in the height of the water. About ten P.M. it began to pour into the first floor where we were. Some of the old-timers kept saying, "The weather ought to make a change about midnight," and it was about midnight when a change came. The deafening roar lessened rapidly as the water began to recede. The terrific wind ceased to a complete calm, and at that point some of the party tried to sleep.

As soon as it was half light the men went out to search for those in the boat and found them all safe. Shortly after daybreak they returned with six awful, cold, wet folks. There were few dry eyes in the party. We could hardly believe the story they told of their experience.

They said that after a long wait for the men to return, they knew they had to do something to save themselves. The wind and water were so bad they didn't think they had a chance, but they started out holding tightly to each other and began walking through the storm in absolute darkness. After a short distance they were exhausted, and at that point they found a one-room shack. Once inside they barred the door with furniture and put anything they could find on the table and placed the three girls on it. The others stood and held on to the table.

When the water was about shoulder-deep the shack began to float, twirling and wobbling toward the north. They realized they were being washed toward the bay and had little hope left when a sudden jolt stopped the floating of the shack. Uncle Charles said, "There is a small briar thicket that may have caught us, if only it will hold." It did, and the shack stayed there. The men found them inside.

Father then turned his thoughts to grandfather and said, "Now I must go and search for my father. We left him alone in our house." Again the men went out. It was now full daylight, and as the men trekked eastward everything seemed to be washed away. They knew an eighty-one-year-old would have had no chance to survive. When they were on the verge of giving up, they saw in the distance the bent figure of a man walking toward them, in the lee of the cedar trees.

He was the only living, moving thing in sight. They were dumbfounded because they hadn't even seen a plant left by the storm. When they met my grandfather they asked him how he managed to stay alive, and he told them a simple story.

He said, "The railroad tracks were forced against the house and gradually crumbled it like kindling wood, so I ran upstairs, taking the dog and cat. I carried two feather beds, put one on top of the other and crawled in between them with my two violins and flute. When the house was crumbled away, the roof settled to the ground and pushed the second floor up near the rooftop. After the storm died down I stayed in the bed until daylight, when I looked around and saw an opening in one corner, so I crawled out, and here I am."

The marvelous thing about this whole experience is that he fared better than any of us. He was completely out of the storm and didn't even get wet. He reminded father of what he had said about never leaving a sinking ship.

I remember looking out the second floor window at sunrise and cannot forget the awesome sight that greeted me—a land of desolation. The whole picture gave the appearance that we were on a narrow island.

Of the dozen boats kept at anchorage at Rollover only two or three weathered the storm. Father found his on the other side of the bay. It was intact except for the loss of the rudder. Father replaced it, and on the third day after the storm he took all of us on the boat across the bay and over the flooded prairie. We sailed up beside the railroad, where a train was waiting for refugees, a few miles north of White's Ranch. The railroad was using boxcars to transport people inland. We had lost everything including all household goods and clothes, so all we had was what we were wearing. Mother and the young children went on the train to Hamshire, and father and I sailed back to the peninsula.

We needed everything badly, and especially money. Father had only thirty-five dollars to his name, so he left right away and went to work in Galveston. He was away about seven weeks and returned the latter part of October. In the meantime I stayed at Uncle John's, and we heard that clothes were being sent to Caplen for the refugees. They sent a large barrel of clothes, and there was a pair of boy's pants tacked over the top. The crowd ripped these pants from the barrel and threw them on the ground, and everyone rushed in and grabbed something—like wild Indians. When it was over I picked up the pants, and Aunt Ellen mended them so they could be worn. A few days after that father and I left Uncle John's by horse and wagon and rode to Hamshire where we joined the rest of the family at Uncle George's.

15 / Kate Hughes

Kate was born in Dayton, Texas, on December 15, 1894. Her family moved to Bolivar Peninsula just before the 1900 storm; then they lived in Beaumont for two years after the 1915 storm. Kate's husband, Buddy Hughes, was the great-nephew of Louis George Hughes. As a young wife, Kate came back to Port Bolivar in 1917 and devoted much of her time to improving education in the community—founded the P.T.A., *boarded teachers in her home, planted trees in the schoolyard, and raised money for better school facilities. Everyone on the peninsula loved her and called her "Aunt Kate." When I visited her at Turner Geriatric Center in Galveston, she brought out an old photo album of Bolivar and started to talk about her adventures—it took three visits to hear them all, and I believe she has many more.*

I went to live on Bolivar in 1914 when I got married. Our house was a one-room place back from the road at Caplen.

We used to raise melons, and we had a stand right by the highway. Buddy, my husband, would take loads of cantaloupes and watermelons to Port Arthur, and I'd be by myself with the kids. We didn't have any electricity, so we kept a lantern lit by the stand.

Buddy would go off to Port Arthur and Houston to take melons and leave at two o'clock in the morning, and I'd stay by myself. I never was scared of anything. We had screens all around, you know. One night I heard a noise and looked out by the road, and there were two black men, all dressed up with a great big car, and they were looking at the melons. I thought to myself, "You go ahead and take all you want. I'm not even going to let you know I'm in here." They each took one of the ninety-pound melons and put them in the car and went off. The next morning I went out there and found the money under a melon, stuck just so I'd be sure and see it. A lot of people wouldn't have done that.

My husband would go hunting with his nephew when my kids were little. Neither one of them was old enough to go to school. At night we could hear the wolves hollerin' all around us, but I was never afraid. I knew they couldn't get in the house. I worried more about my husband being out there. The kids got scared, though, and I said, "Well, if you're too scared to lay in the bed, get under it." So they'd get under the bed.

I used to take the kids out in our little truck to go crabbing in the bay. While we were crabbing the alligators would come up on the bank, so I just put the kids on top of the truck and kept crabbing. Just kept an eye on the alligators. I never was afraid of anything.

When I got married and came to Bolivar, everything was new to me because I had lived in Galveston. I didn't know one end of a mule from the other, although I had been goin' over there and had known my husband since I was six years old. My husband broke horses and had a lot of animals. Everybody had horses and cattle. Buddy had some beautiful riding horses, but he didn't have one gentle enough for me to drive with my buggy. They had little old spring buggies, you know. And this old mule was gentle—you could ride him, and he was my "buggy horse." His name was "Old Jack," and he died just before the 1915 storm. I cried like a baby.

Before we got electricity [1948], we used coal-oil lamps for light. The children did all their homework by lamplight, and the men used lanterns for floundering.

My daddy had a hunting camp, and the wealthy men from Galveston would come over to spend the weekend and shoot ducks and geese—all they could kill, because there wasn't any limit then. The camp was just one great big room, and my daddy did most of the

Cattleman Buddy Hughes, Kate Hughes's husband, with small son Harry riding in front. Most farmers on Bolivar owned cattle, and all the herds ran together. 1920s. (Courtesy Harry Hughes)

cooking for it. He was a good cook. There was one part of the room that was a kitchen, and then there were bunks all around.

I have two feather pillows that my mother-in-law gave us when we got married, and they were made out of duck feathers. Everybody had feather beds—there were so many ducks, you know. A big heavy one was used to lie on, and a lighter one for cover.

There were no doctors on Bolivar, but we had a midwife, Miss Alice Sosby, and whenever she went out to bring a baby into the world, she'd say, "Come on, Kate, and go with me." And I went with her and helped birth the babies. I was married and had my own children at the time.

After the 1915 storm we moved to Beaumont and lived two years, then we came back down to the peninsula. My father-in-law bought a house down there and we rented one till we built ours up by the school. I helped build it. My daddy was a carpenter and contractor and I used to help him with his blueprints and all. Yes, I put on a pair of pants and got up on the ladder and did all the hammerin' and the knockin' and puttin' up sidin' and everything.

My husband and I lived with an old couple and took care of them, and when they died, an embalmer came over on the ferry, and I helped him embalm the bodies. There was nobody else to do it. We had to draw all the blood out and put something else in there, then take it out in the back yard and dig a hole and bury it. There was a boy who blew the side of his head off, and there was no one to help with it, so they called "Aunt Kate." I helped fix up two boys who had committed suicide by shooting themselves and some other people who died.

There was an old cottage down near the lighthouse—there was no road to it, and an old man was livin' there. After he died they didn't find the body until later, when it was so deteriorated the health officers came from Galveston. They asked my daddy to help, and they found some money on the old man, but the body was so rotten that they washed all the money and hung it on the clothesline to dry. Then they burned the house down with the old man in it.

I used to be a substitute teacher at the school in Bolivar. I never did teach a subject. The kids didn't want me to teach the lessons—they wanted me to tell about the old times, about what Bolivar used to be and what they used to do, and whatever. I went along with it. One day I told the principal, "I don't know whether you're going to like it or not (we had a three-room school), but I didn't teach any of the lesson today." He said, "I heard you." He was in the next room, and he went on, "Well, they got more out of that than they would have from the lesson." It really did 'em good.

We always had a lot of fun. We would have "play parties," and we had a big old house with a porch all the way round it, and the front was one big room with a fireplace. The two Adkins girls lived upstairs. We had a "play party" at the house two or three times a week, and we'd play "Shoo-la-lay." A boy would get a partner to dance, and they'd make a line while everybody sang a song called "Shoo-la-lay," and they'd go up and down and swap partners.

We had all kinds of other games we'd play like "Drop the Hand-

Burning home near the lighthouse. The decomposed body of Lawn Gokey had been discovered there, and health authorities set the house afire when they could not locate any relatives. (Courtesy Kate Hughes)

kerchief." Everybody would blindfold himself and one would go around and drop the handkerchief behind somebody and say, "Ready," and then whoever had the handkerchief had to chase and capture the one who was "it" before he got back to his place. Of course the men dropped it behind the women and the women behind the men.

We went swimming a lot in Galveston, and the beach there was beautiful. You went to a bathhouse and rented a bathing suit for a quarter; they had ropes on posts in the water that you could hold onto. We wore stockings and tennis shoes and wool bathing hats with our suits.

I never danced a step in my life until I got married, and I had to learn or else be a wallflower. There were dances at people's houses and at the hotel at Caplen. When we had a dance at someone's house, the women would make a cake, and the men would furnish the coffee; and sometimes we'd have sandwiches. The first time I ate any hogshead cheese was at a dance.

The music was a fiddle and a guitar; some had accordions. We had one man, Jim Gallagher, who rigged up an outfit to play the fiddle, mouth harp, and pick the guitar all at the same time. My husband played the guitar and fiddle, all by ear. There was hardly anyone that didn't play music of some kind. We danced the waltz and the two-step, and when the one-step came out, we couldn't do it because it wasn't nice.

We used to have a barbecue every Fourth of July. The whole community would go together and have it. The men would kill the animals and barbecue them, and all the families went. In the afternoon they'd take what was left and go out to the beach for a beach party, and everyone would play baseball.

Eddy Carr and my husband used to trap a lot. They used to go up toward High Island back in the prairie where they had muskrats, and a bunch of the men would camp together, and they'd muskrat. They put traps out for 'em, and then they'd skin 'em. And when they skinned 'em they'd put the skins inside-out, all together, with the little open places for the head and feet, and the meat part would be on the outside. They'd put 'em on a stretcher thing and hang 'em around on the trees and let 'em dry. The fur was beautiful—you couldn't tell it from beaver on a coat. Oh, they used to trap 'em—there used to be so many around High Island and down at Caplen.

Every Sunday we'd go horseback ridin' down at Patton woods. Buddy's brother Frank Hughes told about the time they were there once and found a buzzard's nest. Frank was goin' to take the eggs home and hatch 'em. He said they got to cuttin' up and runnin' the horses on the way home, and he forgot the eggs till they started runnin' down the legs of his suit.

The first time I went horseback ridin' they said, "You can't go astraddle—you've got to ride sidesaddle." And Percy Harrington lived up there, and I like to fell off because I never had been on an animal before except that old mule, and if I did, he'd stop and let me back on. I said, "Buddy, I'm going to fall off this thing (I was sittin' sideways), so I just put my foot over on the other side, and of course it was uncomfortable, but I went home like that. Percy

Harrington said, "Next time you go and wear a divided skirt when you ride astride." We didn't wear pants, you know.

The men used to go brandin', and everybody's cattle ran together. We'd follow 'em—the ladies and girls would take dinner up to the branders in wagons 'cause we didn't have cars, and then we'd all spread it all out together, and all the men'd come eat dinner. And the women and kids, too. Brandin' was good for the kids, and after everybody ate we would get up on the fence and watch 'em. Sometimes we rode the calves for fun.

And the way they did in brandin', they didn't know which calf belonged to which cow. But you know if you put a bunch of cows together and a bunch of calves together, the calf will go to its mother. And that's how they knew who belonged to what. And the ones they couldn't find any mother to they called "dogies." And they'd brand them with a certain brand that they had for dogies.

When they'd get through with that place and brand, the next day they'd start there, get all the cattle and brand at another brandin' pen till they'd get the whole Bolivar Peninsula branded. And the ladies would follow, and every time they branded the ladies would take dinner to 'em. Oh, we had wonderful times.

All the cattle run together. One bull could be a father to your cow, my cow, or somebody else's cow. Father to their calves. Our house had a barbed-wire fence around it. We just had two rooms on our house, and there were two bulls that roamed the country—one was a Brahma and one was a black Angus. Everybody watched out for 'em 'cause together they were mean, but by theirselves they wasn't much. But we'd sit there at the window and watch them bulls fight at the corner of our house many a night. And they'd knock one another into our barbed-wire fence. It never did bother us, but I guess it'd scare us to death now.

I remember one time Westcott Kahla's grandpa, Barney Kahla, and some other men went together and bought a fine stallion to put on the prairie up there so the mares would have a chance of gettin' good horses. I never will forget Westcott at the branding. He was just a teenager. They had just got through eatin' lunch, and the men were sittin' around against the fence restin', you know, and Westcott come from around where they were brandin' the colts. He was just dyin' laughin', and we were sittin' up on the fence. He said to Barney, "Grandpa, you know what you got around there? You got six jackasses!" There wasn't a good animal in the bunch. Somebody had put a male jackass in there in the pasture, and all the mares had colts by him. The stallion they had bought didn't have a single good animal. Everybody just died laughin'.

16 / R. C. Bouse, Jr.

When I interviewed R. C. and his wife Oca (Shaw) in April 1987, they had been married sixty-four years and had spent their entire lives on the peninsula. The Bouse (rhymes with "goes") family is one of the most well known, having run the only general store and post office in Port Bolivar for many years. R. C. was born in 1903, and at the age of fourteen he took his first job for the federal government, building a gun battery at Fort Travis. R. C. did a lot of fishing in his time but said it was hard work, not a sport. In 1918 he played second base for the Port Bolivar baseball team and still enjoys watching major league games on TV.

My dad, R. C. Bouse, Sr., was born in 1875, and he knew everybody in the bay part of the country. He used to help make saddles over at Harmon's at Hankamer—one of the biggest saddle-makin' places around here. My dad was just a young fellow, startin' out to work, and they'd go out in the woods, and you've heard of a "saddle tree"? Part of that saddle is chopped out of a tree—the frame. The seats, the sides, and the front is made out of a tree. Old man Charlie Harmon was the originator of that.

    I had one of the last saddles and best saddles he ever made. I owned it. Barney Kane had that saddle made—I don't know what year, and he had on the side of the saddle, you know, the skirt, where it comes down, he had pockets made on them skirts. And saddles was sellin' for around forty-five and fifty dollars, and it cost him sixty-five dollars to have that saddle made, just like he wanted it. Well, he used it just a short while, and that's when the High Island oil boom started. He went to work in the oil field and left that saddle with Casey Sullivan, and I was up there at Boyt's ranch. For some reason or other I didn't have a saddle, and Casey said, "Hey, use Barney's saddle. You know, you could buy that saddle for forty-five dollars." And I bought it. That was around the early twenties.

I was born in Stowell and was two years old when the family moved to Caplen in 1905. My dad went broke rice farming, and his wife's people were living at Caplen, and they had been after him to open up a store. There wasn't no store between High Island and Bolivar. My mother's name was Laura Hughes. Grandpa Hughes' daddy, he was ninety-nine, and his wife was ninety-eight when they died. They homesteaded land in the 1830s. Daddy had the store at Caplen and got the post office put into the store—it was in a four-room house first, and then he moved the building back and put that concrete slab. Between 1908 and 1909 he built a big store, and the post office was right in the corner of that store. They had a concrete factory where Rollover Pass is now, and they built concrete blocks, and my dad made the building out of those blocks.

There was some guy at Morgan's Point that had a little gasoline launch. In those days they all had sailboats. They didn't know what an engine was. This guy would tow the sailboats with a load of vegetables up to Houston for four or five dollars, and if they caught the wind right they could sail back, but they couldn't very well sail against the wind with a load. They had to get a tow. But they could sail into Galveston. Sometimes they'd have to lay out two or three days till the wind picked up. That's the way my dad got groceries for his store over at Caplen. This country was so level at that time that my dad could look out the window at home and see down the bay. My grandpa owned a sailboat, and when Dad would see the sailboat comin' he'd know to meet him to get the groceries off the boat when he'd bring 'em from Galveston. That was back around in around 1907, '08, and '09.

Raymond C. Bouse, Sr., and wife Louise Hudnall Bouse in their carriage on Bolivar beach just before 1915 storm. No roads existed until 1930. (Courtesy Dixie Bouse Shaw)

I started school at Caplen. The schoolhouse had just one little room—it was the first school. The first teacher I remember was Mary Sandal.

I never will forget the day I quit school. It was the day that old Dr. Stephens started the school at Port Bolivar. We had moved to Bolivar after the 1915 storm and was livin' in the old place that had this big mulberry tree, and naturally nothin' didn't grow on the ground under that tree; we had cleaned the well out, and there was some clay mixed with that stuff we cleaned out of the well. I was ready to go to school, and my dad had a little car that he was going to take the kids to school in, and I come runnin' off of those steps and my feet slipped out from under me, and I went plum under that mulberry tree right plum on my back into that mud. I told my dad I said, "That's the end of it, 'cause I ain't goin' to school no more." I was fourteen, and that was the last of my school 'cause I didn't go no more.

Most of the original people in Port Bolivar left after the 1900 storm. A bunch of people came in from up the peninsula, near Patton and Caplen. There wasn't anything left up there.

Only the Gordon place was standing after the 1915 storm. I stayed at the Stephensons' house, and it went down in a hole, and after the storm you could step out from upstairs—it was that deep in the ground. Turned it completely around. And it taken four brickbats to level the beds. The house was leanin' so bad on that side, we had to put brickbats on one side of our bed so we could stay in it. Me and Ernest and Frank did that.

They moved the house completely. Old man Joe Stephenson got a contractor out of Galveston, and he brought some long, big sills, and they raised that house on the back and pushed them sills under it, and I don't know what they used to pull it with, but they moved the house back and filled that hole. It did that in the 1900 storm, and done it again in 1915. Later on the Boyts bought it. There's about five or six houses on Bolivar that's been here since 1900.

In the early 1900s cattle and farming was the main things. There was all cattle pasture along the peninsula, and they would take 'em out to the high land around Stowell in the summer and bring 'em back to the marsh grass in the fall. They'd go on horseback and spend a night or two on the road. Some never did take their cattle out.

The Cades had a fence from bay to gulf at Rollover, and their cattle were on that side. All the rest of the people's cattle ran together on this side. There wasn't any fences, and the cattle ran through people's yards—but there wasn't many houses either.

There wasn't any road here on the peninsula till 1930. When you went anywhere, you went on the beach. That was the only way to go. My dad had half interest in the contract to build this road from here [Port Bolivar] to High Island.

There used to be passenger boats run over here all the time; the main one was the *Silver King*. It had a deck, and they could haul about fifty, but there never was that many to haul. There was seats on each side, and you could sit downstairs or upstairs. Captain Fredericksen started it, and the ferry run him out of business, but he'd still run it when the ferry broke down.

All I did for years was hunt. We used to have a hunting camp up there at Caplen and take duck hunters from Galveston up there.

Bouse's Store at Port Bolivar with Texaco gas pump and the town's only telephone in 1930s. Mr. Bouse sold groceries and ran the post office there for many years. (Courtesy Odessa Mouton)

The hunters were mostly streetcar conductors that used to come over—they wanted to get out of town. We had that Cade land, and we leased it from Charlie Holt. We knew Charlie Holt real well. He was a surveyor here for years.

We trapped muskrats back in what they used to call Long Point marsh—that's back before they even thought about building the canal. At times there were a lot of muskrats, if the season was right. One of the best deals I ever got into—Frank ("Ank") Kahla and I caught twelve hundred dollars worth of rats in two weeks. That was back in 1927, and that was big money then. We got a dollar and a half apiece for the pelts.

Ben Bright was a local bootlegger—he made his own whiskey, and the rest of 'em just hauled it back and forth. I tried it once, and it was powerful. It was a poor grade. Most of the bootlegged stuff was unloaded on this beach, brought across and put in launches and taken different places—anywhere a boat could land; that included Texas City, Houston, Galveston, and everywhere else. That was in Prohibition, back in the early twenties. It was strictly against the law to even own whiskey.

At the concrete factory they built concrete slabs. That's what started the jetties. They put the slabs down to make the jetty, because the cross tide filled the channel and ships couldn't get in and out. That was back around the time that fort was built—that big fort was built in the early 1900s. It was a small gun batt'ry at the time—they had two eight-inch guns and two three-inch. When the war started in 1914, then they built them big places. I worked there when I was fourteen years old. I helped build them batt'ries—they had twelve-inch guns—two of them big guns that come up and shoot and go back down. I worked there, and men were scarce then, and I went out there with some mules and would dig out where they was gonna pour concrete. They'd drive concrete pilin', then they'd have to clean between them pilin's to make a concrete slab. That slab was about three feet thick. That seawall outfit was built all at the same time. The dredge boats filled that in, and the fort was built up on top of that. It's supposed to be seventeen feet above sea level.

When we worked on the gun batt'ry, after they put in the concrete pilin', we went in there with mules and a slip (a scoop), and we'd dig that dirt out where them pilin's would stick up, and they'd run iron rods all through there and pour the concrete. They had about a hundred-foot tower, and they'd mix that cement at the ground, and it'd go to the top, and they had a dump and chute thing, and they'd run them chutes all round to where they wanted to pour it. After we got all of that put down, then they wanted the fort covered up with dirt, and we did it up with mules and slip. We hauled the dirt from out of them sand hills.

They didn't have many soldiers out there then—just a few lookin' after the small guns.

After that storm in 1919 a boat out of Freeport come ashore up at Crystal Beach, where Patton used to be. My dad went to the coast guard, and they told him he could salvage it, and if nobody didn't pay the cost or claim it, they'd give him clearance papers on it, and they did. Him and Mr. Hudnall patched a hole in it, and my dad brought it down here, and he traded that boat for a house. It was a strong house. It had iron rods all the way through it and was bolted so it wouldn't go to pieces in a storm, and that's the one a tornado picked up in Hurricane Carla, and there wasn't nothin' but splinters left.

17 / Agnes Blume Stephenson

The day I went to the Stephensons' house I wanted to see both Agnes and her husband Ernest, who was at that time the oldest person born and raised on Bolivar Peninsula. They both had had similar experiences, living so long together, and it was difficult to decide whose story to write. Ernest helped Agnes recall her family's harrowing days in the 1900 storm, when the Blumes ended up at the Stephensons' house, and I chose her episode to tell about.

Agnes was born in 1904. Her parents, the Blumes, came to Port Bolivar in 1908 and built a house with lumber they brought in a boat from Turtle Bayou. "We didn't have a care in the world when we were children," she says. "Daddy used to make us help him in the fields, but we didn't do much. He just wanted to get us out from under Mother's feet."

My great-great grandparents were the Samuel Parrs. On my daddy's side they were the Blumes from Germany. Samuel Parr had a land grant, and he must have been a surveyor, because a lot of this land still has his name as a surveyor. My great Grandpa Parr was one of the men on the ship that brought lumber back and forth from New Orleans. That was before 1900. They carried lumber and iron ore, I believe. My husband Ernest's daddy had a boat that carried produce to Galveston. It was called the *Columbia*. Lots of people had boats then.

My grandfather's people on my father's side, the Blumes, landed in Galveston, and the yellow fever struck there about that time, and the parents died leaving three children. They had started to go to a German settlement near Chocolate Bayou and didn't get there. My mother was a Parr, my father a Blume. They lived on Bolivar on some land that was left to my grandmother, named Statham, from the Parr family. They were early settlers down here.

We kids didn't have toys; that was unknown. We played with conch shells, and we'd get the ones with long tails, and those were our cows, and the round conchs were bulls. We used corn cobs for horses. Sometimes we'd hitch up a horned toad to a matchbox and get a straw and punch him along to make him go. Sometimes us kids would go down to the bay shore, and there were little fiddler crabs, and we'd build a fence and herd them up—that was our cattle.

We'd go out to the beach, and our mother didn't know where we were, and we'd strip all our clothes off except our underdrawers and go out in the water as far as we could go and jump the big waves over our heads.

Half the time we didn't have any shoes, and when it froze, we'd get an old pair of Daddy's and go slide on the ice in the ponds. We were playing one time, and we had a tub with a rope tied to it, and we'd get in the tub and push each other out as far as it would go, then pull it back in. My older brother was playing with us, and he got in that tub, and he was a little heavier than we were, and we pushed him out there, and the tub broke through the ice. Down he went. He was so mad at us. We ran away. We had all kinds of fun doing things like that.

We would go out in the corn patch when our daddy wasn't watching, and you know how corn grows that silk? We'd find one with that pretty silk, and that would be our lady doll, with pretty hair. We'd fix the hair all up in knots and do all kinds of things with that silk. The boys used to smoke the cornsilk, too. Our daddy didn't like for us to pick too many ears because that was his corn crop.

We raised cotton, sweet potatoes, corn, cabbage, and watermelons. Most of it went by train to Beaumont. They'd bring a boxcar, and the farmers would all load the car. All the children helped their parents with the farming.

We used to take a cast net and go to the bay shore and catch a tub full of shrimp, bring them home and boil them. We never had any ice, but we ate those shrimp, and they never did kill us. There was a big oyster bed just back of Parr's Grove, and we'd go out in a boat and catch oysters by the basket. Mother would make crab stew on the wood stove, and we'd get the fire wood on the beach.

When the 1915 storm came, my father first moved us all out of our home to an old vacant house; when we got there my daddy lit a lantern and put it on the table. We all gathered there with our suitcases of clothes. It was back by the canal and my daddy thought it would be safe. We went there on Monday during the day. The water then started to come up, and something bumped against the door. My daddy said, "That's somebody trying to get in." He looked out, and there was a pig swimming along. Daddy said, "We've got to get out of here."

Then Daddy started carrying us, one at a time, back to the trees. Everybody used to get into the trees when storms came. I remember going back there; the rain was so hard it cut you. My sister-in-law had a little girl about two years old, and she was expecting another one. Daddy carried them out and the rest of us—my mother, my sister (about seven), my brother who was eight or nine, and my younger sister. He put us all in one tree, and I was among the last to be carried out. I was eleven years old then.

Daddy had left my brother and a colored man in the house, and he went back and got them, and when he came back he missed the tree we were in and took them to another one. There were nine of us holding onto one tree. My mother sat in the lower part, in the water, because she said it was warmer. It was blowing and raining horribly. As soon as we had all gotten there, a big wave came and knocked the house down. We could see the kerosene lamp being swept off the table, and the whole house piled up by the cedar row. The miracle of it is that all the debris that came through those trees missed the ones we were in and landed further back, and it really was piled up in there.

For two nights we stayed in that tree. I don't remember ever getting hungry, but I remember getting sleepy, and I tried to crawl out of the tree, and they woke me up, so I crawled back again because I didn't want to get in that water.

Every one of us escaped. We got out of there, and the water was still pretty high, but my daddy said, "You all hold onto me," and we formed a chain and started to walk. We went to where our home had been. It was still there, but it was down in a hole and all washed out with nothing inside, no clothes or anything, and all we had left was the clothes we were wearing. The kitchen part was separate, and it was still standing there, and our stove was in it, and a shelf in the corner still had coffee and dry goods. The stove didn't have any stove pipe, but we found some wood scraps, and there were dry matches on the shelf, and Daddy lit a fire. We found a pot on the shelf and got some water out of the rainwater holders, and we made black coffee and drank that. My mother had canned plums without sugar and had put them on the rafters. They were still there, and we opened them. To me, it tasted like candy. That's all we had, the black coffee and sour plums.

We were all tired out and didn't have anyplace to sleep. There was no furniture left in the house except the sewing machine, and the pedal was gone. My mother crawled up on that thing and went to sleep.

Ernest and his daddy came looking for us, and we went up to their house. Their house was down in a hole, but they still had a lot of supplies, so we stayed there. They had dry clothing and food they had carried upstairs. There was plenty of food, and my sister was old enough to cook, so she did the cooking. She made biscuits and rice, and it tasted *so* good.

18 / Dixie Bouse Shaw

162 / THE PEOPLE

Dixie was born at her grandfather's house in Galveston on June 17, 1917. Her mother decided to leave Bolivar to have the baby because there were no doctors on the peninsula. She spent her life on Bolivar and remembers how everyone used to depend on each other. "The closeness of the people in the community was a special thing," she says. Dixie was the only student in her tenth-grade class and sometimes double-dated with her teacher, who was eighteen.

I looked forward to interviewing Dixie because she was known as one of the best historians of the area. She lived up to all my expectations—not only did she remember many details, which are treasures, but her enthusiasm added a warm touch to her narrations.

After the 1915 storm we were washed out at Caplen and my father, R. C. Bouse, Sr., went into Beaumont and rented a place on the outskirts of town, and he was contemplating buying another grocery business there, but the older kids persuaded him to come back to Bolivar. My dad had been postmaster at Caplen, and when he bought the old Crockett store in Port Bolivar he automatically became postmaster again, because the store had a fourth-class post office, and Mrs. Crockett said she was GONE and to do what they wanted with the post office. My dad went out either on horseback or in the old Model T, when it would run, twice a day to get mail and put it on the train. They paid him forty dollars every three months for the job.

The post office was in one corner of the store, and at night we'd close up and go back in the dining room to read the paper and set around the table and get lessons, and somebody'd come by and say, "I didn't get my mail today—would you open up?" Somebody, usually one of us kids, had to go open the door and let 'em see if they had any mail. Or they forgot their chewin' tobacco, and we had to go let them in the store. You know, that used to aggravate me to death.
   We played with horned toads, and we saw our parents dipping the cattle because the ticks were so bad, so we'd dig a little vat and put water in it and make the horned toads go through the dipping vat.
   The beach was always a big part of our lives; we spent at least one afternoon a week there. It was our relaxation. We'd all swim, come in and build a big bonfire, then sit around and roast wieners and marshmallows and just talk.
   There would be times that fish were plentiful, and my dad always had a little seine. We'd go out to the beach on holidays with Crisco and a skillet and some cornmeal and a loaf of bread. They'd pull that seine and get fish and crabs to eat. During the wintertime we'd go up on the bay around Caplen with our cooking supplies, build a fire, and the men would get oysters out of the edge of the bay, and we'd fry oysters.
   Once in a while we'd have home dances. They would usually clear out somebody's living room. Everybody took the family; the little kids danced as well as the adults, and the babies were put in the bedroom. Vera Miller's dad and my father-in-law played the fiddle, and Harry Hughes picked the guitar. I remember Aunt Lil and Uncle Frank Kahla's house—it was an old-fashioned one that the kitchen and dining room were built separate from the main house and a walkway between them. I can remember them dancing at Miss Minnie Kahla's big old two-story house, in the living room. They used to dance at a dance hall up over a store that Vernon Kahla ran, and there was a dance pavilion out near the bay.

Unidentified couple frying fish on the beach, a favorite pastime. Fish, crabs, and oysters were plentiful and easy to catch. (Courtesy Dixie Bouse Shaw)

A lot of people played the accordion, because you could buy one and learn to play it. My dad's first wife, Laura Hughes, played one and everyone was fascinated because they didn't get a chance to hear music very often. To be able to play was a real treat to people. No one had a drum because they were too expensive.

We'd play ball sometimes out in front of the house after all the chores were finished—after the cows were milked, after the evening meal was over and all the dishes were washed and everything done.

The cattle would bed down on the beach at night, and just about dark we kids would take a big gunny sack and tie a string on it. We'd put the gunny sack on the other side of the road, and we'd set on the porch of the store. My dad would get a bucket, put green grass and a sack on some live coals, because the smoke would keep the mosquitoes away from us. We'd set there, and as the cows come down the road, we'd let a cow get her front feet over this string, and we'd jerk the string, and the sack would come up underneath the old cow and she'd jump straight up in the air and run. The ones that would come behind, they'd stop out on the road for a while 'cause they didn't know what happened, and that gave us a chance to put the sack back.

Because there were no electric pumps to pump water, everybody had their own well, and you drew your water. You bathed in a number three washtub every Saturday whether you needed it or not.

Even at school they just had a pump, and each fellow had their own little metal collapsible cup, or was supposed to have. If the teacher wasn't lookin', you'd put your hand over the mouth of the pump and drink out of your hand.

Everybody ordered what they needed by mail from the Sears and Roebuck catalog. The mail came by the train, and people ordered linens for the house, curtains, and all. The train was very important in our lives. At one time there wasn't even a highway through here. We had to drive on the beach, and if the tide was high, you just had to stay home or ride the train.

Grandfather Bouse lived at Fannett, which is a heavily wooded area, and he always cut our Christmas tree and sent it down to us on the train. My dad would give the baggage men seafood so he could send fish and notes to Grandpa, and the baggage men would throw them off at Grandpa's place, because he lived about five miles out of Fannett, where the depot was. The train went right by the edge of his property, so my dad and grandpa would send things to one another and just use the train as a ferry service.

The baggage men accommodated people along the way, and sometimes people left cookies on the fenceposts for them. There was very few communities right on the railroad track, just scattered houses.

People would get on the boat and go into Galveston to buy things like furniture or shoes. Everybody quilted their own quilts and made their own clothes, and all the material was ordered through the catalogs—Montgomery Ward's and Sears. They would come to the post office and make out a money order to pay for their stuff; they didn't have checks—there was no bank. They ordered seed to plant and practically everything.

There wasn't any ice here until after the ferry started in 1930. Now my dad used to get ice across on Captain Fredericksen's boat,

Vera Miller, *Silver King* captain Alfred Fredericksen, and his daughter-in-law Ora Shaw Fredericksen. The *Silver King* provided Bolivar people transportation to Galveston before the ferry started in 1930. (Courtesy Ora Shaw Fredericksen)

the *Silver King*, to keep meat and butter and cheese in his ice box in the grocery store.

People had cabinets with screens on their porches, and these were really for milk. You'd milk the cow in the afternoon and churn your butter and buttermilk, and at night the night air would keep the milk from spoiling. If it did spoil, you let it clabber, because it wouldn't rot like it does now, and you had a mold, and you'd pour that clabber into it, and there were tiny holes in the sides, and the whey drained off, and the solid part made cottage cheese. You could skim the cream off the fresh milk and put it on the cottage cheese with sugar. We had regular cream cheese molds, but if you didn't have a mold, you could put it in a cloth sugar bag and hang it on the clothesline. To have a cow in the family was very important. You were almost rich if you had a cow.

Captain Clarence Fredericksen, son of Alfred Fredericksen. The *Silver King* made one trip in the morning to Galveston and came back in the afternoon. (Courtesy Ora Shaw Fredericksen)

It wasn't until ever so long that milk was delivered here because everybody had their cow. When they finally started deliverin' milk, nobody milked cows anymore. Delivery started after electricity came, in 1948, because there was a way to store it.

There was no ice cream except on Saturdays, when my dad would order five gallons in a big container packed with ice, and cones; they would send it over on the *Silver King*. Some of us kids would sit out out on the front porch of the store and sell ice cream cones. But mostly we ate it. With our big family, we rarely broke even on five gallons of ice cream 'cause we ate most of it. But we did give the other kids a chance to get a little.

My dad was always the one people called in emergencies. He knew how to take care of anything, and none of us kids went to a doctor till we were way up in age. He had a little penknife that he kept sharp as a razor, and he performed more surgery with that penknife than a lot of doctors.

When people died, they put nickels over their eyes to keep them shut. When Grandma died, the women took care of her. When Grandpa Kahla died, some of the men bathed him and dressed him in his suit, put coins on his eyes, and had him laid out on boards between two chairs until the coffin was brought from Galveston.

The *Silver King* made two trips a day, and after the five o'clock trip, there was no way of getting out of here at night. In later years when some had shrimp boats, they took people in emergencies to Galveston. There were no phones except one at the fort and the lighthouse, and they were for emergencies only.

There was a man named Bud Lecroy who owed my dad some money for groceries, and he couldn't pay, so he gave my dad a cow for the grocery bill. When my dad sold the cow he got more money for it than the bill, so he gave the difference back to Bud.

People were important to my dad, and many times we had strangers staying at our house because they had nowhere to go. One night a man and his wife were on their way to Galveston from

Port Arthur, and they knocked on our side door and asked for a place to stay. My dad put them upstairs with all of us, and the next morning after they ate breakfast the man gave my brother Jim a card as they left. When we looked at it we realized the guest was a famous singer from New York.

19 / Vera Shaw Miller

Vera was born on Bolivar Peninsula in 1899 and has twin sisters, Oca and Ora Shaw. Oca is married to R. C. Bouse, Jr., and Ora's husband was Clarence Fredericksen, captain of the Silver King. *The Shaw family lived at Caplen, and the children had to walk two miles to school. Mrs. Shaw was a strict mother. "She didn't let us get too far and kept both eyes on us," Vera says. "Mama made us study at home, and all we had was oil lamps to see by." Vera has four children and doesn't remember how many grandchildren.*

When I went to see Vera in her Port Bolivar home the first thing I noticed was her beautiful face. She smiled often, enjoying her thoughts of the many years she spent on the peninsula.

I was born here on Bolivar, at Patton, in April, just before the 1900 storm in September. I was just a little baby in that storm. My father was from Galveston and my mother from Cedar Bayou. Their house at Patton was wiped clear off the face of the map. We had gone to my grandfather Tucker Shaw's two-story house during the storm. It was in back of the sand hills at Patton. Everyone in the house survived, and I don't know how many people were there—some of the neighbors came because they had small houses, and they figured my grandfather's would be the safest place, and in fact, it was, too, because the little houses were all washed away. We lost everything we had. There was one little house on the edge of the woods that didn't get washed away, and my father moved us there.

Later, my mother and daddy had a railroad car filled with lumber to build a new home and had it on the siding, and when the 1915 storm came we lost the house we had and the car with all the lumber in it.

Just before the 1915 storm, my parents took all of us on the train to High Island and stayed until the storm was over. We stayed at Barrow's, and they had the house packed full. We stood up all night because there were so many people in the house—they didn't have room to sit down; they had one bed there, and they put the babies on the bed. Things to eat wasn't very plentiful, because the people who lived there didn't have food enough to serve everybody very much.

After the 1915 storm my father built a house again. My father, you couldn't have kept him off the peninsula—he had the Bolivar sand in his shoes, and he had to come back. He wouldn't live anywhere else but Bolivar. The Kahlas, the Bouses, and a lot of them just kept comin' back. I don't know why they did 'cause there wasn't anything to come back to. Just a house that had been washed around in a storm, and they had to clean it up and fix it up as best they could till they could build better. They must have just loved Bolivar.

My dad was a farmer, and farmin' was pretty good here. When we were small children we worked in the fields and helped raise watermelons. All the kids helped their parents. We didn't have very long schools—three months, I believe it was. There wasn't that many children—I think we had nine pupils the first year the school started—us, the Stephensons, and another family. We had three *long* months of school. The first year I went to school we had a little house near the beach; we walked about two miles to the school and took our lunch in a paper bag. The parents furnished the chairs and tables, and I remember I had a little bitty table. We didn't have regular school furniture; it all came from the people's houses.

Vera Miller's house after the 1943 hurricane. Paulene Bouse and Barbara Brister survived this storm in their father Andrew Johnson's house. (Courtesy Odessa Mouton)

The children played dolls and paperdolls that we cut out of the Sears and Roebuck catalogs. For Easter my mother used blueing to decorate our Easter eggs with stripes and dots. We was just tickled to death when Easter come.

We played on the beach a lot, and different kind of shells was cows and horses and pigs. We had just as much fun as if they was real.

I remember when they used to ride those big herds of cattle up to the brandin' pens, and they'd come down the reed brake, and they would go MOOOO and MAAAH. They'd make more noise. Remember when the mosquitoes was so thick—those old cows would come up and march around the house goin' MOOO and MAAAH. They was fightin' the mosquitoes.

Our house was back from the sand hills, and we had a bridge across the reed brake to get to the beach. Our first school wasn't until about 1909, and before that my mother taught us at home. She taught us to read and write, and we minded her or else. I just sometimes wonder how we came through it all, living way out there in the country. Mama was a very determined woman.

My mother made us bathe every day. We got scrubbed down every night before we went to bed, and we had to wash our hair, or you couldn't live at Mama's.

We washed our clothes on a rubboard 'cause there was no electricity and we used a big tub in the back yard and hung the clothes out on the line.

We used to have to drive about seven or eight miles to the post office when it was up there at Caplen, and Papa would drive or ride horseback up there to get the mail. He might not go but once a month 'cause he was a farmer and was real busy. I'm tellin' you, livin' here on Bolivar was a chore.

20 / Ernest Simpton

At seventy-seven, Ernest let a bronc get the best of him. His half-wild quarterhorse threw him, breaking his pelvis, so he vowed not to get on that one again. After the accident his son Jerry wrote: "When a little girl in Bolivar heard that Papa had been thrown from a horse and was in the hospital, she asked if it was a real Cowboy that had been hurt. Yes, he was a real Cowboy. He gathered cows when the range was open, ran down wild horses on the prairie, swam cattle across the Intracoastal . . . and owned his own herd for 50 years. . . . He was a thoroughly honest man who believed in helping anyone that asked for it. His word was good, and he had the respect of men that lived by their word. . . . Papa earned the best compliment a man can receive. He was a good man, and yes, he was a real cowboy."[1]

My grandma she was French. She come from France on one side, and her husband from Germany on the other side. On my dad's side my grandma come from Scotland. She come over in a sailboat when she was sixteen years old with some people called Dorsetts, and it took 'em three and a half months to get over here. They come on a sailin' schooner and landed at Galveston, so they went down on the wharf and they cut a watermelon, and she got a spoon or whatever they had then—I think it was a spoon—and she took all the red out and was throwin' it away. They said, "No, you don't do that—that's what you eat!" And she said, "I don't eat the intestines of anything!" She never did go back. She come over about 1886 or somethin' like that.

Grandpa C.W. Kahla come here from Germany when he was fourteen years old. The way he got here, his dad played music, and he said in Germany they didn't call 'em "beer joints," they called 'em "cabarets." He was twelve years old and he played a fiddle, and he said he'd go to sleep, and his dad would reach over and hit him over the head with his bow. He said they was playin' on a ship, and they shanghaied 'em. The ship untied and sailed out and when they come on deck they was on the high seas, headin' for Galveston. When they got to Galveston, Grandpa jumped ship and hid out, and his dad went back to Germany. He stayed on the waterfront—they called 'em "wharf rats" then. He probably worked for somebody's daddy. Then he finally got over here to Bolivar and got him a boat and started runnin' freight back and forth. He'd buy groceries for everybody and charge 'em a little fee for bringin' 'em back. Our family has been here about two hundred and twenty-five years.[2]

My mother was a Kahla. She was raised right over here in this old two-story house. Pike Kahla's daddy and my mother were brother and sister. Me and my brother own that old two-story house that Grandpa Kahla built in 1886, and one day a lady come here, and she said, "You ought to buy insurance on that house." I said, "Yeah, I know insurance is good when you have trouble, but suppose we had been payin' insurance on that house since it was built in 1886. How much insurance would we have paid y'all, and that house went through the 1887 storm, and it went through the 1929 and the 1942, and about seven or eight major storms—the most damage it ever had was the front door blew off." They built 'em in those days.

Grandma Kahla said when she come here, there was nothin' but mesquite trees. She come from Louisiana to Smith Point in a wagon with a pair of oxen. There was some Indians at Caplen and some Mexicans around Bolivar. She said a little Mexican boy was

Ernest Simpton (left) and his father, Leslie, in front of old Kahla home, circa 1955. (Courtesy Elgie Simpton)

born and the mother died, and her mama took this little Mexican boy and raised him.

Once when there was a dance somewhere, the boy wanted to use the horse and wagon—he was sixteen or seventeen then—to go to the dance. But her daddy wouldn't let him go because they had to work the horses in the field next day. One night later on her mama and daddy got in the wagon to go to a dance, and this boy was in the bushes, and he jumped out and knifed her daddy. He killed his foster grandpa who helped raise him.

Grandpa owned a freight boat that went from Anahuac to Smith Point to Galveston to sell vegetables and get groceries, and I imagine he met Grandma on one of those boats. They got married in Port Bolivar, and Grandpa built this house—went to Louisiana, bought the lumber, put it on a schooner, sailed the schooner over here, unloaded the lumber, hauled it up there and cut out every piece of lumber on the ground before he built the house. It's made out of long-leaf yellow pine, and the sills it sets on are twelve-by-twelve sills. It ain't like they make 'em now, two by six, or four by four or somethin'.

Grandpa Kahla lost everything he had three or four times in the storms, but he ended up with thirteen hundred acres of ground, three hundred head of cattle, and fifty thousand dollars in the bank. Carried his money in a BB sack. They used to load their shotgun shells, and they bought the BBs and black powder. The BBs came in a little sack about three inches long, and Grandpa put his money in it, rolled it up, and stuck it in his front pocket.

In the storm of 1915 I was three and a half years old, and we lived at Caplen. Our house was brand new—about a year old. It had a kitchen and a little dining room and a hallway and a bedroom over here and a bedroom over here. It didn't have no front room, you know. People et and talked in the dinin' room, I guess, mostly. Grandpa Kahla built it, and Marrs McLean he come by here and said to my mother, "You want to sell your house? I'll buy it." I think he told her he'd give seven or eight thousand dollars for it—and that was a lot. You could build a house for about two thousand dollars. She said, "No, we don't want to sell it," and it wasn't three or four months until the storm come, and we never did go back there. We went to Port Bolivar.

Grandma Kahla lived in Port Bolivar, and I don't know how many babies she delivered. When I got a little bigger my mother started deliverin' babies. They called me "Buddy" when I was little. They used to wake me up and say, "Buddy, get up!" I'd say, "Where are we goin', Mama?" "We're goin' to deliver a baby." And we'd take off—dark, rainin'. I'll never forget one night she woke me up, and we took off and went over to little John Kahla's. My job was goin' in and puttin' the water on the stove, you know. It was a wood stove, and you open the door and stick wood in it, find you an old big pot, put the water in there, and after a while you'd hear a big "WHAAAANH!" Mama'd come in there and the first thing she'd do was tie its navel cord, then take an old towel and put around it after she bathed it. I don't know of her ever losin' one.

I used to raise watermelons. The family raised watermelons ever since I can remember. My dad raised 'em, and I've been raisin' 'em ever since I was big enough. So I went to sell some melons over here at Seabrook. I had some nice big melons, and this guy had some little old—we call 'em "chunks"—in his store, and I said, "You want to buy some good melons?" And he starts out to tell me all about a watermelon. I said, "You could tell me all about that store, but you can't tell me nothin' about a watermelon." I said, "We've been raisin' 'em for two hundred and twenty-five years, and I've been growin' em ever since I was big enough to get in the field." My dad gave me a pair of horses and told me to go out there and plow the ground, and I wasn't quite eight years old, and I plowed the ground. We could plow about an acre a day with a pair of horses. Now you can cut up twenty acres a day with a tractor.

We kids would go up to Caplen on a horse. The only way you could get up there in them days was to get in a wagon or ride a horse—didn't have no cars or nothin'. There was a road that went past the graveyard, and where little Andrew Johnson lives, on this side, the railroad had a cattle crossing, and you crossed over the railroad, then you went up to Patton to about the old Blalock place, then you hit the beach, and that's where you went to High Island. After you got to Patton there wasn't no more roads—you went on the beach. If there was an east wind blowin', the tide would get high and you'd ride up on the sand hills and cut back—sometimes you made it.

There was a hotel at High Island they called the "Cade Hotel [Sea View Hotel]," and they had a little railroad track that went down to the beach. The railroad train would go by there in the mornin' and come back in the evenin', and on the weekends people would ride down on the train and stay at the hotel. There was a little ole mule hooked up to a wagon, and they had boards for a track, and he'd take off down to the beach, unload, then come back to get some more. They'd walk up and down the beach. That's all you could do, I guess.

We went to a dance in that old hotel one night. I was about seventeen, and we danced till about two o'clock—then we all started home. COLD! Man, it was cold. We dressed up then—you wore a suit and tie and you looked decent. And we started down the beach. This truck had a magneto on it—and a magneto has got fields on it, and the flywheel turns and picks up the current that makes your lights, see. You get lights off this mag. No batt'ry. You crank it to start it, and it had three pedals on it: your clutch, your reverse, and your brake—and you could really haul. You want to go ahead, you push this; you want to back up, you push this, and man you could go WHOOP WHOOP.

And this thing, when we hit this little old shell bank, the guy drivin' pushed on the pedal and pulled the throttle and burned all the light bulbs out. It was about a quarter to four, and COLD! There was a bunch of us back there, and we just laid on one another in that old wooden truck bed and tried to stay warm. We made it about half way, and there was somebody on the beach with a big fire. (There used to be logs all along there.) And that's where we stayed till daylight, then we come on home. Mama said, "Where in the world have you been?" She was worried about us.

We used to go to dances down here—right across that little bayou. Daddy and Mama could really dance. They used to do the waltz a lot—the old-time waltz where you go one-two-three, and you turn around one-two-three, and you turn around. And when they would play the waltz there would be fifty couples on the floor, and everybody was goin' the same way and everybody was doin' the same thing. Same way with the schottische—you'd go one-two-three-kick, and spin around, and you'd go one-two-three-kick, and spin around. Everybody schottisched the same way. Then for the square dance, they'd call it slow. And you can't be drunk and square dance.

The same way with rodeoin'. I rodeoed for years, and you can't drink whiskey and rodeo. You drink your whiskey after you rodeo. I've seen more people hurt tryin' to ride bulls, ropin' calves half drunk, see.

They used to have dances in people's houses, and they danced till daylight. In those days, nobody worked on Sundays. On Saturday they'd say, "We better get cleaned up for the dance tonight." The musicians would pass the hat after they played—just enough to buy strings and stuff. They played the fiddle and guitar, and my dad would knock out time with the spoons on his knees. A lot of 'em played the mouth harp.

One night they was all dancin' at the Joe Altmans' place, and the Harringtons and the Paytons got in a big fight; the Harringtons was all little men and the Paytons was all big men. They was dancin' upstairs, and they had to come down the stairway to get out, and one of these Paytons was standin' down at the bottom, and he'd hit the Harringtons and knock 'em plum out the door. Papa had one of the Harringtons workin' for him and had borrowed Papa's coat to wear to the dance (everybody wore a coat to the dances), and they didn't cut him, but they cut the coat and ripped it plum down, and it had two tails instead of one. But finally one of the Harringtons got to one of the Paytons and knifed him and laid him out, and that stopped the fight.

Uncle Buddy Hughes was scared of the dark, so he went to a dance one night ridin' a horse. Comin' back, just before daylight, somebody knowed he was comin' back, so they got ahead of him and hid in the bushes. When he come along on his horse, they jumped out and fired their guns in the air—he took off and ran that horse FAST as he would go and run him right up to the kitchen steps. The door was open and he dove off and just slid into that kitchen. His mama said, "My Lord, what's the matter?" He said, "Somebody was shootin' at me!" It was just a big joke, you see.

Then one night there was a bunch stayin' up at our old home, after we had left there, and they were goin' to hunt. They heard somethin' hollerin'—like a woman screamin'. Uncle Buddy was there, and he didn't know what it was and got scared. Turned out it was a panther back at Long Point somewhere, and it was goin' EAAAAEH.

Then another time they were stayin' up there and in the yard was a jug with the stopper out of it, and the wind was blowin' so hard that the jug was makin' a WOOO WOOO sound, and Uncle Buddy got scared again. They finally went out in the yard and discovered what it was.

You talk about the jug—they used to play it, too. A fellow would blow in it BLUMP-BLUMP-BLUMP, and make the down-beat with it. Just an old gallon brown jug, you know. I think whiskey come in it. They had whiskey in them days. If you know how to drink out of a jug, you turn that jug right up and drink out of it. I've seen people in Georgia do that a good deal. They're noted for that.

Grandpa Kahla was in partners with old man Davison, who had a feed store in Galveston, and they had cattle together here on Bolivar. Grandpa never touched no kind of liquor—he didn't believe in it. So they started brandin', and each fellow would brand a couple of hundred calves apiece, and about halfway through the brandin', Mr. Davison brought out a keg of beer, and they all started drinkin' that beer, and they all got about half drunk and messed up all the brands on the calves. Got the wrong calves with the wrong mamas, and Grandpa Kahla said, "No more of this." Mr. Davison said, "Oh, I'm sorry. This will never happen again."

So about a year later at the next brandin', in August, when it was hot, about halfway through, Mr. Davison come out with a keg of beer. They started messin' up, and Grandpa Kahla shouted, "Hey, stop everything!" So they stopped the brandin', and Grandpa said, "We are goin' to dissolve this partnership right here." And he took his cattle, and Mr. Davison took his cattle, and that was the end of the partnership.

They started fencin' here in about 1932, or whenever the ferry started runnin'. When they built the shell road beginnin' in 1928, the county would put up fencin' if the landowner gave the land.

The reason I know is I bought a blue 1929 Ford Roadster, with a rumble seat. Drive-out price was six hundred and eighteen dollars, and I didn't have no way to get it over here, so a fellow had a shrimp boat, and we went to Galveston, took some boards, and we run it down on the deck and I brought it across. About a year later they put the ferries in.

I courted my wife in that Ford. She lived down in Frenchtown, and you might get there and you might not without gettin' stuck. My uncle Wescott Kahla always dressed up in a blue serge suit with a tie on. And every time I'd get stuck, instead of gettin' on the side of the car, he'd go around and get behind the back wheel, and I would just throw mud all over him. Then we'd go to their house and get a damp rag to wipe the mud off.

You could get about twenty-five miles to a gallon of gas, and it would run seventy-six miles an hour, a four-cylinder Model A. It had metal lights that never rusted—you just wiped them off with some kerosene. Lube was two bits a quart, and the station had it in these little old pumps you pump. One would be fifteen cents, the other twenty-five cents, and all the poor people would buy the fifteen-cent lube and the big shots would buy the two bit, and it all come out of the same barrel. And one time gas was six cents a gallon.

The shrimpin' business got started here when a fellow from Biloxi named McKellum opened up the shrimp factory. Back before the nineteen hundreds, they used to build barges in Port Bolivar and shipped 'em to Cuba. I guess Cuba and somebody else was fightin'. When all this died down, they left these big long sheds—three of 'em—and they must have been a thousand feet long. This man come from Biloxi and opened up the shrimp cannin' factory, and times was rough, so a lot of people from Louisiana come down here. They called it "Frenchtown." The girls would go there and peel shrimp. They made up to about twelve dollars a day—about twenty cents a bucket.

They would take the peeled shrimp, put 'em in little cans and steam 'em—had a big old boiler out there—then when whoever ordered a carload of shrimp, they would send their own labels. The shrimp were all the same, but the labels were different. All this was in about 1928. And shrimp was two and a half cents a pound off the shrimp boat.

In 1929 everybody went broke—a lot of the Kahlas went to Winnie to farm rice, and they all give up and come back here later.

Uncle Frank owed something like fifty thousand dollars, and that was a lot of money. So he bought a boat to run whiskey in from the big schooners—they'd take little boats, run out to the big boat and take the whiskey to Galveston—Johnny Jack, Joe Varnell, and them people. It come in towsacks, and I believe there was four or eight quarts in a towsack. Well, it got so hot on 'em they throwed it overboard, and when you'd get a strong east wind, it'd wash ashore. So every time it'd blow a strong east wind we'd get in the truck or somethin' and we'd go up there and find us some whiskey, you know, on the beach.

Then they started haulin' at night. A schooner would lay out there and the signals they had was flashlights. You could take a flashlight and hold it up to a quart jar, and it would magnify it, and they used that to make the signals.

They used the same thing to operate the ferry boats—they didn't have no phones, and when a car would come, the ferry would be on the other side, and they had a spot where you walked out on the dock. You'd flash your flashlight with the quart jar so many flashes, and he would answer over there, and they would send the ferry over. It was two and a half miles across the channel.

The cars used to drive up on the fort seawall, and they had a ramp that ran out to the ferry. It used to cost two bits a car to go to Galveston—it was private owned.

When Grandpa Kahla built his house in 1886, land cost about fifty cents an acre. My mother and daddy bought two hundred acres for fifty cents an acre, and there wasn't no such thing as "minerals." When you bought the land, it was yours. After the 1915 storm nobody could buy any land because they didn't have any money. The banks wouldn't finance it 'cause the land wasn't worth nothin'. And a lot of this land was just limitated—you got it if you moved on there and run cattle on it and said, "That's my land,"

and started payin' taxes on it. Taxes was so cheap then that you could have a hundred acres of land and it would cost a dollar an acre. Some of the old settlers just claimed it and for years didn't pay no taxes—just said, "That's my land, and I'm runnin' cattle from the other side of High Island to Port Arthur." But if you had a Spanish land grant, nobody would question it.

Where Bolivar got started, old man Adams bought all this country up one time, and he advertised in the New York paper, "Land on the sea two miles out of Galveston." And people in New York and Chicago bought land—they'd never seen it and they never seen it since and didn't pay any taxes on it. There's land around here yet that hadn't had any taxes paid on it in a hundred years.

One time I used to rodeo a little—I rodeoed a lot as far as that goes, and they had goat ropin' once in a while. I was a calf roper, and a goat is altogether different to rope than a calf. I had a little gray horse, and this goat come out of the chute, and I just went out there and cut away from it and roped the goat, and won the tie-down.

So Pike's daddy died, and he had twenty-some-odd goats. Goats was cheap then—about four dollars—and I bought 'em and put 'em up on the Intracoastal.

Then one time in Port Bolivar the men had about three hundred horses, and they got so many and the horses got so cheap—twelve or fourteen dollars apiece—and I'm talkin' about just a prairie horse, you know, a mare. And a guy from Marshville come down here, and we give him ninety-some-odd horses. Everybody pitched in and give him horses to get rid of 'em, and he was gonna raise 'em on shares. If the mare has two colts, you git one and he gits one. And so we stayed out here a year or two, and one day somebody says, "Let's go see what the horses done." So I had a car and we got the car, me and George Standley and a couple more. I think Pike Kahla went, but anyway, we got out t'ere, and I think I gave 'em somethin' like fifteen or sixteen, and I said, "What happened to the horse deal?" "Well, yours died over there by the tank, and the other one got in the ditch." Finally I said, "How many we got left?" And he said, "Well, you got five or six." And I said, "How much is the goats?" He said, "A dollar and a half apiece." So I said, "Well, just give me enough goats and you can have the horses." So that's the way I got started back in the goat business.

I had the goats up here across the canal from Crystal Beach, and I went back 'ere one day, and I had sixty-some-odd, sixty-six, I think. I went back again, and I had forty. I went back later, and there was twelve, and last time I went back I found eight. Then one day a fellow said, "You ought to had gone to the barbecue they had last night." I said, "Where'd they have a barbecue?" He said, "Up at Crystal Beach." I said, "What did they barbecue?" He said, "Oh, a whole bunch of goats." We found out the fellows in the barge tow boats was puttin' trammel nets across the canal, and they'd run the goats in and tie 'em up. So, I guess that's where my goats was goin'. We finally just run out of 'em and give up.

21 / Jim Bouse

Jim lived next door to his sister, "Sis" Mouton, in Port Bolivar where the old Crockett store used to be. Sis was one of the few people who could get Jim to talk, so she decided to get some of the close relatives over to help inspire him. One afternoon she arranged for Jim, their brother R. C., his wife Oca, and Arnold and Ora Kahla to meet at her house. I sat at a table with the six of them and recorded their anecdotes, arguments, and meandering recollections, wondering how I would sort them all out later. Fortunately, they had distinctive voices, and some talked more than others, so I was able to pick out Jim's and R. C.'s stories.

At one point in our discussion Jim was carrying on about how much he used to hunt, and I asked him what kinds of animals used to live on Bolivar. "Oh, Shaws and Kahlas," he said.[1]

When we were kids we used to eat a lot of candy from my dad's store, so we all had rotten teeth. There wasn't no dentists on Bolivar, but every once in a while one would come over from Galveston to go huntin' at my dad's huntin' camp at Caplen. Dad would pick up the hunters at the boat landing on Friday night and drive them up there in his Model T. When they got through and came back to the store on Sunday to wait for the boat, my dad got the dentists to pull all our bad teeth as payment for the huntin'. We never heard of fillings—they just pulled 'em. Later on my dad found a pair of those tooth pullers on the way to a funeral and then he yanked out our teeth himself.

I used to hunt a lot—ducks mostly. I followed my dad when I wasn't that high out there, dove huntin' and such as that. My dad told me I couldn't kill any more if I didn't eat 'em, so I had to learn how to eat the durn things so I could go huntin'.

We had an old Dutchman that stayed there at the huntin' camp to do the cookin'. He cooked everything in one pot, I don't care what it was. He had some junk piled up there one day, and I asked him what it was, and he named it off. I said, "You got any eggs?"

"*Ja!*"

I said, "How 'bout cookin' some eggs?"

And he broke them eggs and dumped 'em right into that other mess. Sausage, cabbage, potatoes, everything he could find, in one pot.

My dad was married three times. The first two died. My mother, when my youngest sister was born, died in childbirth, along in 1913. They didn't have doctors around—just midwives. There used to be an old lady lived across the street from us—Miss Sosby—and she delivered 'em around here, all over the place. The only way you could get a doctor over here was to get a boat and go pick one up in Galveston. Them boats were slow, anyway, but most of 'em had those little old car engines in 'em or somethin' like that. The car would fall to pieces, and they'd take the engine out and put it in the boat. The *Silver King* was runnin', but it just made two trips a day.

The big attraction was on Sunday night when that excursion train come through. The barge brought the train across, and they made it up on this side as an excursion. Come down Sunday morning and went back Sunday night. The kids used to all jump on the barge and go up and get candy and cakes off the train while it was makin' up.

In summertime when I was a kid we would have to go out on horseback and set fires so the cattle could get in the smoke to keep the mosquitoes off. We had to get wrapped around our face and arms. It was a mess. The farmers had to wear flat-rimmed hats,

Jim Bouse. (Courtesy Odessa Mouton)

and they'd put screen wire on them to be able to go out in the field to pick melons.

At our old store we had to put boards across the front at night 'cause them cattle would come up there and get on the porch to get out of the mosquitoes. They'd be stompin' and carryin' on.

At one time there wasn't any pastures fenced off. This was all open range from here to Gilchrist. They had a cross fence there at Gilchrist, and then where the fence went out on the beach they had a gate, and of course there wasn't but very few cars, and an old man lived out there. He'd kinda watch it for us.

You know they didn't spray for flies or mosquitoes or anything, and they'd get so bad, and when there'd be a little north wind them cattle'd go against that wind and they'd go till they come to a fence, and boy, they'd stop. They was tryin' to get away from them insects. Sometimes the little calves would die from mosquitoes— they'd get in their nose so thick it'd strangle 'em.

In the thirties, there was a big problem with the ticks in Texas. Everybody had to dip each animal fourteen times in two weeks. The first vat they built was concrete, and there was a little slope to it, and them cattle would slide down and skin themselves all up. Then they built wooden vats, and where they'd go in, they made 'em jump in so their head would go under. If the head didn't go under, they had a bucket on a rope to pour the stuff on their heads. Them vats was long, and the cattle would run and jump, and they'd go plum under. Even when the weather was freezin' we had to do it, and them cattle'd come out of there just smokin'.

They was so strict about it that some pens was built at the old Flake depot, and the walls was solid. They wouldn't even let you take a horse in there—kept the gates locked, and they had a long chute with pipes and inspectors on each side. I mean, they would check the cattle underneath the legs and the neck and everything before we could load 'em on the railroad cars.

Bouse's store was the only one in Port Bolivar till Kline's variety store opened. Then Vernon Kahla opened a drugstore—it was more of a soda fountain than anything else. Sold ice cream and soft drinks and things like that. He's been into everything. Later on Vernon sold all his cattle and built him a beer joint and dance hall out on the beach at High Island, and he had a rodeo arena there, too. It was a big place—you could do most anything there. The name of it was "This Is It." A storm come along and just cleaned the whole mess out, and Vernon went and put up a sign that said, "This Was It."

At my dad's store they sold a little of everything, like an ole time country store. All twelve of us kids worked in the store. When we moved down here in 1915 the old store that my dad bought was pretty well stocked with all kinds of hardware and stuff mostly, and we had that stuff for years. After that storm there wasn't too much farmin' or anything around here anymore. Everything was cleaned out.

We had one phone, and it was the only one here for years except the one at the lighthouse. They used to have a cable that went across the channel, and everything was all right till a ship would anchor out there, and when they'd pick that anchor, lot of times they'd pick up that cable and just cut it. But now it's some kind of a micro deal or somethin' with a big antenna.

The phone was a big old square box and you had to wind the handle and give the operator your number. My parents lived up over the store; it was a big two-story place—used to be the Crockett store.

There was a bunch of barrels out by the back door—kerosene barrels. We sold it for stoves, lanterns—they used the kerosene to light the wood stove. Practically everybody used wood stoves up till we got the butane tanks before electricity come in 1948. Mama used to have a butane refrigerator—you lit the pilot on it.

We sold Texaco gasoline—it was brought over on the boat in fifty-five gallon drums. The drums sat on a rack with a spigot, and you got your gas out of the spigot.

In the 1943 storm I was in the service and got an emergency furlough to come home. We had light plants [generators] then—that was before electricity, and I got the light plants goin' for refrigeration and everything. Bought a new windmill from Mr. Simon Johnson. He had a new one he never had used. I got up there and got the old mill down and put the new one up for 'em so they'd have water. The electricity come as far as Caplen years before it come to Port Bolivar.[2]

22 / Stella Suhler

Having heard tales about Frenchtown, a small Cajun settlement at Port Bolivar in the Depression era, I was anxious to find someone who knew something about it. When I discovered Stella Suhler I was elated because not only did she live there as a youngster, but she had several photographs of the people and houses. She had no problems recalling her days there and talked about them with obvious fondness.

Stella is a Galvestonian now and visits Bolivar often. Her best memories of childhood are those in the Port Bolivar grade school. She says the children liked their teachers and enjoyed studying their books because that's about all there was to do. They had no movies or TV, so they played baseball and ran up and down the beach for fun. "Life was simple then," Stella says.

We came to Port Bolivar in December of 1926. I was born in 1922 and was four years old—we came by train from Biloxi. There were quite a few families in Bolivar from Louisiana or Biloxi. My daddy came to work for the cannery. His name was Gaston Roberts, and he had a shrimp boat. Mr. McCaleb was running the cannery, and he came from Biloxi, too. My mother worked there picking shrimp and shucking oysters, and my sisters worked in the packing room where they steamed the shrimp and oysters and put them in cans and labeled them. It was quite a big thing at the time.

There was a big slip where the boats docked next to the cannery and on the other side was the railroad. There were four-room

Stella Suhler (left) and her cousin Warren Comeaux in front of their Frenchtown home, 1928. (Courtesy Stella Suhler)

houses for the cannery workers. Most of the people who worked there were from Louisiana. That's why they called it "Frenchtown"—everyone spoke French. My parents only spoke broken English.

I used to go down with my little bucket and help my mama and them pick shrimp. I went to elementary school in Port Bolivar, and it was a good life. There weren't many roads, so I walked along the bay shore about two miles in all kinds of weather.

There was no electricity or running water. The cannery had two or three outdoor faucets for the people for bathing and washing dishes and clothes, and our drinking water came from a cistern at the depot. We used to go there with buckets and haul it home across the tracks. We washed our hair at the faucet outside and took baths inside in those big old washtubs—and we'd have to run everybody out of the room when it was cold and use the wood stove to heat the water.

We had outdoor toilets and for light we had little kerosene lamps. For ironing we had those little flat irons that we heated up on the wood stove; Daddy used to chop down mesquite trees and Mama would find driftwood on the beach for the stove. It wasn't quite *Tobacco Road*, but nobody ever complained. Everybody was really excited when they finally got electricity in 1948. Then we gradually got indoor plumbing.

Ulysse Norris used to do barbering in Frenchtown. There wasn't any barber shop—he just did it at his house, out on the porch.

My sister worked for the Bouses doing laundry. They were the only ones in town with a washing machine because they had electric generators. My sister had a generator to charge the batteries for her radio—we all gathered there to listen to it.

When a storm would come we'd have to go to the forts. There was no way of getting out or anything. We had warnings, but not like it is now. A lot of people didn't even have radios—they'd send word from the train station. When I was about seven, my baby sister had just been born. There had been a hurricane warning and they brought a train from Beaumont and stationed it there ready to board. My sister was a tiny baby and they had wrapped her head to protect it and they brought a cot to carry my mother. We had packed our bags and were waitin' like a bunch of refugees. They were supposed to blow the train whistle so many times as a signal. My poor daddy and uncles were waitin' to carry my mother on the cot, and all of a sudden the word was out the hurricane had gone another way.

We didn't know any different. That was just the way things were. In about 1933 or '34 there was a hurricane coming, and a friend was going to drive us to the forts in his Model A, and we made it up to the railroad track and a tidal wave came up all of a sudden and we couldn't go any further, so we just got out and held hands and walked through the waist-deep water—ended up at the lighthouse-keeper's house.

So many years we ran from storms ten or twelve times a summer—we'd rush up to the forts because we had no protection except there. When you heard about it, you just took off—you didn't wait to see well, it's goin' this way, it's goin' that-a-way. At one time the railroad station had a telegraph and they got the news and would come tell people, or else you'd watch across the bay at the quarantine station for the signal flags. It was fun.

Things started slowin' down in the cannery about 1932, and a lot of the men started workin' on boats or W.P.A. projects or the county. But that was the end of the cannery then. A lot of people started into the crabbing business, selling crab meat over in Galveston.

Nobody had a car but Mr. McCaleb, and we all just walked everywhere. My father bought an old car once, but he was so used to his horse and carriage in Louisiana that he never did learn how to drive the car.

Mr. Tommy Daniels, the one who ran the cannery after Mr. McCaleb left, he and his wife used to make "home brew." A lot of the women in Frenchtown and Port Bolivar used to be so mad at 'em 'cause the men would go over there to drink that "home brew" beer and get drunk.

At one time there was a Mr. Van, the dirtiest person—he had all kinds of dogs, and he had a little lunch counter near the cannery, and he made the best hamburgers. All greasy, but to us kids, to get a hamburger from Mr. Van was really somethin'.

The men had a lot of fights, but in those days, if they knocked a man down, they'd step back and let him get up. They didn't jump on top of him. I can't ever remember any murders or robberies. Everybody left the house wide open, never locked anything; you just didn't have that much traffic through there. Once in a while maybe a hobo came by on the train, but right away you could spot 'em. Everyone knew what everyone else was doing.

It was a bleak, bleak day for us when we first arrived in Bolivar and got off the train. It was wintertime, and we saw all those wide open spaces and nothin' movin', and we thought, "What are we going to do here?" In Biloxi we had had theaters and concerts and things to do. But there was a group of people at the station—our aunts and uncles and some young people who made us welcome. After that, it wasn't nothin' but Bolivar, even after we moved to Galveston. Bolivar and Louisiana—that was the only places on the map.

23 / Vernon Kahla

Vernon is one of many Kahlas and lives in Stowell. He has moved there four times—in 1931, 1935, 1956, and 1960, and wants to live in High Island again. "I've been married twice and half-married three times," Vernon says. "The last one I married for the baby. She had a cute little baby. She's up in Michigan somewhere, I hope. I hope she's still alive and somebody ain't killed her."

Talking to Vernon is somewhat like having a pillow fight—one is constantly buffeted by unexpected whacks. Without smiling he delivers a string of outrageous anecdotes, starting the next one before the first sinks in. "He never tells a story the same way," his son George says. "When I remind him the tales are getting unbelievable, he says, 'Go to hell.'" It would be fun to listen to Vernon all day, and I'm sure he could go on talking for a week.

I was born in High Island in 1909, and old lady Hughes was the doctor, Aunt Cindy Hughes. I was mostly raised down in Port Bolivar and Patton. We moved back and forth from Bolivar to High Island about four times. My mother was the daughter of Charlotte E. Smith and George Smith of High Island and married Barney Kahla.

Grandpa Smith, my mother's daddy, had a store in Galveston where they outfitted people with mules and harnesses to go out west. It was at Twenty-ninth and Avenue N. Grandpa had liquor there, too, and Grandma moved him to High Island to get him away from the liquor. Then he put in a liquor store there.

In those days they had auctions of damaged and unclaimed freight in Galveston, and Grandpa was there one day with a friend named Bob Thornton. Grandpa bought a carload of merchandise and made a deal with Mr. Thornton to trade it and a mule for 180 acres of land at High Island. Turns out the "merchandise" was a carload of corsets.

Grandpa Smith had one bad fault. Know what it was? He liked to drink whiskey too much, but he was a good old man. My grandma would bring him a drink, and she'd say, "Now, George, that's the only one you're gonna get." Well, it was. He'd keep fillin' it up. Use the same cup.

Did you ever hear of the mineral water in High Island? Grandpa discovered it on his land and put it up in little glass bottles with his name etched on 'em. I helped him bottle it right there by the well. He claimed it could put hair back on bald heads, stop dandruff and pimples, and cure hay fever and asthma. Grandpa would go over to Galveston and sell it on the beach for fifty cents a bottle, and everybody thought he was makin' a lot of money, but he was doin' that to get away from Grandma.

I never will forget old man Granville Shaw as long as I live. We was out there buildin' a road goin' around High Island. Granville come out there carryin' a singletree [crossbar to which harness of draft animal is attached] on his shoulder, walked up to my daddy and said, "Barney, I ought to hit you with this and knock your brains out, 'cause you're the first one that brought me here." He had done got tired of High Island.

A lot of people come from Fannett. There wasn't nothin' up there but pine trees. There wasn't no flounder and there wasn't no crabs and there wasn't no watermelons, so they moved to Bolivar. That's what they did.

What would you think about a girl named Ida? She was out in the field diggin' sweet potatoes one day, and she just started walkin' down the railroad track at Patton. They never did hear tell of her for about twenty-five years. I went over there one day and Granville asked me, "Have you ever heard about my sister that left?" He talked about how pretty she was and said she went to Dallas and never did come back.

We were living in Patton just before the 1915 storm and farmed, raised watermelons mostly and okra and cantaloupes. We came down to Grandpa Kahla's house in Port Bolivar when the storm hit. I was six years old. We went in a wagon 'cause they didn't have no car. We found trunks full of clothes after the storm and spread 'em all out in the yard. There wasn't no water to wash 'em with, but sure enough it started rainin' and cleaned all those clothes up so we could wear 'em.

We could get enough drinkin' water out of the old cisterns, but there wasn't no food. About the only thing we could find was them old canned peaches on the beach and other stuff that come ashore like tins of bacon. That's all we had. People learned to like things they never had eat before.

When I was first married I had my wife workin' for me in the drugstore in High Island. Guess how much I was payin' her a day? I was givin' her fifty cents. We moved down to Bolivar in 1927, and we put in a drugstore and a dance hall upstairs. We lived in a little room behind it. When she was pregnant with Claud she wanted to move the heck out of that place, so we went and shut the door on it. No tellin' how long people got the drugs out of there and bottles of Castoria and cigarettes and Cokes.

We went to High Island and I got a job roughneckin'. The only reason I got the job is because the Gulf Oil guy wanted baseball players, and I could play ball. We never had no basketball or football, but we did play baseball. That's how I made a livin' during the Depression.

They hit oil at High Island in about 1923, but it was cheap then, about thirty cents a barrel. Marrs McLean was an old lease hound then, and I never will forget one time, they caught him over there in Liberty, speedin'. The policeman said, "We're goin' to have to give you a ticket," and he told 'em, "You better give me two of them, 'cause I'm goin' to be back in about thirty minutes."

Before they built the railroad, the only way we could get over to Galveston was on a little sailin' boat. There was no roads, so we used to go to dances at Bolivar in our Model Ts by drivin' along the beach, and if the tide was high when you come back, you had you a job gettin' home. We didn't get no road here until about 1931, about the time they put the swing bridge at High Island. Before then, if it rained, you didn't go to Beaumont. We used to have to get out and push. Before the swing bridge, you'd drive on this ferry and pull yourself across with ropes. Then when you got halfway to Stowell, you'd run into that mud. Old man Monteau and George Sievers used to keep a team of mules out there. One would work twelve hours, then the other would work twelve hours pullin' cars through the marshy part. Then you'd go a little ways further and you'd run into some more mud. We'd have to get two people out on each side pushin'. It was bad.

We used to ride from High Island on a horse to Patton to buy whiskey from old Ben Bright for seventy-five cents to take to dances at the Sea View Hotel. Ben worked for W. D. Gordon and bootlegged for about twenty years. He could *make* that whiskey.

That old Ben Bright was cute about that bootleggin'. He'd bottle that whiskey just like it come out of the factory, in old "Flytox" bottles. That's what you put on horses to kill the flies, so we asked for some "Flytox." All them Beaumont lawyers knew about the whiskey—they'd come down here to get it and haul it back to Beaumont.

When Ben first moved here I think he was kind of under probation. You know, a lot of people did that. I asked Mr. Meynig once, "Whatever give you the idea of comin' to High Island?" He said he wanted to get away from Galveston 'cause he was under surveillance over there, so he got on a boat and come over to High Island. They all did that—and when they got here they'd find 'em a woman and marry 'em. They'd find either a Cronea or a Payton or a Rivea or Dailey, or somethin'. They were under probation for every damn thing—fighting, they'd get out on the dock and stab somebody with a knife. They was longshoremen, and they'd get into fights about who was supposed to be loadin' the boats. Did you ever hear the name of Sullivan? This old man Sullivan one time bit one of the other fellow's lip off. He spit it out right in the guy's face. And they'd eye gouge—pull somebody's eye out.

Old man Henry Sullivan—he was somethin' else. If he was in a good humor he'd say "Hey, Joe, such and such," but if he didn't like you he'd say, "Hey, guy." He raised three families—seventeen kids, with three wives. In about 1895 he come over from Cade, Louisiana, on his horse. When he got to the Sabine River he took his clothes off and put 'em up on the saddle and let the horse pull him across holdin' onto his tail. He rode down the ridge to "High Islands" and stopped at the Payton house to get a drink of water. Molly Payton was there, but he didn't like her looks, so he went around in the back yard and met Lou. That was the other sister. He set his cap for her and took all them brothers with him the next day and asked Lou to marry him.

Henry took Lou to Galveston in his sailboat next day so they could go to the preacher's, but the boat got stuck on a bar, and they had to spend the night. Henry took three of his brothers with 'em, Jeff and John and Jim, and they got in a fight. Most of 'em ended up overboard. They had to wait till the tide come up for 'em to get to Galveston and get married.

Old Henry and two of his sons, Tom and Skinny, used to fight all the time. Once there was a rodeo in Winnie and Tom and Skinny whipped two other fellows with them hard-boiled hats. They broke the hats in two, and used 'em to cut just like a butcher knife. They raked 'em across the face and eyes and clothes, too. There were dances at Fannett all the time, and the Sullivan boys would go out there just to fight.

For fun we used to drive our old cars out on the beach and rope cows from the hood. Then we'd ride 'em. We put one girl on a bull, and he run clear back to Mud Lake with her.

One time me and my brother left High Island on horses, ridin' to

Bolivar, and the only place you could get water was over at W. D. Gordon's house and down at Boyt's ranch, and Andrew Johnson's. Those were the only three houses on the beach after the 1915 storm. Old man Peterson had a little house by the cut in about 1925, but he wouldn't let you have no water. Said it was too hard to get. But you could get it at Gordon's if the hogs hadn't opened up the faucet on you. I never did know why they had the faucets so high up—to get a bucket under it, I guess. But hogs would get there and rub the faucet to scratch their fleas and open the faucet up, then you wouldn't have no water.

You know who learned us about usin' a boat for trappin'? A Frenchman who couldn't read and write. I used to use a team with a harness and walked out in the marshes, and he come along and said, "Why don't you get a little boat and pull it along to carry the muskrats?" So we started usin' a boat to trap with. We used to take a bag on our back to put the muskrats in. We got about fifty cents apiece for a pelt.

In World War II we had some kinfolks workin' in the coast guard and they'd ride up and down the beach lookin' for submarines. I used to call 'em "draft dodgers." What would you call 'em? They'd park their horses behind my place, and we'd have to pull the curtains down where there weren't no lights. They was supposed to be watchin' for submarines comin' ashore, but they'd come inside and dance. Four of 'em got their wives down 'ere. We had about eight of 'em got married while they was coast guardin'.

A lot of our ships got blowed up right out here in the gulf, and bodies would wash ashore. That's why the coast guard had the patrols.

John Payton was the constable, and he made one arrest in twenty-five years. It was a girl at a dance one night at the Green Light. He was standin' in the door with his gun on that he never had shot. That little ole girl was real cute, had on her shorts, and she was just as drunk as a skunk. He looked at her and said, "Let's me and you waltz," and she said "You mean you're askin' me to dance with you, you old big-bellied sucker?" So he arrested her, put her in the car and took her down the road. So me and another boy, LeRoy got in our car and followed 'em to the ferry. LeRoy told John that he'd take him in Joe Massey's store and buy him a cigar, so while they was in the store, I got the prisoner and put her back in our car. That's the only rescue I ever made. Ole John come out there and thought she had run off. He didn't know we had loaded her in our car and hauled her back to High Island. He was plenty mad.

We had a jail right behind Pop's house. There was a fellow from the sheriff's department that built it, a cripple named Smith. I never will forget Henry Kirkpatrick. We went down one day to help build the jail, and the next day they locked Henry up in it. He was drunk. I think they only had one or two arrests. Henry was about the only one I know of. That jail stayed there three or four years, and I don't know what they did with it. Might have burned up.

We sold ducks all our lives. We'd sell ducks in the winter, then oyster a little bit and shrimp a little bit. We had a fellow came to High Island, said he just wanted ducks for a hotel. He was lyin' to us. He just wanted to catch us. Anyway, he caught us, and I spent two months in jail.

What's funny about it, that's the way they lived years ago. We didn't have no muskrats then. We'd take out hunters, and when they'd come in, if they had little old teal or spoonbills, they'd just throw 'em away, so we'd get 'em and sell 'em. We thought we had a sucker when that fellow come along.

I went to jail in Texarkana. I enjoyed it—I mean, it didn't bother me a bit. I had people comin' in there from ten or fifteen miles away to talk to me about that deal. They said the guy that caught us went on across the water, and they like to got him over there. They was tryin' to kill him.

Bonnie and Clyde come to High Island once. They spent about a week. She was cute, Bonnie was. I seen her picture. They was travelin'—runnin'. One of their main hideouts was over at Liberty and Dayton, back in that country. They just come over here lookin'.

One day they went in the High Island cafe to eat, and Pop Payton was sittin' there with a friend, and after Bonnie and Clyde left, the friend said, "Pop, do you know who that was?"

Pop said, "Yeah, Bonnie and Clyde." And the friend said, "How come you don't arrest 'em? Don't you know they're wanted?" And Pop said, "They ain't wanted here."

24 / Anne Broussard Mouton

212 / THE PEOPLE

Since I had never met Anne, Sis Mouton and I walked to Anne's house in Port Bolivar, and Sis introduced me. We wasted no time getting into the past, and Anne confessed that she had always wanted to put her memories in a book. She has a Cajun sense of humor that has helped her through many hard times and spices up her stories.

Anne's favorite recollection of Bolivar was walking on the beach. She found such treasures as a brass water kettle, cans of shrimp and oysters, buckets of paint, coconuts, sea horses, and hundreds of seashells. Another of her pastimes was catching big blue crabs at the Santa Fe slip. Her mother, Eloge Broussard, always made gumbo, stuffed crab, or crab patties and taught Anne how to cook seafood Louisiana style.[1]

We came here [Port Bolivar] in February 1928, and I never will forget it because it was so foggy—we couldn't see nothing for three days, and not used to being by the water, the ships would blow and ring the bells and everything, and it went on and on. We was anxious to see what it was like, you know? Three days, and we couldn't see nothing but a little bit ahead of you. When we finally saw everything, I thought, "This is the end of the world." That's exactly what I thought.

What we hated, though, was leaving our place in Louisiana. My daddy was working at the rice irrigation pumping plant there in Milton, and he was the first one hired, so he was the first to go. He had built us a real nice bungalow, everything was paid for, and we wasn't rich, but we was making it. We was about three blocks from the school and about two blocks from the Catholic church. The church is what Mama missed so much.

We come here for one year, and we never went back. We was happy here. We wasn't making all that much money, but when we come in 1928 it was the Depression. The cannery paid for our transportation to Bolivar, so we put the bare necessities on the train and left our good furniture—marble-top dressers, family pictures, and other things—because we just had a little four-room house we were going to live in. We thought we would just be there for a little while. When we sold our house later, we lost all that.

This building where we was working was five hundred feet long, and the cannery was in the back part. It used to be a lumberyard, I think. This man who run it from Biloxi got people from different places to come work—Louisiana, Biloxi, and Lake Arthur. He had quite a few people working there.

Our house was across the tracks from Frenchtown. It was the only vacant house there was when we come here. There was three houses close to each other, and we had to bring our own furniture. We didn't have electricity—it was just like a few camps here. They furnished the houses for us and the pine wood to cook with on our wood stoves. They brought the wood on the Santa Fe Railroad from Beaumont.

There wasn't anything here but the factory and Frenchtown. Port Bolivar had only that grocery store and post office—later on there was a small Methodist church. There was the Kahlas, the Bouses, and the Simptons living here. From Port Bolivar to Patton you couldn't see a house, and old man Blalock had a house there, and then from there to High Island there wasn't nothin'.

We came on the Southern Pacific train from Lafayette to Beaumont, then we had to get on this Santa Fe train from Beaumont to here. When we come here we thought it was terrible. We was used to goin' to dances in Louisiana. They had orchestras, not that cheap stuff you have down here. We'd go to Youngsville and Lafayette, and, man, we had a good time. When we come here we thought this is *it*. There wasn't nothin', we didn't think. We finally got acquainted to the girls and boys and it was better. When we didn't work, we'd walk the beach all the time.

I was twenty years old when we came here, and I'm seventy-nine now. I worked at the cannery pickin' shrimp and in the packin' room. We opened steamed oysters, too, and they canned them, and they'd wet-pack the shrimp and dry-pack 'em, too. The train come over here every other day and they shipped 'em out on it, and the barge took the train over to Galveston.

At the cannery they had a wharf built of two by eights, and it had big cracks in it. We wore aprons with pockets to put our dimes in—they paid us in dimes. They had barrels on the wharf to wash our hands, you know, to get that shrimp stuff off, or oyster, and we wouldn't think—we'd pick up our apron to dry our hands and many a time the dimes would all fall overboard. It looked like we'd learn, but it happened many times—we lost our day's work. The dimes went through the cracks down in the water. Shoot, during that time, if we made a dollar and a half a day we were doin' pretty good.

We had running water out in the yard from a deep well, and there was a great big cistern over at the Santa Fe depot, and we used to get the water to drink from it. In fact, I remember my daddy bought some big barrels that used to have pickles in 'em, and he burned the inside to get rid of the pickle taste and make a kind of charcoal filter. We'd save our rainwater in 'em because for us it was cleaner than that big cistern. The neighbors used to come steal our water, would you believe? Instead of walking to the Santa Fe depot they'd dip their bucket in our water.

My brother had built us a little shed like an outside restroom, but it was a shower. We didn't have hot water, and Mama used to boil the water on her stove to take baths—we'd take 'em in tubs. But in the summer the water would get so hot in that pipe to the shower, sometimes you couldn't even take a bath. But we went out there and took a shower before we came in the house—it kept us from bringing in all that shrimp smell.

You know the lighthouse. At night we used to wait till the light would turn so we could go outside and see. When they cut the light off at the lighthouse, we missed it. It was bright, bright, bright. If we had to go out and get a bucket of water or use the restroom, we'd wait till the light came. The light turned slow—if we'd wait a minute, it would come again, you know. We depended on that light, and we hated it when they cut it off. We only had kerosene lamps. But after the light went out, we got the water before dark. We had to use our heads.

When we first come down here my daddy'd go shrimping, and in his spare time he caught some fish, and he'd bring it home already cleaned. We never got tired of fresh fish—we could have ate it every day. During those times you could catch fish and crabs—you'd just drop a net down and the great big crabs would just be falling over it. The bay was coming in at the back of our place, and my stepdaughter and I would get a gallon bucket of oysters. We'd open 'em up at the edge of the water and come home with 'em. We loved all that fresh seafood.

At our house we had meat, chicken, roast, pork, and everything. We had our own garden, our own cow, our own milk, butter, eggs, and chickens. Oh, we never got hungry. We may not have had as many nice clothes as some people, but we never got hungry. My daddy always had food on the table.

Mother fixed gumbo, good soups, chicken and rice. We used to buy the bent cans for ten cents a can, and we made the best shrimp salad with it. You could put several cans in the salad for ten cents each. Yeah, we ate beans, black-eyed peas, rice—that was the main thing. My daddy loved rice.

Mama had a six-burner wood range. You talk about makin' the biscuits and cornbread. She'd make her biscuits with sour cream. You know, we had so much cream, we didn't use it all for butter. She was a good cook—she could take little or nothin' and make a good meal, you know. We had a icebox. At the factory they had ice to keep the shrimp and stuff, so they gave us ice. We had to put it on the top shelf in the icebox. We bought the box in Galveston and carried it over on the boat. In Louisiana we kept the food in a safe with screen doors in the kitchen. Mama used to cook three times a day, because we couldn't keep no cooked food.

Here, we bought a few groceries from Bouse's store, or we went to town and bought it. The *Silver King* boat brought fresh bread and the mail every day from Galveston, and vegetables for the store. They raised vegetables over here, too. Mr. Bluch Kahla's father used to raise cabbages, and they'd bring it down to the boat at the slip, and they was those little pointed heads, you know. We'd follow the durn wagon, and the cabbages would fall off, and we'd pick 'em up and eat 'em like apples. He had 'em heaped so tall he couldn't make 'em stay up there.

My daddy used to catch five-gallon buckets full of redfish or trout. He worked on a shrimp boat as a helper for a share. They worked on shares. Then when the cannery closed he worked for the W.P.A. in Galveston. I asked for a job there, too, and the lady told me that if I ate at the same table as my daddy, he was entitled to work before me. I said, "I have to feed myself and my baby," and she said, "I don't care, the head of the family gets the job first."

I remember distinctly that the factory was destroyed in '33 in the storm. A lot of it got knocked down, and it damaged the machinery and stuff, so they did away with it. We had to do somethin' else, you know. That's when I went to work for Mrs. Bouse. She always had three or four girls there. Everybody from town would bring their clothes to Mrs. Bouse's to wash and iron, and the bus stopped there, so it was really a busy place. You really had a job. I worked for Mrs. Bouse for fifty cents a day washing, scrubbing, ironing and doing dishes. The only thing I didn't do was cook. I told her I didn't know how.

You get five dollars and you could go to town and buy a nice box of groceries, like rice and potatoes, lean meat, bread, coffee, and

Harvesting cabbages on Marrs McLean's farm at Caplen in 1914. Rich Bolivar soil produced excellent fruits and vegetables. (Courtesy Ruth McLean Bowers)

sugar. You had a big bag of groceries, maybe beans, for five dollars. Coffee was twenty-five cents a pound, and bread was about fifteen cents a loaf.

When Mr. Bouse would give a barbecue every Fourth of July he'd furnish the beef, and we'd all get potato salad and vegetables and cakes and pies and stuff, and every year we had a big barbecue. At Christmas, they had this little Methodist church, and Mr. Bouse'd buy oranges and apples and bananas and nuts and candy, and everybody got a bag under the Christmas tree at the church. That's true. I used to help fix the bags. It was on Christmas every year. We used to be just like one big family. It was nice.

We used to dance a lot, at Kline's, and other places. When they had a storm, we'd go to the fort and dance. We didn't have no better sense. Some of 'em played the guitar and fiddle and accordion, and we'd dance out there on that round concrete place to pass the time till the storm got there. Many times we rushed to the fort when a storm was comin'—I can't count the times.

We went to Galveston on the *Silver King* to see a movie and shop, and we'd have to spend the whole day because the boat came back in the late afternoon. They had excursions on the train, too.

The barge would come and get the train cars and bring 'em to Galveston and unload 'em, but the train crew slept in Port Bolivar one night, and the next morning they'd go back to Beaumont, and the following day they'd come back here and sleep. There was only about three or four men, and it was a small train—a putt-putt train. It had a little engine and carried passenger cars and freight cars both.

The Santa Fe had little houses where the people who worked on the railroad lived. One was a little yellow one over by the lighthouse for the Mexicans that kept the rails, and then there was the depot. Around 1940 the Santa Fe people had an auction and sold everything; they sold the houses they had for railroad people to live in and the depot, and they took up all the tracks.

We paid eighty-seven dollars and fifty cents for this house and two tons of coal. What you did is you put your bid on a piece of paper, put it in an envelope and give it to 'em. The highest bid won, and you paid for it, that's all. My brother had the first chance at it, and he said, "Oh, it ain't worth it. Do y'all want it?" We said, "Yeah, we want it."

There was a pot-bellied heater in it that went with the house, and there was a garage, and we got the well, too. We burned the coal in the heater and heated the house with it.

There was a shed room for a kitchen, and they had beds all over the big front room, and the train crew used to sleep in it every other night.

When we bought the house, there was one window that was cracked, and we went through storms and storms, and that window never did fall. And the wood was still good on the outside.

This house used to be in the middle of a pasture near the ferry landing, and Mr. Guidry had a moving outfit and he moved it for us. The outfit was big sills on wheels with a tractor. They had a rig of lumber—they'd put that under the house, and they had wheels and they'd roll it. Yeah. Charged us thirty-five dollars. We thought that was high after paying eighty-seven dollars for the house. Yep. At the time it was all it was worth, I guess.

This house is not settin' square with the world. In '43 the storm knocked it off the blocks, and the blocks went through the floor. We didn't have any shingles left on the roof, either. My brothers was in the service, and my son and my two stepsons was too little to help, and my husband and I got on top of that roof; my daddy showed us how to shingle. My husband and I shingled the roof. I had a black pair of slacks, and I want you to know I wore the seat off I was so afraid to fall. Really. Yep. Oh, we went through hell here, and I don't know why we stood here, but you got problems elsewhere, so what are you goin' to do?

There was a beaded ceiling in the livin' room, and the outside was two by eight boards, cedar, I think. That pine floor didn't have one knot in it. When them blocks went through the floor and pushed it all up, my husband asked my daddy, "How are we gonna fix that floor?" He said, "It'll fall back in place." He put every board back in place, tapped it in the groove, and it didn't tear a board. It went right back where it was.

After the '43 storm—talk about nuts—we washed all the clothes by hand we could find. Hung 'em on the line, and it started raining—talk about goofy—went and took all the clothes in, put 'em in the house, and it rained more in here than it did outside. You're so upset you don't think. It's a wonder we got our right mind back.

We lost five hundred and some-odd chickens. The wind blew the chicken house down, and the chickens all got under our house—it was so high off the ground. My husband had raised some potatoes on the corner lot there, and he had twenty-two bushels of potatoes under the house 'cause it was a nice cool place to put 'em, you know. Well, the house fell down on top of them chickens. You talk about somethin'. We had rotten potatoes and chickens under the house. God have mercy. Whooo.

We had two or three hens left—I don't know where they had hid—and our kitchen was gone, so we had an old kerosene stove in the living room and a box of potatoes and onions on the floor that the Red Cross had given us. Here comes this old hen—we didn't have no doors, even the doors had blown off—come this old hen and gets in the corner. I looked over there and saw that old hen tryin' to make a nest in the potatoes, and my stepdaughter said, "Aaanh, poor thing, she ain't got no place to go. Let her stay there." After that, if she had a chance, she'd come lay an egg in there every day—in the potatoes and onions. I feel so sorry for her, she don't have no nest—she don't have nowhere to go.

The table and chairs we had in that kitchen, we never did see where they went. The wind picked 'em up. My daddy had a mare with a little colt in the yard over there. That wind come, and it was blowin' so hard like a twirl, and it picked up that mare and the colt off the ground and raised 'em up in the air and put 'em back down. I saw that from here—with my eyes. It raised 'em up pretty high, but it didn't kill 'em.

But that table and chairs went. And I had canned a lot of stuff—it was all down on the ground and crushed, and my silverware was all buried in the sand. The kitchen had a shed roof, and both of the ends of the kitchen had busted, and that roof fell, too, you know. The floor was still there, but the roof had kind of fell on top of that. I had to go and dig my silverware in the dirt. Some of my preserves looked like it was good, but the Red Cross told me not to eat it, so we had to throw everything out.

For a kitchen, the government loaned us a tent. In the daytime we'd cook on that kerosene stove—we straightened it out, and we could use it, and we put two sawhorses there and a door on top and a clean sheet over it and made us a table, and that's where we ate. The Red Cross loaned us some blankets and cots to sleep on. I said then, "I don't know how we stay here through the years." My sewin' machine peeled off like a potato. It was veneer. All our furniture was wet and ruined. Oh yeah, we had to start over—I don't know how many times.

25 / Mary Silva Dafonte

Mary was born May 6, 1920, in Silsbee, Texas. When I talked with her in October of 1987 she was living in a neat little white house in Port Bolivar. As soon as I arrived, she took me on a tour of every room, pointing out her prize pieces of antique furniture. She remembered well her long life on the peninsula and reiterated that her favorite times were helping her family through the Depression and dancing on Saturday nights at the Frank Kahlas' house. The Silvas were the only Mexicans in Port Bolivar for many years and proud of it. When Mary reminisced about her family and all the good food her mother cooked, I yearned to taste some of Mary's famous enchiladas, but time ran out before I could make the request.[1]

My parents' name was Silva—Jesús and Eudocia—and they were from Morelia, Mexico. They left Mexico walking in about 1910 and landed up at Saratoga, Texas. From there they kept on comin' down the line; he had started workin' on the railroad, and it's a wonder they didn't get picked up. God knows how they made it, but they did. Every time they moved, they'd leave half their stuff. It was just one thing after the other, like gypsies. My daddy worked hard for the Santa Fe Railroad puttin' down them ties and rails and makin' repairs.

In 1925 the family came from Caplen to Port Bolivar, and the Santa Fe had a section house here. It looked like one of those shotgun houses, you know. They had it for the workers to live in, and it was divided into sections for different families. Inside of it all they had was a heating stove and a cooking stove; the rest you had to provide.

Then they had the boss's house and a depot. All that's gone now. Everything was painted yellow—canary yellow. At the depot they had a big water tower where the train used to fill up the steam engine and where the barges came and loaded the railroad cars. There was a cannery there where the shrimp boats unloaded. In later years my mother and I worked there picking shrimp; that was the only activity in Port Bolivar in the Depression.

We had a big family, and my daddy used to make a garden to keep us goin', because they wasn't payin' all that much on the railroad. Then he got a few sheep, goats, chickens, and a couple of cows. But my mother and daddy struggled. My daddy used to go out huntin' and flounderin' and fishin' to bring us stuff to eat. He was a good hunter and fisherman, too.

When you come to this country, it's hard. The Immigration people wanted to try and send him back to Mexico, but then they said, "No, you've got too many kids. We can't afford to send you back."

When my daddy was out workin' on the tracks, the mosquitoes was so thick they could take you away. One day I got him a straw hat and put some screen wire on it and some cloth below so that he could tie it around his neck. That way he wouldn't swallow any mosquitoes. They was so thick. And he said it helped him immensely. The other men all wanted to know who made it. I was always thinkin' of things to do for my parents, but my most [main] role was to help my mother with the children, which was a handful.

My parents went through hell and high water to make a go of it.

In the wintertime we had to use the wood heating stove, and we heated our bath water on it. We had a washtub, and everybody could take their turn. Sometimes we had to start early, with the little ones. We kept 'em clean. That's one thing we believed

Mary Silva Dafonte. (Courtesy Pat Frederick)

in—cleanin'. I used to get on my knees and scrub all the dirt out of the cracks in the floor, and those floors came out snow white.

Our water had to be hauled for cookin' and bathin', but that's one thing we did do—we kept clean all the time. Didn't matter how far we had to go for water. We went. We used buckets, wheelbarrows, or whatever we could get our hands on.

The crossties that were replaced from the tracks, well, my daddy used to save all of those, and we'd haul 'em to the house, put 'em on a sawhorse, and we had one of those saws with the big teeth and a handle on each end, and we'd cut wood like that. In sections, and then chop it. To put inside the cookstove and heating stove. My daddy would sometimes split the ties in four pieces, and we'd put up a fence for the garden. We all helped with the garden. I had to clean my section out, and I had to clean my brother Rudy's section. A lot of the kids wouldn't do it, so it had to be me. Mama'd come help. We made all the rows where Daddy was going to plant all the stuff. He made a beautiful garden.

Mama cooked on the wood stove and made tortillas and beans and rice and chili, and when we made tortillas we had to make plenty. I've seen two stacks of them sittin' on the table about sixteen inches high. To feed all those nine. Yeah.

At the time we were the only Mexican family here. The rest of 'em took off, the ones at the section house. We stayed here, and it was a struggle.

To tell you the truth, when I was young, I didn't have any time to play because I was always tryin' to help my mother. I was always tryin' to see how I could improve the house, 'cause the house that we lived in didn't have nothin' except rough wood walls with splinters and cracks so big you could see the daylight. So my brother Rudy and I we'd go to those boxcars out there and we'd get that big thick paper. The boxcars had thick, thick paper lining on the walls; it was brown, like paper bag brown. I told Mama, "I'm goin' to cover those holes up," and I'd make some flour and water, and we'd cook it and make a paste and put alum in it so no roaches or nothin' could get behind it. We covered all our walls with it, like wallpaper.

When Rudy and I would go to the boxcar, I'd say, "Rudy, I can't reach," and he'd get down and say, "Okay, now get on my shoulders," and he'd boost me up so I could crawl inside. And we'd get corn, we'd get wheat, and we'd get a whole bunch of stuff out of there, and Mama'd say, "*Where'd* you all get all this?" I said, "Out of the boxcars." Papa said, "Leave it up to them kids." We'd bring the corn home and give it to the chickens. Rudy and I always got into stuff.

When the Santa Fe went out of business, my daddy worked at the canning factory. He was the one who boiled the shrimp and steamed the oysters. Oh, those shrimp were delicious. I'm the only one that got away with it—I'd go over there to the factory and hold my little apron out and they'd give me a little bunch of shrimp. I said, "I brought too short of an apron. Next time I'll bring a big one." And they'd start laughin'. They all liked me.

Daddy used to make home brew out of that Blue Ribbon malt and five pounds of sugar and three cakes of yeast. I know, I made it myself, and I used to go in there and get stoned. Blew all that foam off and drank it 'cause it was sweet, and we was lookin' for somethin' sweet. That was the only sweet thing, and I come out of there stoned one time and Mama said, "I know where you've been!" And it was delicious. We put it in brown bottles—first we'd wash 'em, then cap 'em. I helped my daddy with all that. We used to get 'em real cold and people would come to our house especially to drink that beer. And I mean, they'd drink.

A lot of people made home brew—the people next door, and there were some that lived in a boxcar. That was "Yardy" Jenkins and "Pistol." I don't know their real names. They were here when we came here. There was three houses in a row—us, the Broussards, and the Clevelands, and the Jenkins lived in a boxcar near the track. He worked for the cannery. They used to make home brew and those people off the Santa Fe, the ones that worked there, they used to go to the Jenkins' and drink that stuff. I think they sold it, but I don't know. All them people would go there, and Yardy would holler at me. She used to call me and my brother "Maggie" and "Jiggs" 'cause we was always together. She'd yell at me, "My dear, come over here. These men want to see you dance." And I says, "I'm not gonna dance for nothin'." They'd throw money at me—they liked the way I danced—the Charleston and all that, and I'd pick up a few dollars. She'd keep callin' me and callin' me, and I said, "I'm gettin' tired of comin' over there." They all thought of me just like I was theirs, you know. They treated me good.

I been treated good by a lot of people here, 'cause they know I worked hard.

The only time I got to play was when I went to school. To me, school was fun. When I came to Bolivar I was close to six years old, and the pretty part about startin' school was that I didn't know a word of English. A little boy that I knew said, "Come on, you're goin' with me," so finally Mama got me dressed, and I said, "Well, I'm goin' to try to go to school today. I don't know how I'm goin' to turn out." But finally I picked up the English, and it didn't take me long.

They was all so nice to me. Our teacher had three different classes to teach all at the same time. After she'd give us the lesson and tell us what to do, she'd go to the next class, and it was hard on her. If I wanted to go to the bathroom, I wouldn't even ask, I'd just run out of the room because I had to go. She called me to her desk when I came back and told me I had to ask to go.

And my mother would fix me those round little tortillas with beans in 'em for my lunch. They were good. So all the children at that school was always wantin' to give me their lunch for those tortillas, and I'd say, "No," 'cause, you know, I was ashamed. But finally I traded, and they loved it. So then Mama would cook some extra ones for the children who wanted some. The school just went through the sixth grade, then we had to go to Lovenberg in Galveston on the bus, across the ferry.

You know that lighthouse. What we'd do, we'd go roller-skating underneath the keeper's house. We didn't have nowhere else to go. I wasn't too much on skating. Man, I had more spills. I thought sometimes I didn't have no bottom left I slipped and fell so much. We'd climb up into the top of the lighthouse, too, and when you got to the top, you was out of breath. The keeper, Mr. Fox, let us go in there.

We had many a good time. Here in Port Bolivar, if you wanted to go to a dance, Mrs. Frank Kahla used to give dances for the different people, and they had fun. She had one big room that she kept empty for that purpose. She gave dances for the people that wanted to go dancin' on Saturday. She sure did. That house is still here—on Overton Street, at about Sixth. That was all the recreation there was.

There was a colored guy they called Jim, Jim Cleveland, and his broad Lizzie, and I'm tellin' you she was a character. He played the violin and she played the guitar. They made good music together. Just the two of 'em. They lived not too far from where we used to live, near the depot. They had a little hole-in-the-wall, too.

We had a little store, Mrs. Kline's, where they sold medicines, ice cream, candy, material, sewing notions and just about any little odds and ends that people needed. The only place that had meat was Bouse's store, when they butchered. Otherwise we butchered our own. Mr. Bouse would butcher regular.

There was an old man named Mr. Van who had a little place where he used to make pies and doughnuts and sell drinks and stuff like that, and that man could make the pies. I know because I spent most of the money I made on pies. They were sweet, and I used to love sweets. He used to let me eat what I wanted even when I couldn't pay for it. The people from the cannery would go to his little place and buy his pastries.

When I had to go to Galveston, they'd take me on the pilot boat. Papa told them to take me across, and they would bring me back. But other times we had to go on the shrimp boats, or later on the *Silver King*. I was the one that had to go to Galveston because Mama had all those children and couldn't go. I'd get lost sometimes, but I'd find my way back. I was the one that did everything for the children. Had to go when they needed shoes or something that we wanted to pick up. For their shoes I'd take a piece of paper and mark their foot on it, put their name on it, then go to town and put the shoe on the paper for the size. Oh, you don't know.

Sometimes I'd have to bundle one of the kids up when they were sick and go across in a pilot boat or shrimp boat to Galveston. I'd have to walk down the path to the docks, then go about a mile from the landing to get to the hospital. I did that many a time. It was a lot easier when the ferry came in—then we could get a nurse to come over.

After I was older, about sixteen, I worked sewing for the W.P.A. and the National Youth Administration, two weeks in each place, and it was nineteen dollars for the two weeks. But every little bit helped. I was on the cutting machine where we cut the cloth, and I made shorts.

We received relief, too, from the welfare, to help clothe the children. Mrs. Weaver always came over to see what clothes we needed. What I'd do is fix the old clothes so they'd look different, change buttons, you know. I'd buy me a bunch of buttons 'cause they was cheap. Sometimes the welfare lady would bring mattresses for us, too. But one day she said, "You come over there and pick out the clothes you want." I never will forget. She'd give us food sometimes, too.

One day Mrs. Weaver brought us several bolts of cheesecloth and said, "Maybe you can use this for something." And I did. I made curtains out of it, and they come out beautiful. Everybody thought I had gone to some extremes to make 'em. But it's *hard* to work with cheesecloth.

I used to work around Port Bolivar, too, for Mrs. Simpton and others helpin' 'em to can and stuff like that. They'd always give me different things to take home. Ironin'—I ironed for different people up and down this territory, cleaned houses and did just about everything.

I used to work for Mr. Segura in his crab shop, and there weren't any regulations then. Nowadays there are so many rules about the seafood business, but nobody used to get sick. Mr. Segura processed crabs, boiled them, picked the meat, and everything so he could go sell it, and there was only a little bit of ice. Sometimes he'd throw it over his shoulder in a sack and go sell it in Galveston to get money for his family. He was blind. I worked for Mr. Segura for twenty-five years, and nobody ever got sick on his crabmeat.

The storms is what used to keep us messed up here. All the time, those different storms. In the '43 storm we lost just about everything. The Red Cross came and picked us up in army trucks and took us to Galveston. We was tryin' to get to the fort—that was the only place to go. We were out there in the middle of nowhere tryin' to walk through waist-deep water. I lost my shoes—oh, I got all cut up.

When the storm came we was in the house and the walls was shakin', and pretty soon, ping! Some of the window panes would come flyin' in, and so my husband took blankets and quilts and nailed 'em on the windows because the glass just missed my daughter and I. The Red Cross picked my mama and daddy up in their house 'cause my husband told them to get them first. They finally picked us up, too, but I was on the side of the road for a long time. I had told my husband to go on and take the baby to the fort. My mama and daddy's house was completely gone and we had to rebuild another one. Here you gotta really look after yourself, be on your toes, 'cause you never know.

Sometimes we stayed in the forts. It was not a pretty picture. You had to go clean the area and watch for snakes and rats or whatever it was. But we'd take cots and blankets and eat canned food. One time we stayed there about three days. Like I said, it's *something* out here when it comes to storms.

Those years back, I wouldn't take nothing for those years. Everybody helped one another, and what one couldn't do, the other one could, and it was like a great big old huge family. We knew we was Mexicans and all that, but it didn't matter. They liked us.

26 / Paulene Johnson Bouse
Barbara Johnson Brister

The Bouse family was celebrating the Fourth of July in their beach cabin across the street from their father's old house when I went to see Paulene and Barbara. They cleared out all the children and grandchildren so we could talk, and the two sisters regaled me with tales of hurricanes and their father, Judge Andrew Johnson, for whom they had the utmost love and respect. Paulene, Barbara, their sisters Paula and Cora Beth, and their brother Andrew helped their father tend cattle and sheep, pick watermelons and do other rugged chores. The girls rode horses everywhere and acted like tomboys, although Mrs. Johnson wanted them to be proper ladies. Paulene and Barbara thought Bolivar was a wonderful place to grow up. "It was like heaven," they said.

Sometimes the sisters finished each other's sentences, and it was obvious that they agreed on everything, so I have blended their accounts as though one person were speaking.[1]

Our daddy, Andrew Johnson, was justice of the peace for forty years, the longest in Texas history. Before every election he would say, "You know what I stand for, I've enjoyed being your judge, and I would like your support again this time," and no one ever defeated him.

Daddy was born in 1894, and when the 1900 storm came, his parents tied him up in a salt cedar tree, and he rode out the storm in that tree. He was six years old. That's probably why he planted salt cedars all over the place later on, around the house and up on the levy behind the house. They withstood storms.

He and our mother were very strict, and Mother would whip us with a switch. She would make us walk barefooted through the grass burrs to go get one, then say, "That's not long enough." Mother had been a school teacher before she married Daddy, and she was a very social person. She was always trying to teach us manners.

Daddy tried to settle people's arguments before they got out of proportion and had to go to court. He made peace between the cattlemen and fishermen a lot of times, and he never talked to anyone else about it.

Sometimes the fishermen would use illegal nets (the net size was too small), but that was their livelihood. All they had was their fishing. Daddy was supposed, by law, to destroy their nets, but he would tell the officials to put the nets in his garage and that "he would take care of it." Then he'd tell the fisherman, "Now, I'm not going to be home, and your net is in the garage, but you're going to have to cut it down. You will have to abide by the rules or next time it will be gone." Daddy was forever preaching a sermon in the most gentle, kind way. He never said a cuss word or was ugly, but if someone was brought up to him drunk, he'd say, "Just put him in jail till morning 'cause I don't want to fool with him."

We had court in our house every Friday, but we never did hear a word. We were not allowed in there, because that way we could never repeat anything. And our parents didn't repeat anything, either.

Court was always at two o'clock, and there was a big old constable from High Island who always came on the eleven o'clock bus—he'd always get here in time for dinner. Court started at two, and he'd stay through court, and then he couldn't leave until the next bus, so he had supper. No matter what Mother fixed, he ate everything. His name was John Payton, and Mother couldn't stand him.

Daddy was a real gentleman, yet he had authority over the

whole community, because when people had problems they'd go to him. If they had money troubles or were about to get a divorce, they'd come to him, and he would just smooth things out. He would help them in so many ways. He had a unique personality, and he gave his time to every group in the community—the school board, church, and many others.

In the 1943 storm, the U. S. dredge *Galveston* went to pieces on the Bolivar jetties. Eight people survived—they were brought to our house and stayed there through the rest of the storm. During the lull of the hurricane many bodies washed ashore.

We had a little fish camp down by the slip and a shrimp boat run by Mr. and Mrs. Meyers. When the storm started to come, they tried to get to our house in their truck, but they couldn't get it started, so they opened the doors, and the wind blew the truck up the road all the way to our house.

We couldn't get any weather information because the war was on and they said it would help the enemy. Out on the beach there were little look-out towers, and soldiers were stationed in them. The wind got so strong the army sent a truck up to get them, and the men got in the truck and started back down to the forts, but couldn't get there so they pulled in and parked right at the base of our front steps. The tin on our roof started coming off, and the back of the truck was covered with canvas—the tin was slicing the top of the truck. The soldiers got out and crawled, holding onto whatever they could, into the house.

Daddy went out to the barn to check things, and I remember him crawling across the yard to the back steps to come up. There were no ferries running, and you couldn't get help from anybody. We were stranded.

We had twenty soldiers, eight men from the dredge boat, Mr. and Mrs. Meyers and their son Skippy, all five of us, and Mother and Daddy in the house. The men from the dredge were injured, and some of the soldiers were banged up a little bit. Mrs. Meyers was an R.N. and she treated the soldiers; she stripped the men down and poured hot cocoa and coffee in them and wrapped them up to get them warm. They had been in the water so long they were shriveling up.

During the storm we shoved our big upright piano against the front door to keep the wind from blowing it open. The soldiers and dredge men helped keep everything in place, but most of the windows blew out. Mother had a great big bread box above the refrigerator in the kitchen, and the bread box flew out the window into the pasture. We thought everything else was going, too. I remember us sitting on the couch and the couch moving across the floor. The house had pilings that went from under the ground all the way up to the roof, and the floor was shaking a lot. The piano kept moving away from the door, and the men kept shoving it back.

After the storm, Daddy and Mr. Meyers took their horses down to the beach and walked back with bodies piled across the saddles. They brought the bodies to the house and put them in the garage down below.

We rode down the beach with Daddy to gather up the cattle. His diary said, "We were short half the herd—lost over twenty thousand dollars worth of cattle, one hundred cows, fifty calves, one hundred fifty sheep, the wool, the feed, the barn, the pens, and so forth. Mr. John and I were on the beach and we spotted a man in the water. We got somebody to go out and get him, but he had been out there so long his mind was gone."

That's the first time we saw Daddy cry. He was glad that we children and his folks had survived the storm, but having to bring in all those dead men and losing most of his farm . . . There were masses of dead animals everywhere—everybody's cattle. When the wind came from the north, it shoved the water way out and blew the cows onto the beach. Then the lull of the storm came, and the tide reversed and swished back in, drowning all the cows up and down. The men had to burn and bury all of them. It was terrible.

There were only three churches—Baptist, Methodist, and Catholic. The Methodist church was completely destroyed and the other two badly damaged. The school was off its blocks, and all the water wells contaminated. We all had to have vaccinations for typhoid fever.

Later on when we were teenagers and could go to the forts during storms and be together in a community situation, it was fun. We almost prayed for it. There you could be with all the kids your age. We went when we had warnings, but in 1943 there was no warning. In fact, the day before, Daddy and Mother had been in town for something, and I was crabbing down by the slip. It got really sultry—hot and still like an Indian summer. That afternoon Daddy was putting a new red roof on the hay house. The other children penned up some sheep, gathered some watermelons and picked up posts from the railroad right-of-way. Daddy wrote in his diary the next day, "The wind had first come from the north, and the barometric pressure was 28.60. Children and I rode to the pasture and could not find cattle. Later, the wind came from the south, at approximately one hundred twenty miles per hour."

When we had warning, though, we went to Port Bolivar. We'd drive the cattle as a herd and put them on top of the forts. We couldn't leave them there long because they would get hungry. Sometimes the cows would panic and jump off and drown.

Everybody took their belongings and children to the forts—bedding and food to live on for a few days. The Bouses always hauled everything they could gather up from their store and put it in one room, and if anybody needed anything, they got it. I know the Bouses never were paid a cent. Everyone brought kerosene lanterns, fuel, and bedrolls. You hadn't lived until you'd been through a storm at the forts. There were individual rooms and tunnels from one fort to the other, but we never went in the tunnels because there were snakes and everything else in them. Each family had a designated area that they went to each year.

We teenagers had a lot of fun. While the grown-ups were sweating out the storm, we were hanging onto the side of the building trying to keep from being blown away and chasing the boys.

The unity of Port Bolivar and closeness of the older families is something almost akin to a big, big family. A long time ago, it was a security blanket. I'll bet you to this day there's not a single old Port Bolivar family that's ever taken a penny of welfare or food or medical attention or anything. It's a unique community. The people want to help the other person, and they just come out and they do it.

27 / Herman Johnson

240 / THE PEOPLE

Herman is the great-great-grandson of Charles Cronea, Jean Lafitte's cabin boy. His great-grandmother was Cronea's daughter; she and her husband John traded a rifle and scabbard for ten acres of land at High Island, where Herman now lives.

I discovered Herman one day in the fall of 1989 when I was photographing old houses in High Island. Thinking his was the Cronea home, I knocked on the door and was greeted by Herman in his carpentry clothes. He explained that this was the ancestral Meynig place, and that he was restoring it to live in. When I asked Herman if he would share some of his past for the Bolivar book, he readily accepted, and I made a return visit a few days later. Our first interview took place in the living room, sitting on sawhorses.

I was born in Beaumont, October 3, 1932. My mother went up there to the doctor. My daddy's a yankee and he lives in Indianapolis, and all he ever did was race cars. He was a chief mechanic, and he had cars in the Five Hundred about fifteen, sixteen years. He used to break every bone in his body all the time, and he never did make any money. He's somethin' else.

My grandma's mother was a Cronea. Molly Payton. She was a midwife. She delivered every kid on this island. You go down to the courthouse, and all them old settlers used to put down "baby"

Cade or "baby" Johnson or "baby" Dailey. It might be a month or two before they ever named him. That's how them old timers used to get so messed up on Social Security and stuff, because they just had "baby" on the records.

My aunt was born at Star Lake. That's near a ridge that runs from Big Hill to High Island. That used to be the only way you could get to High Island. In 1898 the biggest snowstorm that ever hit the state of Texas came along, and she was born out there in a tent in that snowstorm. The family was out there marketin' ducks. They'd kill ducks, put 'em in a barrel and salt 'em, then send 'em to Galveston to sell 'em.

When I was a kid I used to trap for Challie Holt. We used to trap everything—gators, muskrats, nutria. My whole family trapped and hunted all their lives.

Challie Holt come down here once a week, him and Mr. Kirkpatrick. He was his overseer. They'd ride around here in the oil field checkin' things out. I was just a kid. I'd be down at Mr. Kirkpatrick's pool hall, and I'd see 'em down there.

We had fur sales in the pool hall. When the fur buyers were here, that was the *thing*. That was like a fair come to town. There was a lot of money goin'. All buyers brung cash money, and you'd have five or six buyers. They come mostly from Beaumont, and Mr. Britt from Alvin, Pappy, and Mr. Knight from Beaumont, Mr. Rosenquist from Silsbee. They come from all over. You'd have about thirty people sellin' rats [muskrats]. You ain't never seen so much money in all your life.

They had a little house out back about twenty by twenty, and they'd skin 'em and hang 'em up and dry 'em by a fire. Then after the hide dried, they turned 'em wrong-side-out, put 'em on stretchers and the heat cured the meat, and they stack 'em up in hundred bundles and put 'em in sacks or boxes.

They used to have five grades, but they don't do that no more. They don't grade. You had your kits, your trash, your seconds and thirds and top rats. Old man Rosenquist had a big old coat on, and he'd sit there in the pool hall right in the middle of the floor. He used to give us kids a nickel a box, and we'd take them rats and just pour 'em on him, and he'd grade 'em. He was the buyer and the grader. Oh, yeah.

It took all night. Sometimes it'd be one or two o'clock in the mornin' before they'd get through, 'cause they had so many buyers, you know. And those buyers would go back and grade every one, and they'd give you so much a round. The highest I can remember, I think it was back in '48, they gave a dollar sixty-five, and, man, that was like fifteen dollars a rat then.

We'd see 'em drinkin', gamblin', playin' dominos, shootin' pool. They'd see us kids and say, "Hey, kid, want a dollar?" They'd give us a dollar, and you could get a cold drink for a nickel, so we'd hang around.

We didn't have no TV or anything like that. Our fun was goin' to the pool hall. We had three of 'em here. There was lots of drinkin' and lots of characters—roughnecks and such. We'd watch the old men play Moon or Forty-two. They played all day long. If we'd sweep the floors, they'd let us play a game of pool. Sometimes we'd have rat skinnin' contests, too. See which one could skin a muskrat the fastest.

I was raised with old alligator hunters, my buddies and my uncles. I'm an old gator hunter from way back. It's better than cattle. You don't have to feed 'em, vaccinate 'em, or worry about any kind of a fence, or nothin'. So, I mean, it's just profit, you know?

People kill 'em just for fun. We used to call 'em "freebies." We used to go gator huntin', and we'd get in the boat about twelve o'clock in the daytime, like on a Saturday, and we'd find two or three dead ones floatin', and we'd pick 'em up and skin 'em. We got 'em before the sun hit 'em. As long as his toenail was stickin' up, he was still good.

All my old hide buyers are dead. I had one in Alvin, Mr. Treadwell. He was a sweet old man. And we had one in Beaumont we called Pappy. That's all he ever done, and he was a prince of a man. He'd always give you a fair price and never try to cheat ya. The rest of 'em, you had to kinda watch 'em. But they're all dead now, though.

Pappy was eighty-seven years old when he died. He come from Oklahoma, and he was buyin' skunks when he was ten years old. He got hung up with them boys down in New Orleans, and that's when he got his start. He was workin' in the warehouse sackin' and gradin', then he started buyin' for 'em.

Durin' the war they had about two hundred and fifty coast guards here patrollin' the beach from Bolivar to Sabine Pass. There was a bunch of ships blown up out there, and there was a U-boat sunk right off of Sabine Pass. I got a buddy that scuba dives, and three years ago, he went on it and drownded in it. There's all kind of boats been sunk out there.[1]

The government wouldn't let you go on the beach down there when a ship was sunk. When we was kids we used to have to go get our firewood off the beach. Everybody in High Island did—they all had wood stoves. But they wouldn't let you on the beach, so you knew somethin' was up. They sunk a ship. Or a sub.

"Pop" Payton was my uncle. He was the constable. He had an old Chevrolet, but he couldn't drive it. He could make it go ahead, but he couldn't back up 'cause he was too fat to turn around and look behind him. Most the time he'd get my brother to drive him, but sometimes he'd get me. I was about twelve years old, and I couldn't drive either.

We used to go over to Galveston, and the thing that scared me the worst was the ferry. I was afraid I'd run into somebody. We went to the Galveston police station on Nineteenth Street, and I didn't know how to park, so I just left the car in the middle of the street. The police would look out the window and say, "Hey, there's a car parked illegally out there." Somebody would say, "Oh, it's okay. That's Pop Payton's. Just leave it alone."

We'd go to see old Mr. Moody, and I was scared to death of

him. He was *Galveston*. Pop and him were buddies. All them old-timers was.

Old man Henry Sullivan, what he done, he married a Cronea. He couldn't read or write, and he used to go to Galveston to get supplies for people. They'd give him a grocery list, and he'd go to Galveston and buy it. He sailed through Mud Bayou out to the bay. A lot of people didn't have no money, so they'd trade land for groceries.

Mr. Sullivan was a big Irishman. He was about six foot three—a big old man. Those old-timers used to bite and gouge. His eyes was pulled out so many times, boy, they was in real bad shape. That was the only thing wrong with him, you know. They'd pull your eyeball out and lay it on your cheek.

He used to work on the wharf. Them old Irishmen and dagoes, they used them just like niggers. They'd import 'em, and they considered 'em dumb and ignorant. That's how the Irishmen got in Galveston. Some of 'em was stonecutters, and they cut the stone for all them fancy homes—that Bishop Castle and rich people's houses.

This is the old Meynig house I'm workin' on. I been doin' it for about four years. It belonged to Mrs. Meynig, and she was a hundred and two when she died. It was about '63 or '64, I think. I bought it about five years after that. It was all run down. Nobody had done nothin' to it—the grass was up, the tallow trees was takin' over. It took me six months to pull all the tallow trees up. You got to pull 'em up, dig 'em and cut 'em. They just keep poppin' up.

They claim this house was built in 1900. I can't remember who built the thing. Local people built it. But it's an old box house. They built 'em all the same. They put the two by fours on the sills, and it was square. And they did it all by hand. I tell you what, though, them boys was real good, but they weren't the carpenters these boys are now. This house was cut out with a handsaw. That's all they had. They'd buy the lumber and two or three of 'em, they'd saw it all out, then they'd start puttin' it together. It'd take 'em about three or four months to saw it all out. But they did wonderful with the tools they had.

When I sell enough alligators I rebuild another room in this house. I've done one room every season. Year before last was bad. We didn't get hardly any gators, and I had to turn my permits back in. That like to killed me.

28 / Monroe Kahla, Sr.

"Uncle Pike" Kahla, born in 1904, still works in his garden, uses chicken fertilizer, and grows seven-pound turnips. Every year he supervises the goat roundup on Goat Island and directs the slaughtering behind his house, tends to the calf brandings, raises turkeys and guineas, and distributes government cheese and butter to the older folks. Pike and his wife Elaine live in Port Bolivar in a modest green house with red geraniums and pink flamingoes in the front yard. Last Halloween the grandchildren put a dummy of Elaine sitting on the front porch and one of Uncle Pike perched on the roof, then hid behind a tree with a rope. When trick-or-treaters came to the front door, the pranksters jerked the rope and Uncle Pike's dummy fell off the roof, scaring the little ones out of their wits.

There was eleven of us kids, and I grew up on Bolivar. Papa and them lived right above Crystal Beach, and when the 1915 storm hit, it come at night when they didn't know nothin' about it, and the house floated on the tide about three or four hundred feet on yonder down where the canal is. They had to climb into the attic to keep from drownin' 'cause the water was all up inside. There was Papa and Mama and three of my brothers and two girls. Mama had a baby one week later in the attic. We lost everything we had then. All our cattle was killed, and we had to start all over again.

We all stayed at Grandpa Kahla's a good while till we built us a house over here, you see. Papa had to build a house and barn, and he used lumber off the beach. All us kids had to get out and help, then we moved in. We started farmin', and in them days we'd get some wild horses and break 'em. Boy, that was a mess.

There wasn't hardly any houses left, and no food. We would find a big one-hundred-pound sack of flour that only got partly wet, and we'd pick it up and bring it home, and Mama would make bread out of it. There wasn't no way to get meat, but there was canned goods we could find on the beach, and there was a bunch of asparagus—cases and cases of it. I never will forget it. I ate that stuff till it made me sick. Oh, man.

There were some potatoes we found, too. For water we had wells, and that wasn't a problem. There was snakes everywhere—them old black moccasins and rattlesnakes. You had to watch where you was goin'. They'd be blind, 'cause that salt would get in their eyes, and you get anywhere near around 'em and they'd start bitin'.

Only thing we found that come ashore was a big white sow. It was alive, and we said, "Looky yonder—a live hog." And Papa said, "Well, go and get the poor thing." And we went to get it, and the hog was so gentle. We petted it, and then drove it on home from the beach. Just the luck, she was bred already, and just two or three months afterwards we found a bunch of little pigs. I was born in 1904, and I was about eleven years old then.

We was buildin' us a house after the storm, and my dad and I was pickin' up lumber on the beach, and we come up on two little girls. They was tied together. We just dug holes and pushed 'em in and covered 'em up. There wasn't no names on 'em or nothin', and they was smellin' so bad. They might have come from Galveston, but we didn't know.

I picked up a big piece of board I had dug out, and there was a big woman layin' there, and I said, "Papa, here's a woman." And he said, "Well, we'll just have to dig a big hole and lay her in it." We buried her and the two little girls along in that big sand hill. They didn't wash out, and I imagine if you'd dig over there you'd find 'em.

We had some of 'em, though, they wouldn't bury people. They

would just go along there and look for trunks and stuff, and they was there for the money. And I won't say who they was, but one had a hatchet, and he cut a woman's finger off and took her ring and put it in a sack. My dad wouldn't let us take none of them trunks and break 'em open. But all of them headhunters did, and they got a bunch of money and stuff. Papa said, "We ain't that kind of people."

After the storm we only had two old milk cows left, so every now and then we'd buy a cow or horse and bring 'em home from Galveston. Papa was bringin' a bunch of ole wild mares on a sailboat, and one of 'em kicked him and knocked him overboard—we thought he was goin' to drown, but we got him in. When we started to unload the horses, one broke the plank, and down they all went, just like a bunch of kids. My brothers was ridin' along the shore and helped round 'em back up.

We helped Daddy with the cattle—every mornin' we'd leave here about daylight on our horses and go check on the cows. Sometimes we'd find a cow that the little calf was gone and she had a big bag on her, one of those wild cows. Me and the other boys would bring 'er home and gentle her, you know, make a milk cow out of her. We'd go plum up yonder to Caplen and all 'round. In them days there wasn't no houses there, and everything was just wide open.

When we had big freezes, a lot of the cattle would die and we'd skin the hides and get two or three dollars for 'em in Houston. We loaded 'em in barrels and hauled 'em up there on boats, then put 'em in ole Model As or Ts. Sometimes Daddy took dried hides, cut 'em in little strips and made cattle quirts and whips.

When I got big enough we'd go out for a whole week brandin'. We kids would get played out, but we knew better than to say somethin' 'cause them old men would whip our butts with them cow whips. They'd holler, "Boys, get up!" And when they hollered, "Get up!" you better get up, 'cause look out for them whips. We didn't holler at 'em or talk back to 'em, 'cause they was right if they was wrong, by gosh.

We'd start up at High Island. We'd brand some of 'em up there, and we'd work on down and pick out the calves and brand 'em on the back. They'd say, "You all boys, we'll bring you somethin' to eat after while or in the mornin'. Take your saddles and get by them cattle guards and don't let them cows go through it. You all stay there all night."

We knew a damn sight better we better stay there, too. Many a night we slept on them ole wet saddle blankets. There wasn't so many mosquitoes then, but them ole wolves was a-hollerin', and us kids was about half skeered. We knew a durn sight better than to leave. And that ole guy, Uncle Barney, was hell on tryin' to skeer everybody, you know. One night we was right by the graveyard at the cattle guard, and I said, "I believe Uncle Barney's gonna come out and skeer us tonight."

About twelve or so o'clock we was all layin' there sleepin', a couple watchin', and Uncle Barney tied his horse way down there and sneaked up and started hollerin' and raisin' heck like a cow, and boy, those boys jumped and started yellin' "Look out, here come the cows!" And I said, "Hell, that's Uncle Barney!" And he started whoopin' and laughin' then. And the boys'd tell the older folks, and they'd raise heck with Barney 'cause they wanted us boys to get a good night's rest so we could hold them calves down and brand.

We used to have these rodeos. When I was young, Papa didn't want us to ride the steers because we might bruise 'em up. They didn't think about us, the hell with us. We'd sneak outside, my cousins and all of us, and we'd go out at night and round up a bunch of cattle and put 'em in a big arena. We was supposed to just get the milk cows, but Papa had told us to bring everything so we could use the fertilizer for the fields, and we'd pick out a bunch of good-looking steers and bring them, too.

Boy, nighttime would come, and we'd get out there and ride 'em, and some of us would get all full of cow fertilizer, and we'd be in a hell of a fix next morning. Mama would get up raisin' heck—"You all boys, where you been?" I guess I was about fourteen years old then, and it was a wonder we didn't get killed. We did it at night 'cause Papa would whip us if he caught us—and we finally made him let us have a rodeo.

We had a little rodeo back of our place, and George Standley, from Anahuac, he got in there with us, and he was brave. He said, "I'll ride one of those big steers." In those days they wouldn't let us ride the bulls. He broke his leg, and he was wearing a pair of boots he had borrowed from Vernon Kahla. I said, "Well, we can't do anything but cut his damn boot off." And George said, "No, you can't cut the boot off, because it isn't mine, by gosh." We just held him down anyhow and cut the durn boot off, and boy, he was mad as heck at us. Old Vernon, he cried about it 'cause we cut his boot off.

In the rodeos we rode the steers and milked the wild cows and everything else. We built a rodeo pen up there this side of Crystal Beach, and we used to call it Patton then. My sister Ethel says, "Pike, if you ride one of them bulls, I'll ride it with you." And like a damn fool, I didn't know. Mr. Henry Sullivan, a big guy, says, "Yeah, I'll take care of you all." And I got on the durn bull's neck, and Ethel got on his back. A big yellow bull—I never will forget him—and boy, he come out there and was really jumpin' and raisin' heck, and Henry come up on his horse and grabbed Ethel under her arms and took her off. I said, "God durn, what am I supposed to do?" And he said, "Get off the best way you can!" And I just turned loose and fell off, and the bull took after me, and I had to outrun him to the durn fence. Boy, everybody was laughin' at us.

And them old cows was so wild that come out of the woods—we would gather a bunch of 'em up, and some guys would rope one while the other ones milked her. We was supposed to get a little milk in a soda water bottle and take it back to the other end while that old cow was kickin' and carryin' on. Them cows would tear our clothes off and everything else. They had hardly ever seen a rope or a human before. They come out of the woods behind Caplen and Long Point.

Us kids had to help dig the sweet potatoes—about ten acres of 'em. I mean they was pretty. We worked like a bunch of slaves plantin' them things. That ground was so durn hard—whoo. Your feet'd be blistered at night. We didn't know what shoes was, and we wore short pants. We never wore no long pants till we was about twenty years old. Wore those knee pants with a button. And we'd wear those old striped overalls that made us look like convicts out there in the field workin'.

We got everything out of the catalogs, and Mama made the dresses out of them spotted feed sacks. Later on I used to make my own pants out of canvas, so when I'd kneel down for oysterin', it wouldn't hurt my knees so much. It'd be so cold in the mornin' with ice on the ground, and you'd leave your pants on the boat, go in the cabin and strip off, get them pants and there'd be ice all over 'em.

Every Saturday and Sunday was our days off, and boy, we used to have a hell of a time. We sometimes went swimmin' in the bay. We had a wagon, and Papa would hitch up a pair of horses, and we'd go out into the water till the horse was pretty near swimmin', and we'd have a lot of fun divin' out of the wagon. Papa would hold the horses while we'd play out there in the water.

There used to be plenty of oysters all along the shore, till they built that canal [Intracoastal]. There was oysters as big as your hand, and we used to take the wagon out in the wintertime when it was cold and there was nothin' else to do, and we'd pick up a bunch of oysters. Everybody took a sack, and we'd pick up sacks full and load them in the wagon.

And crabs. We used to go along at nighttime with a light—one of them old smudge pots. You'd take a five-gallon can and cut it open and wing it out on both sides and have a bunch of old rags tied in there and fill it full of kerosene. We'd have a light to go along and catch flounders and big old male crabs. We'd bring them home, and Mama would make crab gumbo. Our faces would be all full of smut from that ole pot.

We used a sharp rod with a broom handle on it to stick the flounders. Those redfish would be swimmin' along there, and we'd gig them, too. When you saw the fish, you'd hold still, then hit him in the side and hold him down, and the other boy would hold the light while you picked him up.

We had a seine about eight hundred foot long, and we'd haul it down to the bay in a wagon and wade out with it in water over our neck, come around, and bring it in. That's how we caught our fish and shrimp. In them days you couldn't sell shrimp 'cause everybody caught their own, and we'd fill that wagon up with big shrimp and dig us a trench, shovel the shrimp in it and make fertilizer out of 'em. Boy, that stuff would grow.

Mama would peel shrimp and pickle 'em in vinegar, and they'd keep year-round. We'd clean all them little fish good, cook 'em down, and you could eat the whole thing, bones and all, just like sardines. Mama would steam the little six-inch mackerel and can 'em—we canned lots of things and made our own ketchup, too.

We bought our coffee for about five or ten cents a pound. Papa used to bring home about fifty pounds of green coffee, and we hated to parch it. We had to put it in the oven in a pan and roast it till it got dark, then we'd have to grind it up.

The women did the ironin' while the men worked outside. They had to heat the iron on top of the wood stove. Sometimes they'd get smut all over the shirt and have to wash it all over again. Them lids on top of them damned wood stoves was all black. Those girls would catch hell.

Back there by the Indian graveyard the wolves would be all over that place. One day we counted twelve of 'em. They would catch the little calves and eat 'em. On Sundays we'd get on our horses, and we'd run wolves and kill 'em. Some of us would get so far that way, and some of us would get the other way, and we'd run 'em down. Sometimes we'd shoot 'em and sometimes we'd rope 'em.

There was a watermelon field out there by the graveyard, and we chased two wolves till they jumped the big high fence to keep the hogs out, and they got in there, and we roped 'em, we did.

Them old wolves would throw their heads up and grab the rope, and you'd jerk it out of their mouths. They was mean, I tell you.

Me and my brother Slim used to give them wolves a fit all the time. They were big and brindle-lookin' timber wolves. Some of 'em would get after a cow if a calf was there, and after they run the cow off, some of the other wolves would kill the calf. Sometimes they killed pigs and rabbits, but they never attacked any humans.

Mr. Hudnall had a hunting camp about where Sun Oil is now. There used to be so many mesquite bushes you couldn't hardly ride through there. And on the ponds there was big rushes as tall as a house. Crab Lake was nothin' but a rush pond. We used to run wolves, and they'd hide in there. Old man Henry Sullivan, he'd have some dogs, and we'd wait for him till he got there, and we'd send in the dogs, then he'd go in there with clubs and kill them wolves. He was a big ole husky guy—he wasn't scared of a bear. He'd just go in on his horse and beat the wolf to death. He wasn't scared of nothin'. He lived at High Island.

At Caplen we used to have a bunch of sloughs and ponds, and anybody could go there and hunt in them days. One time we had some bears here. We never did get to kill 'em, but we seen 'em. I seen 'em a couple of times when I was ridin' a horse, but I didn't have no gun. One time I seen a big ole black bear here [Port Bolivar], and ole Ben Bright seen two up at Crab Lake.

Ben used to make moonshine up there and had a bunch of hogs. That was some ole black man, he was. He was friends with half of Bolivar. Every Sunday me and a couple of the boys would ride up there, and that's when they had all them big rushes. Ben had big barrels and all in there, and he was foolin' with it one day, and there was a bunch of hogs runnin' around everywhere squealin' and raisin' heck. We said, "What's the matter with them hogs?" He said, "I dumped a bunch of that durn mash out, and I guess they're all drunk." Boy, they were goin' around hollerin' and squealin', they was. He said, "Next time I'll have to watch myself and dump a little at a time."

But he'd make that ole white corn whiskey. Boy, it was pretty whisky, but you better not drink too much of it, 'cause it'd knock you on your can. He'd tell us, "Go on and drink all you want." But I'd say, "Nun-unh, not me. I might take a swallow if I'm cold, but not that stuff. I might not be able to find the way home."

The law never did get him. I think he was in with the law. We had an old fellow who lived at the lighthouse, old man Brooks. He'd get in his ole Model A and go up there and tell Ben, "Look out, the law's comin' over tonight on the boat." And Ben'd lay low till it was over, then he'd go again.

Most of the time they'd take the stuff over to Galveston on Twentieth Street where that big whiskey joint was and sell it. They had them bottles with three corners they'd put in a canvas bag and make it a square bag. And heck, they knowed me, and I'd go by, and they'd say, "Kahla, want to take some whiskey home?" And they'd give me a bag, and I'd bring it home to Papa and them, and they'd use it for medicine.

That's what our medicine was in them days. You'd get a cold and you'd take a sip of sugar and whiskey. And they'd put all kinds of stuff in it to rub you with if you was feelin' bad. They'd get those camphor balls and mix it together, and boy, they'd rub it on your chest and your back, and next morning you were ready to roll again. Take off and go to work, by gosh, you were well now.

They'd catch a coon and take the fat off and make grease out of it, too, to rub on your chest if you got a cold. In them days they didn't know what Vicks Salve or Vasoline was. And pole cat musk, it's pretty and green, and if you take a match to it, it blazes way up. You could inhale it if you got a real bad cold, and your nose would start runnin' just like an ole horse, and next day you wouldn't have no cold at all. But you couldn't smell for a week.

Ole Ben Bright first come in here to help Uncle Frank and Uncle Fred. They was farmin' up there at Caplen—raisin' watermelons. And Ben come in there ridin' on a horse, he did. They had a couple of old shacks up there, and Uncle Frank made him stay there and help pick watermelons and stuff. Uncle Frank had some hogs, and first thing you know, ole Ben had some hogs. He'd steal Uncle Frank's hogs and put his mark on 'em, but my uncle wouldn't say nothin' about it.

After ole Ben had stayed around there four or five years, first thing you know he started havin' some calves. One day Raymond Bouse wanted a couple of butcher calves for his store, and Ben said, "Okay, I'll bring you a real good one." And Ole Ben hauled a calf down here in his Model T truck, and they went to skin it, and it had Mr. Bouse's brand on it. Mr. Bouse said, "God damn, I bought my own damned calf." Ole Ben said, "Aw, I guess I made a mistake. I'll bring you another one tomorrow." So next day Ben brought him another calf, and it had Uncle Frank's brand. And Ben said, "Well, these was two good calves, and you wanted two good calves, so I sold you two." Boy, we really hoorahed Mr. Bouse. It was about nine or ten dollars in them days for a calf, and that was good money.

When I was a kid some of 'em used to bootleg whiskey across. That was back in the twenties when it was dry here. There was big money in it in them days, and I wanted to do it, too, but Mama and Papa wouldn't let me.

They'd come in with them ships, bring the whiskey to shore in little boats; meanwhile, Mansel Shaw had a tractor and Uncle Bluch had a pair of ole mules and them rice field wagons that had sides on 'em. About where the fire station is now in Crystal Beach, there's a hole in the sand hill on this side, and they'd get the whiskey off the beach at night and haul it up and put it in that hole. Then they'd load the wagon and haul it down Stingaree Road, where boats would meet 'em to take it to Galveston.

There was always a man watchin' at the hole. It was deep, and they'd put weeds and stuff on top to hide it. The Prohibition men would come across on the *Silver King*, and Mr. Brooks, the lighthouse keeper, would talk to them and keep 'em off. Then Mr. Brooks would come get a couple of bags of whiskey and take it home. He liked that stuff.

I was ridin' out to check on a couple of cows with one ole boy, and we had to ride right by the hole. He seen that whiskey and wanted to take a bunch of it. I said, "No, you don't. Look over yonder in the grass and you'll see a man's head ever once in a while. If you want some, I'll just get you one of those bags, and that fellow won't say nothin', but you start fillin' up, and you might not leave here. They'd just as soon shoot you as look at you, by gosh." He got him one of them quarts, and that was all, and he got so damn drunk I had to bring him back home.

Me and Uncle Leslie and Arlie Shaw went rabbit huntin' at Uncle Wesley's camp house near where the Sun Oil Company is. We had an ole Model T then, and in them days you had to drive up the beach. We went up the beach, and the tide was low, and there was a bunch of that durn whiskey along the beach; somebody had got scared and unloaded it, and it floated to shore. Well, we picked up about a dozen bags of it and Uncle Leslie started drinkin' it, and he wasn't used to drinkin'. We went to go rabbit huntin', and Uncle Leslie got so damn drunk he was barkin' and runnin' around, and we couldn't get no rabbits. He was drunk as a barn owl, and we was scared he was gonna shoot somebody, so we took his gun and hid it in the truck and brought him home.

The bootleggin' went on for two or three years. Uncle Barney and Uncle Fred, they got into it when they was single and runnin' the women. Then that fellow would give one a truck and the other a big car to help haul the whiskey. Well, Uncle Barney, he'd go over yonder and collect, and he wouldn't give Uncle Fred none of the money, you see, and then they'd have a fight about it. And Uncle Fred, he'd get the money and Uncle Barney didn't get none. They went back and forth till that fellow had to take the truck and car away from 'em, cause they was fightin' over the durn money, they was. That was a heck of a mess. It's a wonder somebody didn't get killed on that one.

In them days they didn't care whether they killed you or not. Nobody wouldn't say nothin', you know. You'd shoot a man, and there wouldn't be nothin' to that. Many a one of 'em got killed, and they'd bury 'em out there in a field.

We had a law, but he wasn't no good—old man Payton, from High Island. Ole John Payton. He was supposed to be the law to take care of everything—the sheriff, you know. You'd have to tell him what to do, and he couldn't even write his own name. Boy, he was a cutter, ole John Payton. He wasn't elected, and I think they just put him in there 'cause he wasn't no good for nothin' else. He'd pack a big ole gun, but I don't think he knowed how to shoot it. Ole fool. He was the High Island sheriff, and when we needed him down here somebody'd have to get in a truck and go pick him up and take him back. He didn't have no wagon and he couldn't ride a horse 'cause he was too damned fat, and he couldn't drive a car. There wasn't very much crime then—everybody helped each other, and if there was a fight we'd help get things back together again.

The ole *Silver King* boat was the only way you could get over to Galveston. You had to pay twenty-five cents to go over and twenty-five cents to come back. It was a pleasure boat, not too big, but it had an upstairs and a downstairs, and boy, that thing would like to sink on you when a norther come. But it'd come over every mornin' and go back in the evenin'. And it'd go out there with those ships, and it be a norther blowin', and that thing was top-heavy, and man, people would be hollerin' and screamin', "It's gonna turn over!" "Oh, no," the captain would say. "It ain't turned over yet."

The ole *Silver King* used to come down there by the ferry landin'. They had that ole barge with a tugboat that would take the train across. They called it the *Seaside Special*, and on Sundays we never had anything to do, and we'd haul out and go watch the *Seaside Special* come in. That old train with three or four cars had a lot of people on it, and they'd load it on the barge, and the tugboat would take it across to Ninth Street in Galveston and unhook it.

We just had to see that *Seaside Special* on Sunday. It couldn't go by without all of us watchin' it. It was just like a circus to us. All the people on the train would look at us on our horses, and some of us would holler at 'em. If there was any black people on the train, some of the boys would throw dirt at 'em through the window, but I never would do that.

The train would pick up any passenger wherever he was walkin' along—could have been a duck hunter from Galveston with a bunch of ducks (in them days, all he could pack), and he'd flag it down, and the train would stop so he could get on. I think the fare was about fifteen cents to go back to Galveston.

The hunters used them ole shotguns with that black powder—boy, you'd look out of a smoke screen when you'd shoot. When you fired the gun, that black powder was like a train shootin' out black smoke. Sometimes you'd have to wait a few minutes to see if you killed anything. And that ole shell was about three inches long. Boy, it'd kick ya. Your arm'd be all blue next day. A lot of times we put rags on our arms. The guns were Lefevres and L. C. Smiths.

There used to be a lot of geese here, too, and a lot of people come from Galveston to shoot 'em, as many as they could pack. We used to go out about dark and kill all the game we wanted, but there wasn't no iceboxes so we just shot as many as we could eat the next day.

In about 1931 or '32 me and my cousin was workin' on the shell road at Port Bolivar with Raymond Bouse—he was the boss—and here come an ole Model A car. It was Bonnie and Clyde. We was back in the woods, and I was waitin' for my mules to rest for a while, and they said "How do we get to High Island?" I told 'em, "You have to go back up to the beach and go that way." They said, "Come on over and talk to us." I said, "Okay." He was sittin' in the front and she was in the back. She had machine guns layin' in her lap, and he had a couple of guns layin' alongside him. She was a pretty girl, she was, and they was young. I thought, "Uh-oh, I hope they don't start nothin' here, gunnin' us, by God!" So I just got to shootin' the bull with 'em, and I asked 'em, "Where you all been?" And they said, "We was goin' down towards Galveston, but we didn't think we wanted to ride that ferry, and we turned around and decided to go back and we got lost." So I said, "Well, you have to go up that-a-way." They knew where High Island was but they didn't know how to get to it. I told 'em they had to go up on the beach 'cause there weren't no roads to it. We only had a few dirt and shell roads then.

I asked 'em if they was any kin to the Barrows at High Island, and they said, "No, I don't think we are, but we might be. We want to get on to Beaumont. We never had no trouble the last couple of months—we been doin' good." I said, "Oh, you have?" (Oh, God damn.) They said they just robbed the rich, but they wouldn't hurt none of the poor people. We talked about thirty minutes or so, then they went and spent the night at Mrs. Kline's house in Port Bolivar.

When the law got 'em they were at some poor people's house—they had just robbed some bank or business, and they knew those people's relatives. When they went to stay with 'em somebody blowed on 'em so the law ganged around 'em and shot 'em.

When Pearl Harbor happened, that's when they put those coast guards in the old [Sea View] hotel at High Island. The fellows had horses and patrolled along the beach at night. That's when that ship with big bales of rubber was goin' right out in front of High Island, and a submarine sank it. We was workin' out on the forts when they bombed that thing, and it sounded like a cannon went off. They notified us then and we closed everything down and pulled the sireen, and here come the blimp, airplanes and all.

Before the ship sank, there was shrimp boats all around the ship draggin', and they didn't know what to do, but when they seen the men on the rafts, they picked up all of 'em—must have been about thirty. But the shrimpers saved everyone. The submarine must have torpedoed 'em. All the bales of rubber floated to shore, and we sold one of 'em for five dollars. A lot of things happened then that nobody knows about.

There was blackouts on Bolivar all the time. For a while there, after it got dark, everybody had to put their lights out, cars and everything else. If you wanted to go somewhere you couldn't drive with no lights on. We'd go to town after dark and we'd have to come back with no lights—drive slow, be careful. We was all runnin' in the dark. One time the only two cars in Bolivar run into one another, but it wasn't much of a wreck.

We was workin' out at the fort buildin' barracks for the soldiers. I was kind of an overseer—and after the boss left, I had to go and get the men to unload the lumber off the trucks. The trucks come in about dark, and we couldn't use lights, so we'd just throw lumber comin' and goin'. We had about eleven thousand feet of lumber, and we just threw it as far as we could, and the next mornin' we'd have the crew straighten it all up.

At the fort they had twelve-inch guns with eight-inch guns mounted on 'em. They decided the guns was too big and not needed here, so they made us take the guns down and put 'em in boxes. We thought we was doin' somethin' good, and we was told to grease them all up so they could go on the ship. We took the guns to High Island and loaded them on the train there, and that was at the beginning of the war. They was goin' to ship the guns over to some islands. We put the boxes on the train, but the inspector come along and told us to take 'em all out and clean off the grease because it might cause a fire on the ship. The government wanted us to go overseas with the guns and put 'em back up, but I had just gotten married and said no. The other ones that worked with me said no, they didn't want to go either, and about a month afterward the ship got blowed up, and they lost the crew, guns, and all.

Notes

Chapter 1

1. Dr. Thomas Hester, lecture: "Prehistory of the Upper Texas Coast," April 6, 1990, Rosenberg Library, Galveston, Texas; Dr. Lawrence E. Aten, letter to author, November 13, 1990.
2. Álvar Núñez Cabeza de Vaca, *Adventures in the Unknown Interior of America*. Translated and annotated by Cyclone Covey with new epilogue by William T. Pilkington. Albuquerque: University of New Mexico Press, 1961, 54–57.
3. Ibid., 57, 58.
4. Ibid., 60.
5. Ibid., first quotation 61, second quotation 63.
6. Ibid., 61.
7. Ibid., 62.
8. Ibid., 64.
9. Ibid., 66.
10. Ibid., 66, 67.
11. Ibid., 10.
12. Interview with Dr. Margaret Swett Henson, Houston, November 15, 1990.
13. Fray Agustín Morfi, *History of Texas, 1673–1779*. Translated with biographical introduction and annotations by Carlos Eduardo Castañeda. Vol. 1. Albuquerque: The Quivira Society, 1935, 80.
14. Henri Folmer, "De Bellisle on the Texas Coast." *Southwestern Historical Quarterly*. Vol. 44, 1940–41, 207.
15. Ibid., 211–14.
16. Ibid., 215.
17. Ibid., 216, 217.
18. Ibid., 219.
19. Ibid., 221–25.
20. Dr. Joseph O. Dyer, *The Lake Charles Atakapas (cannibals): Period of 1817 to 1820*. Galveston: privately printed, 1917, 1–6.

21. Ibid., 2.
22. Ibid., 2.
23. Ibid., 2.
24. Ibid., 2, 3.
25. Ibid., 3.
26. Ibid., 3.
27. Charles W. Hayes, *Galveston: History of the Island and the City.* Vol. 1. Austin: Jenkins Garrett Press, 1974, 44.
28. Aten, Dr. Lawrence E., *Indians of the Upper Texas Coast.* New York: Academic Press, 1983, 34, 36, 55–60.
29. Dr. Lawrence Aten to author, November 13, 1990.
30. T. N. Campbell, "Archeological Investigations at the Caplen Site, Galveston County, Texas." *Texas Journal of Science,* Vol. 9, No. 4, December, 1957, 451–57; Dr. Thomas R. Hester (Director of Texas Archeological Research Laboratory), Lecture at Rosenberg Library, Galveston, Texas, April 6, 1990; J. F. Powell, "An Epidemiological Analysis of Mortality and Morbidity in Five Late Prehistoric Populations from the Upper and Central Texas Coast." Master's Thesis, Department of Anthropology, University of Texas at Austin, 1989.

Chapter 2

1. Hayes, *Galveston,* 17; Margaret Swett Henson, *Juan Davis Bradburn: A Reappraisal of the Mexican Commander of Anahuac.* College Station: Texas A & M University Press, 1982, 27, 28.
2. Hayes, *Galveston,* 18.
3. Henson, *Bradburn,* 27, 28.
4. Henderson K. Yoakum, *History of Texas from Its First Settlement in 1685 to Its Annexation to the United States in 1846.* Vol. 1. Austin: Steck Co., 1935 (originally published in 1855), 455.; Eugene C. Barker, "The African Slave Trade in Texas." *Texas Historical Association Quarterly.* Vol. 6, 1902, 146.
5. Anonymous unpublished manuscript, Laffite Files, Rosenberg Library, Galveston, Texas.
6. Barker, "African Slave Trade," 148.
7. Hayes, *Galveston,* 27.
8. Yoakum, *History of Texas,* 194; Hayes, *Galveston,* 34, 35.
9. J. Randall Jones, "A Visit to Galveston Island in 1818." Transcript of notes by Philip Tucker from Jones's memoirs. Rosenberg Library, Galveston, Texas.
10. Ibid.
11. Dr. Joseph O. Dyer, "Lafitte a Schemer as Well as an Executive," *Galveston Daily News,* May 14, 1922.
12. "George Graham's Mission to Galveston in 1818: Two Important

Documents Bearing Upon Louisiana History." Edited by Walker Prichard. *Louisiana Historical Quarterly*. Vol. 20, No. 3, July, 1937, 646, 647.

13. Hayes, *Galveston*, 44.
14. Jean Laffite to James Long, July 7, 1819, Lamar Papers, Vol. 1, No. 19.
15. Hon. Dermot H. Hardy and Major Ingham S. Roberts, *Historical Review of South-East Texas and the Founders, Leaders and Representative Men of Its Commerce, Industry and Civic Affairs*. Vol. 1. Chicago: The Lewis Publishing Co., 1910, 300.
16. Hayes, *Galveston*, 60, 61.
17. Dyer, "Laffite A Schemer."
18. Anne A. Brindley, "Jane Long." *Southwestern Historical Quarterly*. Vol. 46, October, 1952, 220, 221.
19. Dyer, "Laffite A Schemer."
20. Ibid.; Hayes, *Galveston*, 62.
21. Dyer, "Laffite A Schemer."
22. Hayes, *Galveston*, 66, 67, 69.
23. Lamar Papers, Vol. 2, 123.
24. Ibid.
25. Ibid., 124.
26. Ibid.
27. *Galveston Daily News*, January 13, 1907.
28. Lamar Papers, Vol. 2, 124, 125.
29. Ibid., 125.
30. Ibid. Lamar papers did not specify Mr. Smith's first name or his daughter's age.
31. Ibid., 125, 126.
32. Lamar Papers, Vol. 2, 125, 126; Abel Terrill to Jane Long, July 8, 1822.

Chapter 3

1. David. L. Kokernot, "The Reminiscences of David Levi Kokernot." *Gonzales Weekly Inquirer*, June 22, 1878; Kent Gardien, "Kokernot and His Tory," *Texana*. Vol. 8, Texian Press: 1970, 284, 285; Captain Walter C. Capton, *The U. S. Coast Guard*. New York: Franklin Watts, Inc., 1965, 13.
2. Kokernot, "Reminiscences."
3. Ibid.
4. Ibid.
5. Ibid.
6. Ibid.
7. Ibid.
8. Ibid.
9. Ibid.

10. Ibid.
11. Ibid.; Gardien, "Kokernot," 276.

Chapter 4

1. [Anonymous], *A Visit to Texas: Being the Journal of a Traveler Through Those Parts Most Interesting to American Settlers with Descriptions of Scenery, Habits, &c. &c.* Second Edition. New York: Van Nostrand and Dwight, 1836, 1–4. The author's name is unknown, and he did not mention the names of his companion or of the two agents.
2. Ibid., 60.
3. Rupert N. Richardson, Ernest Wallace and Adrian N. Anderson, *Texas The Lone Star State*. New Jersey: Prentice-Hall, Inc., 1970, 69.
4. [Anonymous], *A Visit to Texas*, 65.
5. Ibid., 69, 72, 73.
6. Ibid., 73.
7. Ibid., 86.
8. Ibid., 87.
9. Ibid., 88.
10. Ibid., 89.
11. Ibid.
12. Ibid., 90.
13. Ibid., 91.
14. Ibid., 92.
15. Ibid.
16. Ibid., 93.
17. Ibid.
18. Ibid.
19. Ibid., 95, 96.
20. Ibid., 98.
21. Ibid., 99.
22. Ibid., 100, 101.
23. Ibid., 101.
24. Ibid., 103.
25. Dorothy Louise Fields, "David Gouveneur Burnet." *Southwestern Historical Quarterly*. Vol. 49 (1945–46), 219; Burnet to Williams, April 13, 1831, Samuel May Williams Papers, MS in Rosenberg Library, Galveston, Texas.
26. Fields, "David G. Burnet," 220.

Chapter 5

1. Galveston Customhouse Records, 1835–46. Vol. 1 (1835–44), Rosenberg Library, Galveston, Texas. June 1837.
2. Ibid.

3. *Galveston Daily News*, December 11, 1883.
4. [Anonymous], *A Visit to Texas*, 82.
5. Galveston County Deed Records, Book A, 55, 56.
6. Hayes, *Galveston*, 398.
7. Galveston County Deed Records, Book B2, 41; Book C, 91.
8. Galveston Customhouse Records, 1835-46. Vol. 1 (1835-44); Margaret Swett Henson, "Tory Sentiment in Anglo-Texan Public Opinion, 1832-1836." *Southwestern Historical Quarterly*. Vol. 90, 3.
9. Henson, *Juan Davis Bradburn*, 72-75.
10. Richardson, *Lone Star*, 93, 100.
11. Camilla Davis Trammell, *Seven Pines: Its Occupants and Their Letters, 1825-1872*. Dallas: Southern Methodist University Press, 1987, 33, 34.
12. Ibid., 34; Jean L. Epperson, "Notes and Documents, 1834 Census—Anahuac Precinct, Atascosito District." *Southwestern Historical Quarterly*. Vol. 92, January, 1989, 442.
13. Trammell, *Seven Pines*, 36.
14. Ibid., 39.
15. William Hardin to Sam Houston, December 14, 1836. *Beaumont Enterprise*, December 30, 1934.
16. Ibid.
17. William G. Cooke to William Logan. *Beaumont Enterprise*, December 30, 1934.
18. William M. Logan to William G. Cooke, *Beaumont Enterprise*, December 30, 1934.
19. Ibid.
20. "Some Early Settlers," *Galveston Daily News*, March 26, 1907.
21. Charles Hooton, *St. Louis' Isle, or Texiana; with Additional Observations made in the United States and In Canada*. London: Simmonds and Ward, 1847, 98. Hooton did not give Potter's first name.
22. Ibid., 99.
23. Ibid.
24. Ibid., 100.
25. Ibid., 102.
26. Ibid., 103.
27. Ibid., 105.
28. Interview with Frank Simpton, Jr., Port Bolivar, Texas, October 12, 1985.
29. "Old Pilot Days," *Galveston Daily News*, October 24, 1906.
30. Receipt from Republic of Texas to George Simpton. Collection of Frank Simpton, Jr.
31. Interview with Frank Simpton, Jr., Port Bolivar, Texas, October 12, 1985.
32. 1850 Census, Galveston County, Texas.

Chapter 6

1. Hooton, *St. Louis' Isle*, 6.
2. *Galveston Weekly News*, May 23, 1844.
3. Maury Darst, "Texas Lighthouses: The Early Years." *Southwestern Historical Quarterly*. Vol. 79, 305; Peggy Leshikar, "Lighthouses and Lightships of the Northern Gulf of Mexico." Department of Transportation, U. S. Coast Guard. No date.
4. *Galveston Daily News*, April 17, 1856.
5. Ibid., June 9, 1857.
6. Ibid., March 26, 1907.
7. Darst, "Texas Lighthouses," 305.
8. *Galveston Daily News*, November 23, 1930.
9. Ibid., May 17, 1930.
10. Ibid., May 27, 1933.

Chapter 7

1. J. de Cordova, *Texas: Her Resources and her Public Men: A Companion for J. de Cordova's New and Correct Map of the State of Texas*. 1st Edition. Philadelphia: printed by E. Crozet, 1848, 39.
2. *Galveston Daily News*, November 3, 1895.
3. Ibid., November 12, 1895.
4. Ibid., November 27, 1895.
5. Ibid.
6. Ibid., December 8, 1895; February 19, 1896.
7. Ibid., March 15, 1896.
8. Ibid., November 27, 1895.
9. Ibid., March 15, 1896.
10. Ibid., March 26, 1896.
11. Ibid.
12. Ibid., April 13, 1896.
13. Ibid., April 14, 1896.
14. Ibid., May 27, 1896.
15. Ibid., June 12, 1896.
16. Ibid.
17. David G. McComb, *Galveston: A History*. Austin: University of Texas Press, 1986, 58–61.
18. *Galveston Daily News*, July 26, 1896.
19. Interview with Melanie Holt Speer, Fort Smith, Arkansas, March 3, 1985.
20. Chris Emmett, *Shanghai Pierce: A Fair Likeness*. Norman: University of Oklahoma Press, 1953, 287.
21. Ibid., 289.
22. Ibid., 293.

23. *Beaumont Daily Afternoon Journal*, October 3, 1900.
24. Ibid.
25. Bob Burton, "The Bolivar Peninsula Railroad," *Beach Triton*, May, 1985; *Galveston Daily News*, September 24, 1903.

Chapter 8

1. *Beaumont Enterprise*, July 9, 1898.
2. Ibid., July 4, 1899.
3. Ibid., August 27, 1898; June 3, 1899.
4. Ibid., July 16, 1899.
5. *Beaumont Semi-Weekly Journal*, Sept. 14, 1900.
6. Ibid.
7. Ibid.
8. *Galveston Daily News*, September 12, 1900.
9. *Beaumont Enterprise*, September 14, 1900.
10. Ibid.
11. Ibid.
12. Ibid.
13. Ibid.
14. Ibid.
15. *Beaumont Semi-Weekly Journal*, September 11, 1900.
16. *Galveston Daily News*, September (?), 1900. No date on paper.
17. Ibid.
18. Ibid.

Chapter 9

1. Cade's statement did not appear in letters—the author envisioned him saying it.
2. *Galveston Daily News*, April 28, 1897.
3. *Beaumont Weekly Enterprise*, October 1, 1898.
4. Galveston County Deed Records, Book 183, 200.
5. Galveston County Deed Records, Book 183, 133.
6. *Galveston Daily News*, January 21, 1901.
7. Ibid., January 31, 1901.
8. Ibid., February 1, 1901.
9. Ibid.
10. Prospectus, The Great Western High Island Oil Company. Cade Family Collection, no date.
11. Charles Taylor Cade to Charles Stubbs. James B. and Charles J. Stubbs Papers, 1872–1904. Rosenberg Library, Galveston, Texas.
12. Ibid.
13. Ibid.
14. Ibid.

270 / NOTES

15. Ibid. Sour Lake Oil Field, in southern Hardin County, was opened in 1901 after the Spindletop success. Because of excessive drilling, which caused a decline in gas pressure, half of the original 150 wells had been abandoned by 1903.
16. Ibid.
17. Ibid.
18. Ibid.
19. Ibid.
20. Deed of Trust, Charles Stubbs to John Hanna, September 13, 1910, Cade Family Collection.

Chapter 10

1. *Galveston Daily News*, January 25, 1901; March 15, 1922; February 16, 1908.
2. Ibid., March 26, 1907.
3. Ibid.
4. Ibid.
5. Ibid., February 16, 1908.
6. Ibid.; "Observation Platform," January 1981. Galveston Pamphlet File, Rosenberg Library, Galveton, Texas.
7. *Galveston Daily News*, February 16, 1908.
8. Ibid., June 15, 1909.
9. Ibid., June 16, 1909.
10. "Manufacturers Record," October 13, 1910. Port Bolivar Files, Rosenberg Library, Galveston; *Galveston Daily News*, October 13, 1910.
11. *Galveston Daily News*, January 10, 1910.
12. Records U. S. Army Corps of Engineers, Galveston, Texas. Just before Congress declared war on Spain in April 1898, the U. S. Government purchased land for Fort Travis (February 21, 1898). Battery Davis and Battery Ernst were built in 1898; in 1925 Battery Kimble was built, and Battery 236 was completed in 1943. The fort was used in both world wars.
13. *Galveston Daily News*, May 17, 1930; January 15, 1912; "Manufacturers Record," Port Bolivar Files, Rosenberg Library, Galveston.
14. *Galveston Daily News*, May 17, 1930.
15. "On the Rim of Galveston Bay," *The Earth*, June 1914. Galveston Pamphlet File, Rosenberg Library, Galveston.
16. *Galveston Daily News*, February 11, 1912.
17. *Encyclopedia Britannica*. Vol. 23. London: William Benton, 1962. 769, 779.
18. Interview with Jim Bouse, Port Bolivar, April 2, 1987.

Chapter 11

1. *Galveston Daily News*, August 16, 1915.
2. *Beaumont Enterprise*, August 17, 1915.

3. Ibid.
4. Ibid.
5. *Galveston Daily News*, August 23, 1915.
6. Ibid.
7. Ibid.
8. *Beaumont Enterprise*, August 21, 1915.
9. Ibid., August 20, 1915.
10. Ibid., December 18, 1927.
11. Ibid.
12. Ibid., September 18, 1924.
13. *Galveston Daily News*, August 19, 1915; November 9, 1930.
14. *Beaumont Enterprise*, August 19, 1915.
15. Ibid.
16. Ibid.
17. *Beaumont Journal*, August 19, 1915.
18. *Beaumont Enterprise*, August 21, 1915.
19. *Galveston Daily News*, August 23, 1915.
20. *Beaumont Enterprise*, August 20, 1915.
21. *Galveston Daily News*, August 23, 1915.
22. *Beaumont Enterprise*, August 23, 1915.
23. Ibid.
24. Interview with Tolley Davis, Lafayette, Louisiana, June 27, 1985.
25. *Beaumont Enterprise*, August 30, 1915.
26. Ibid.
27. Ibid.
28. Ibid.

Chapter 12

1. *Beaumont Enterprise*, May 31, 1936.
2. Interview with Monroe Kahla, Sr., Port Bolivar, July 5, 1985.
3. *Beaumont Enterprise*, February 16, 1934.
4. Ibid., May 31, 1936; *Galveston Daily News*, May 17, 1930.
5. Ibid.
6. Ibid.
7. Ibid.
8. Ibid.
9. *Beaumont Enterprise*, March, date unknown, 1947.
10. *Galveston Daily News*, July 22, 1948.

Chapter 13

1. *Houston Post*, April 8, 1987.
2. *Galveston Daily News*, April 10, 1987.
3. Ibid.

4. Ibid., April 11, 1987.
5. *Time*, April 27, 1987.
6. *Galveston Daily News*, May 2, 1987.
7. Ibid., May 7, 1989.
8. *Houston Chronicle*, May 11, 1987.

Chapter 20

1. Ernest was born March 9, 1911, and died in spring 1990.
2. The time period is an exaggeration of 100 years. The Simptons came to Bolivar in the 1840s.

Chapter 21

1. Jim Bouse died in February 1990.
2. Electricity came to the peninsula in several stages and reached Caplen in the late 1930s.

Chapter 24

1. Anne was born in 1907.

Chapter 25

1. Mary Dafonte died in November 1990.

Chapter 26

1. Barbara was born in 1930; Paulene was born in 1933.

Chapter 27

1. The U-boat sinking was, as far as is known, a rumor.

Bibliography

Books

[Anonymous]. *A Visit to Texas: Being the Journal of a Traveler Through Those Parts Most Interesting to American Settlers with Descriptions of Scenery, Habits, &c &c*. Second Edition. New York: Van Nostrand and Dwight, 1836.

Aten, Lawrence E. *Indians of the Upper Texas Coast*. New York: Academic Press, 1983.

Capton, Captain Walter C. *The U. S. Coast Guard*. New York: Franklin Watts, Inc., 1965.

Clark, James A. *Biography of Marrs McLean*. Houston: Clark Book Co., Inc., 1969.

De Vaca, Álvar Núñez Cabeza. *Adventures in the Unknown Interior of America*. Translated and annotated by Cyclone Covey with new epilogue by William T. Pilkington. Albuquerque: University of New Mexico Press, 1961.

De Cordova, J. *Texas: Her Resources and Her Public Men: A Companion for J. de Cordova's New and Correct Map of the State of Texas*. 1st Edition. Philadelphia: E. Crozet, 1848.

Emmett, Chris. *Shanghai Pierce: A Fair Likeness*. Norman: University of Oklahoma Press, 1953.

Gulick, Charles Adams, Jr. et al. (eds). *The Papers of Mirabeau Buonaparte Lamar*. 6 vols. Austin: A. C. Baldwin & Sons, 1921–1928.

Hardy, Hon. Dermot H. and Major Ingham S. Roberts. *Historical Review of South-East Texas and the Founders, Leaders and Representative Men of Its Commerce, Industry and Civic Affairs*. Vol. 1. Chicago: The Lewis Publishing Co., 1910.

Hayes. Charles W. *Galveston: History of the Island and the City*. Austin: Jenkins Garrett Press, 1974.

Henson, Margaret Swett. *Juan Davis Bradburn: A Reappraisal of the Mexican Commander of Anahuac*. College Station: Texas A & M University Press, 1982.

Hooton, Charles. *St. Louis' Isle, or; Texiana: with Additional Observations Made in the United States and In Canada.* London: Simmonds and Ward, 1847.
Linsley, Judith Walker and Ellen Walker Rienstra. *Beaumont: A Chronicle of Promise.* Woodland Hills, California: Windsor Publications, Inc. 1982.
McComb, David. *Galveston: A History.* Austin: University of Texas Press, 1986.
Morfi, Fray Agustín. *History of Texas, 1673–1779.* Translated with biographical introduction and annotations by Carlos Eduardo Castañeda. Vol. 1. Albuquerque: The Quivira Society, 1935.
Richardson, Rupert N., Ernest Wallace, and Adrian N. Anderson. *Texas: The Lone Star State.* New Jersey: Prentice-Hall, Inc., 1970.
Rundell, Walter, Jr. *Early Texas Oil.* College Station: Texas A & M University Press, 1977.
Trammel, Camilla Davis. *Seven Pines: Its Occupants and Their Letters, 1825–1872.* Dallas: Southern Methodist University Press, 1987.
Yoakum, Henderson K. *History of Texas from Its First Settlement in 1685 to Its Annexation to the United States in 1846.* Vol. 1. Austin: The Steck Co., 1935 (originally published in 1855).

Published Articles

Barker, Eugene. "The African Slave Trade in Texas." *Texas Historical Association Quarterly* 6 (1902), 145–58.
Block, W. T. "Jean Lafitte Haunts Southwest Louisiana." *Beaumont Enterprise* (Heritage I). February 5, 1984.
Brindley, Anne A. "Jane Long." *Southwestern Historical Quarterly* 56 (October 1952), 211–38.
Burton, Bob. "The Bolivar Peninsula Railroad." *The Beach Triton.* May 1985.
Campbell, T. N. "Archaeological Investigations at the Caplen Site, Galveston County, Texas." *The Texas Journal of Science,* Vol. 9, No. 4 (December 1957), 448–71.
Darst, Maury. "Texas Lighthouses: The Early Years." *Southwestern Historical Quarterly* 79 (July 1975–April 1976), 301–16.
Dyer, Dr. Joseph O. "Laffite a Schemer as Well as an Executive." *Galveston Daily News.* May 14, 1922.
Dyer, Dr. Joseph O. *The Lake Charles Atakapas (cannibals): Period of 1817 to 1820.* Galveston: privately printed, 1917.
Epperson, Jean L. "Notes and Documents, 1834 Census—Anahuac Precinct, Atascosito District." *Southwestern Historical Quarterly* 42 (January 1989), 438–47.
Fields, Dorothy Louise. "David Gouverneur Burnet." *Southwestern Historical Quarterly* 49 (1945–46), 215–28.

Folmer, Henri. "De Bellisle on the Texas Coast." *Southwestern Historical Quarterly* 44 (1940–41), 204–31.
Gardien, Kent. "Kokernot and His Tory." *Texana* 8 (1970), 269–93.
Henson, Margaret Swett. "Tory Sentiment in Anglo-Texan Public Opinion, 1821–1836." *Southwestern Historical Quarterly* 90 (1986–87), 1–34.
Kokernot, David L. "The Reminiscences of David Levi Kokernot." *Gonzales Weekly Inquirer*. June 22, 1878.
Prichard, Walter, ed. "George Graham's Mission to Galveston in 1818: Two Important Documents Bearing Upon Louisiana History." *Louisiana Historical Quarterly* 20 (July 1937), 619–51.

Newspapers

Atakapas Gazette, St. Mary, St. Martin & Lafayette Advertiser. St. Martinville, Louisiana. May 3, 1844.
Beaumont Daily Afternoon Journal. October 3, 1900.
Beaumont Daily Journal. January 2, 1901; August 19, 1915.
Beaumont Enterprise. July 9, 1898; August 27, 1898; October 1, 1898; June 3, 1899; July 4, 1899; July 16, 1899; September ?, 1900; September 14, 1900; August 17, 1915; August 19, 1915; August 20, 1915; August 21, 1915; August 23, 1915; August 30, 1915; September 18, 1924; December 18, 1927; May 31, 1936; February 16, 1934; March ?, 1947.
Beaumont Semi-Weekly Journal. September 11, 1900; September 14, 1900.
Galveston Daily News. April 17, 1856; June 9, 1857; November 3, 1895; November 12, 1895; November 27, 1895; December 8, 1895; February 19, 1896; March 15, 1896; March 26, 1896; April 13, 1896; April 14, 1896; May 27, 1896; June 12, 1896; July 26, 1896; April 28, 1897; September 12, 1900; September 17, 1900; January 21, 1901; January 25, 1901; January 31, 1901; February 1, 1901; September 24, 1903; October 24, 1906; January 13, 1907; March 26, 1907; May 26, 1907; February 16, 1908; June 15, 1909; June 16, 1909; January 10, 1910; January 15, 1912; February 11, 1912; August 16, 1915; August 19, 1915; August 21, 1915; August 23, 1915; March 15, 1922; May 17, 1930; November 9, 1930; November 23, 1930; May 27, 1933; July 22, 1948; April 10, 1987; April 11, 1987; May 2, 1987; May 7, 1987.
Galveston Weekly News. May 23, 1844.
Houston Chronicle. May 11, 1987.
Houston Post. April 8, 1987.

Manuscript Collections, Unpublished Articles, Maps

American State Papers, Vol. 4.
[Anonymous]. Unpublished manuscript, Laffite Files, Rosenberg Library, Galveston, Texas.
[Anonymous]. "On the Rim of Galveston Bay," *The Earth*, June 1914. Galveston Pamphlet File, Rosenberg Library, Galveston, Texas.

Aten, Lawrence E., letter to author, November 13, 1990.
Burnet, David G. to Samuel May Williams, April 13, 1831. Samuel May Williams Papers, MS in Rosenberg Library, Galveston, Texas.
Cade, Charles Taylor to Charles Stubbs. James B. and Charles J. Stubbs Papers, 1872–1904. Rosenberg Library, Galveston, Texas.
Cooke, William G. to William Logan. *Beaumont Enterprise*, December 30, 1934.
Dunman, Martin Family Files, Wallisville Heritage Park, Wallisville, Texas.
Galveston Customhouse Records, 1835–46. 2 Volumes. Rosenberg Library, Galveston, Texas.
Glass, James. "A Replica Chart of the Galveston-Houston Area Circa 1836." Houston: Kelvin Press, 1986.
Hester, Dr. Thomas R. "Prehistory of the Upper Texas Coast." Lecture April 6, 1990. Rosenberg Library, Galveston, Texas.
Jones, J. Randall. "A Visit to Galveston Island in 1818." Transcript of notes by Philip Tucker from Jones's memoirs. Rosenberg Library, Galveston, Texas.
Leshikar, Peggy. "Lighthouses and Lightships of the Northern Gulf of Mexico." Department of Transportation, U. S. Coast Guard, no date.
"Manufacturers Record." October 13, 1910. Rosenberg Library Pamphlet Files, Galveston, Texas.
"Observation Platform." January 1981. Galveston Pamphlet Files, Rosenberg Library, Galveston, Texas.
Powell, J. F. "An Epidemiological Analysis of Mortality and Morbidity in Five Late Prehistoric Populations from the Upper and Central Texas Coast." MA thesis, Department of Anthropology, University of Texas at Austin, 1989.
U. S. Army Corps of Engineers Records, Galveston, Texas.

Interviews

Bouse, Jim. Interview with author. Port Bolivar, Texas, April 2, 1987.
Davis, Tolley. Interview with author. Lafayette, Louisiana, June 27, 1985.
Henson, Margaret Swett. Interview with author. Houston, Texas, November 15, 1990.
Kahla, Monroe, Sr. Interview with author. Port Bolivar, Texas, July 5, 1985.
Shaw, Dixie. Interview with author. Port Bolivar, Texas, April, 1987.
Simpton, Frank, Jr. Interview with author. Port Bolivar, Texas, October 12, 1985.
Speer, Melanie Holt. Interview with author. Fort Smith, Arkansas, March 3, 1985.

BIBLIOGRAPHY / 277

Public Records

1850 Census, Galveston County, Texas. Rosenberg Library, Galveston, Texas.
Galveston County Deed Records, Galveston, Texas.
Jefferson County Deed Records, Beaumont, Texas.

Private Collections

Cade Family Collection, 1880–1940. (Letters, maps, deeds, and receipts)
Republic of Texas (receipt) to George Simpton. Collection of Frank Simpton, Jr.

Published Correspondence

Hardin, William to Sam Houston. *Beaumont Enterprise*, December 30, 1934.
Logan, William to William G. Cooke. *Beaumont Enterprise*, December 30, 1934.

Index

Abrason, Mr , 62
Adams, Mr , 187
Adkins Family, 141
Akokisas (Orcoquisas) Indians, 6, 7, 9
Alamo, 40, 41
Altman, Joe, 183
Army Corps of Engineers, 100
Assinais (Hasinai or Caddo) Indians, 7
Atakapas (Attacapas) Indians, 6, 7, 8, 9, 39, 71, n.263
Attakapas Gazette, 28
"Aunt Kate" (*see* Kate Hughes)
Aury, Louis de, 12, 13
Austin, (Stephen F), 28
Averill, Mr., 57

Barr, Eddie, 106
"barracoons," 12
Barrow Family, 261
Batz, A. De, 71
Beach Hotel, 81
Beaumont Enterprise, 58
Bellisle, Simars de, 6, 7, n.263
Bielstein Susan, 115
Big Hill, 241
Bill's Restaurant, 105
Bishop's Castle, 244
Blalock Family, 181, 213
Blanchette, Coy, 59
Blanchette, Joe, 62
Bleeker, Rev. J. W., 63, 64
Boddecker, J A., 90
Bolivar lighthouse, 47–50, 74, 88, 104, 168, 215, 226, 227, n.268

Bolivar Point (*see also* Point Bolivar), 25–27, 38, 39, 43, 44, 48, 52, 53, 59, 64, 65, 100
Bonnie and Clyde, 208, 209, 260
Borden, Gail, 38, 73
Borsum, A E., 87
Bouse, Charlie, 113
Bouse Family, 198, 213, 216, 217, 227, 232, 236
Bouse, Grandfather, 165
BOUSE, JIM, 189, 191, n.272
Bouse, Louise Hudnall, 150
BOUSE, PAULENE JOHNSON, 174, 232, n 272
Bouse, Raymond, 257, 260
Bouse, R.C., Sr., 148, 150, 162
BOUSE, R C., JR , 82, 103, 172
Bouse, Sid, 109
Bouse's Store, 76, 91, 101, 152, 192, 193, 216, 236
Boy Scout Troup #2, 86, 90
Boyt Family, 151, 207
Bradburn, Colonel John, 26, 29, 32, 37, 40
"Breakers," 87, 88, 91, 92, 101
Bright, Ben, 152, 205, 255–57
BRISTER, BARBARA JOHNSON, 174, 232, n.272
Britt, Mr , 241
Brooks, Captain, 50
Brooks, Mr., 256, 257
Broussard, Eloge, 212
Broussard Family, 225
Brown (Mayor of Galveston), 48

Brutus, Edward, 21
Burnet, David G., 30, 37, 41
Burnet, Mrs., 30, 37, 41

Cade, Charles Taylor, 56, 58–59, 63–70, 75, 95, 151
Cade Hotel (*see* Sea View Hotel)
Cade, Kitty, 56, 75
Cade lands, 100, 152
Cade, Margaret, 56, 75
Campeachy, 9, 13, 14, 16, 39
Caplen, 9, 10, 76, 77, 84, 87, 88, 91, 100, 121, 133, 136, 142, 149, 150, 151, 162, 163, 172, 175, 180, 181, 189, 194, 217, 221, 250, 252, 255, 256, n.272
Captain Cotton, 29
Carpenter, George, 85
Carr, Eddie, 143
Carroll, Monroe, 69–70, 87
Carter, Keith, 115–18
"Charlie," 30–37
Charpiot, A B., 106
Charpiot, Pat, 107
Chocolate Bayou, 157
Cleveland Family, 225
Cleveland, Jim, 227
Climax, 30, 31, 34–37
Cochran, Captain William 15, 16
Columbia, 156
Comeaux, Warren, 197
Commercial Intelligencer, 45
Cooke, William, 42
Corder, Mrs E.W , 85, 86
Cordova, J. de, 52, n.268
Crab Lake, 255
Crenshaw, Will, 93
Crockett store, 189, 193
Cronea, Charles, 240
Cronea Family, 205, 244
Crystal Beach, 58, 74, 105, 106, 153, 188, 248, 252, 257
Cull, 30, 31, 37
Cybelle, 47

DAFONTE, MARY SILVA, 221, 223, n 272
Dafonte Family, 205
Dailey, Louis, Jr , 107, 108
Daniels, Tommy, 95, 199
Davis, Samuel, 12

Davis, Tolley, 90, n.271
Davison, Mr., 184
Delgado, Captain Pedro, 41
Depression, 196, 204, 213, 222
de Vaca, Álvar Nuñez Cabeza, 4, 5, 9, n.263
Dorsett, Family, 177
Double Bayou, 24, 87
Dougherty, Mr., 11
Dunman, Mr., 49
Dunman, James, 42
Dunman, Joseph, 41
Dunman, Martin, 39, 41–42

Edwards, Amos, 24
Emery, L.L., 66, 67
Enterprise, 15
Esder, Mary, 132

Fannett, 165
Fannin, Col (James W), 41
Featherstone, L E , 89
Featherstone, L.P., 53, 55, 79, 80, 82, 83
Fisher, George, 40
Flake, 89, 101, 192
Flake, Oscar, 89
Fort Travis, 81, 94, 104, 148
Fox, Mr., 227
Franks, Burrell, 24, 25, 38–42, 43
Franks, Elijah, 25–27, 38–39, 41, 42
Franks, Mary, 27, 38, 39
Franks, Russell, 39
Franks, William, 27
"Frederick," 28–37, 39, n.266
Fredericksen, Captain Alfred, 166, 167
Fredericksen, Captain Clarence, 151, 165, 167, 172
Fredericksen, Ora Shaw, 166, 172
Frenchtown, 95, 96, 101, 104, 185, 196, 197–99, 213

Gage, Will, 91
Gallagher, Jim, 142
Galveston, 234
Galveston Bay and Texas Land Company, 28, 29, 37
Galveston Daily News, 53, 67, 80, 84, 86
Galveston Weekly News, 47
Gaslight Restaurant, 106
General Midnight, 36

INDEX / 281

George Washington, 20
Gilchrist (*formerly* Rollover), 100, 192
Gill, Mr., 23, 24
Goat Island, 97, 109, 248
Gokey, Lawn, 141, 142
Gonzales Weekly Inquirer, 27
Goodhue, Mrs., 59
Gordon Family, 77
Gordon, W.D., 87, 91, 92, 205, 207
Great Western High Island Oil Company, 68, n.269
Graham, George, 7, 8, 14, n.264
Green Light, 207
Griffiths, Mr., 69
Guffy (Lucas), 69
Guidry, Bernard, 113
Gulf Bay Hotel, 59
Gulf and Interstate Railroad, 52–60, 65, 79–81
Gulf Oil Company, 204
Gulf State Utilities, 103
Gulf View Hotel, 76, 77, 91
Gulfway Cafe, 115
Gulfway Motel, 105

Hackberry Island, 39
Halbouty, Michel, 70
Hall, Warren D.C., 11, 16
Hampshire, Mr., 49
Hamshire, Asa, 91
Hardin, William, 26, 40, 41
Harrington Family, 183
Harrington, Otto, 92
Harrington, Percy, 143
Heiman, Ernest, 127
Heiman, John, 125, 127, 133, 136
Henshaw Family, 90, 91
High Island, 24, 41, 42, 52, 53, 56, 58, 64–68, 70, 75, 85–88, 90, 91, 94, 99, 100, 104, 105, 107, 108, 114–16, 143, 149, 151, 157, 173, 181, 187, 193, 202–4, 206, 208, 209, 232, 240, 241, 243, 251, 255, 259, 260, 262
High Island Hotel, 99
High Island Mineral Springs, 56, 203
Hogg, Governor (James S.), 68
Holland, Tom, 86, 90
Holt, Charles "Challie," 90, 100, 152, 241
Hooton, Charles, 43–45, 47

Hudnall, Mr., 153, 255
Hughes, Buddy, 133, 138, 140, 183
Hughes, Charles, 131, 133–35
Hughes, Cindy, 202
Hughes, Edwin, 124
Hughes, Eliza, 124
Hughes, Ellen Agnes, 124
Hughes, Felton, 131, 132
Hughes, Florence, 129, 131, 133
Hughes, Frank, 143
Hughes, Harry, 124, 132, 133, 140
Hughes, Henry, 127
Hughes, Jessie, 58
HUGHES, KATE, 133, 138, 140, 141
Hughes, Laura, 149, 163
Hughes, Louis George, 138
Hughes, Louise, 123
Hughes, Samuel F., 48, 121
Hughes, Sidney, 129, 131, 132
Hurricane Carla, 154

Indian graveyard, 92, 105, 254
Intracoastal Canal, 100, 104, 109, 113
Irwin, Mrs., 61–63

Jackson, Hugh, 86, 87, 91
Jamaica Beach, 10
"James," 28–37
Jenkins Family, 225, 226
Jenkins, "Yardy," 225, 226
Johnson, Judge Andrew, Jr., 103, 174, 181, 207, 232–37
Johnson, Cora Beth, 232
JOHNSON, HERMAN, 115, 116
Johnson, Paula, 232
Jones, C. J., 54, 55
Jones, Henry, 54
Jones, J. Randall, 13, n 264
Jones, N.C. "Buffalo" 53–55
Julius Caesar, 22

Kahla, Arnold, 189
Kahla, Barney, 144, 145, 202, 251, 258
Kahla, Bluch, 92, 216, 257
Kahla, Butch, 118
Kahla, Claud, 114, 115, 204
Kahla, Elaine, 114, 117, 118, 248
Kahla, Ethel, 252
Kahla Family, 213

Kahla, Frank "Ank," 92, 152, 256, 257
Kahla, Mrs. Frank, 227
Kahla, Fred, 256, 258
Kahla, George, 202
Kahla, Grandpa C. W., 168, 178, 180, 184, 186, 204, 248
Kahla, Hotel, 94
Kahla, Joe Bill, 102, 109
Kahla, John, 180
Kahla, Leslie, 117, 258
Kahla, Lil, 163
Kahla, Minnie, 163
Kahla, Monroe, Jr., 110
KAHLA, MONROE, SR., "Pike," 99, 100, 102, 108, 110, 114, 117–19, 178, 187
Kahla, Rodney, 110
Kahla, Slim, 255
KAHLA, VERNON, 66, 114–17, 163, 192, 193, 202, 252
Kahla, Wesley, 258
Kahla, Westcott, 144, 145, 185
Kane, Barney, 148, 149
Karankawa Indians, 4, 5, 6, 8, 9, 10, 17
Kearny, Lieutenant Commander, 15
Keith, Alice, 62, 63
Keith, Jim, 91
Keith, Olga, 62, 63
Kelsey, Bill, 106, 107
Kian, 17, 18
Kirkland, Mr. Frank, 86
Kirkland, Mrs. Frank, 86, 87
Kirkpatrick, Henry, 208, 241
Kline, Mrs., 241
Kline's store, 192, 217, 227
Kokernot, David Levi, 20–27, 39, 42, n.265
Kronprinz Wilhelm, 82

"labor," 28
Lacassinier, 13, 14, 15
Lady of the Lake, 39
Laffite, Jean 7, 9, 12–16, 20, 24, 29, 30, 37, 39, 45, 71–73, 101, 102
Laffite, Pierre, 39
Lamar, Mirabeau B., 16
Lecroy, Bud, 168
Levy, Max, 59, 60
Logan, Colonel William, 42, 43
Long, James, 14–19, 73

Long, Jane, 15–19, 73, n.265
Long Point, 152, 184, 252
Louisiana, 48
"loup blanc," 101
"loup garou," 101
Lucas, Anthony, 66–70

Madden, R.J., 90
Majesty, 28
Manufacturers Record, 81
Marmion, W.H., 89
Mary, 38
Mary Hamilton, 48
Margaret M. Ford, 80
Massey, Joe, 208
McCaleb, Mr., 196, 199
McFaddin Family, 91
McGaffee John, 40, 42
McKellum, Mr., 185
McLean, Marrs, 77, 87, 99, 180, 204, 217
Meyers, Mr., 234, 235
Meyers, Mrs., 234
Meyers, Skippy, 234
Meynig, Mr. 205
Meynig Family, 240, 244
MILLER, VERA SHAW, 163, 166, 174
Monroe, President James, 7, 14
Monteau, Mr., 205
Moody, Mr , 243
Morawitz, 89
Morfi, Fray Juan Agustín, 6, n.263
Morgan, Colonel James, 26
Morgan's Point, 149
Morris, Mr., 23, 24, 26
MOUTON, ANNE BROUSSARD, 212
Mouton, "Sis," 189, 212
Mud Bayou, 52, 244
Mud Lake, 206
Myles, F.F., 66

Nash, C.L., 59
National Youth Administration, 228
Nicholas, 16
1900 Storm, *passim*
1915 Storm, *passim*
Norris, Ulysse, 198

Oppikofer, Fred, 68
Orcoquisas (Akokisas) Indians, 6, 9

Pacho, Lieutenant Juan, 40
Padilla, Juan Antonio, 9
Parminter, P E , 85, 88, 90
Parr, Samuel, 43–45, 156
Parr's Grove, 158
Patton (see Crystal Beach) 58, 74, 88, 101, 105, 143, 172, 181, 204, 213, 252
Patton, Charles, 58, 61, 62
Patton, C.R., 48, 49
Patton Hotel, 58, 61
Patton, W C., 55
Payton, Charles, 90
Payton Family, 183, 205, 209
Payton, Jeff, 206
Payton, Jim, 206
Payton, John, 99, 206, 207, 232, 243, 259
Payton, Lou, 206
Payton, Molly, 206, 240
Payton, Skinny, 206
Payton, Tom, 206
Pearl Harbor, 261
Pelican Island, 49
Perry, Colonel Henry, 11, 12, 26
Perry's Point, 26
Peterson, Mr , 207
Pierce, Abel Borden "Shanghai," 56, 57, 79, n 268
Point Bolivar, 11
Port Bolivar, 78, 80–84, 88, 89, 90, 92, 93, 97, 102–5, 138, 150–52, 179, 180, 185, 187, 189, 192, 194, 196, 197, 199, 204, 212, 213, 218, 221, 222, 227, 228, 236, 237, 248, 255, 260, 261
Port Bolivar City Company, 79
"Potter, Mr." 43, 44
Potter, Monte, 107
Pride, 15, 16
Prohibition, 152

Quinn, B.E., 89

Rageur, 13
Red Cross, 220, 229
Redfish Bar, 24
Redfish Reef, 89
Redman, Mr , 23, 26
Reindeer, 38, 39
"Richard," 30–37
Rivea Family, 205

Rivea, Mr., 49
Roberts, Claude, 87
Roberts, Claude, Jr., 86, 87
Roberts, Gaston, 196
Rohacek, J.T., 88
Rolling Over Place, 38, 40, 58–61, 85
Rollover (see Gilchrist) 58, 60, 61, 85, 86, 88, 90, 92, 133, 135, 151
Rollover Hotel, 85, 88
Rollover Pass, 149
Rosenquist, Mr , 241

Sabine Pass, 243
Sandal, Mary, 150
Santa Anna (Antonio Lopez de), 40, 41
Santa Fe Railroad, 74, 80–83, 93, 212–214, 218, 221, 225
Scanlan, Oscar, 85
Schwab, Charles M., 81
Seabrook, 181
Seaside Special, 259
Sea View Hotel, 56, 64–66, 70, 75, 85, 90, 99, 102, 104, 181, 205, 261
Sears and Roebuck, 165, 174
Segura, Mr., 228, 229
Shaw, Arlie, 258
SHAW, DIXIE BOUSE, 84
Shaw, Mr , 49
Shaw, Granville, 203, 204
Shaw, Mansel, 257
Shaw, Oca, 148, 172
Shaw, Ora (see Fredericksen)
Shaw, Tucker, 172
Shrier, Mike, 129
Sievers, George, 205
Silva, Eudocia, 221
Silva, Jesus, 221
Silva, Rudy, 224, 225
Silver King, 151, 166–68, 172, 190, 216, 218, 227, 257, 259
Simmons, Mrs , 59
SIMPTON, ERNEST, 177, 179, n.272
Simpton Family, 213, 228
Simpton, George Washington, 45
Simpton, George, 46
Simpton, Jemima, 45
Simpton, John, 45
Simpton, Leslie, 179
Simpton, Mary, 45
Simpton, Sarah, 45

Singing Sands, 10
Smith, Charlotte E., 202
Smith, Mr., 18, 19
Smith, George, 66, 67, 70, 90, 202
Smith, Peggy, 18
Smith Point, 178, 179
Smith, Tom, 62, 63
Sosby, Miss Alice, 140, 190
Southern Pacific, 213
Spangler, H.S., 65
Spillman, James, 21
Spindletop, 69
Standley, George, 187, 252
Star Lake, 241
Statham, 157
Stephens, Dr , 150
STEPHENSON, AGNES BLUME, 156
Stephenson, Ernest, 156
Stephenson Family, 150
Stephenson, Joe, 151
Stimson, General E.K , 52, 53
Stingaree Road, 257
Stirling, Mayor Bill, 106
Stowe, Mrs , 133, 134
Stowell, 151, 202
Stubbs, Charles, 55, 68–70
Subaru commercial, 107, 108
SUHLER, STELLA, 196, 197
Sullivan, Casey, 149
Sullivan, Henry, 87, 99, 206, 244, 255
Sun Oil Company, 258

Tasso, 129
Tellepsen Company, 100

Terán, General Manuel Mier y, 29, 40
Texaco, 152, 193
Texas War of Independence, 40
The Blue Man, 115
Thornton, Bob, 203
Time Magazine, 106
"Tory Land," 40, 41, 73
Travis, William B., 26, 41
Treadwell, Mr., 242
Tuggle, George, 64
Turtle Bayou, 156

Van, Mr., 198, 227
Varnell, Joe, 186
Vermilion Bay, Louisiana, 11
Vratis, George, 106

Weaver, Mrs., 228
Weekes-McCarthy Bank, 56
Westfield, 49
White Family, 87
Whites' Ranch, 64, 136
Williams, Samuel May, 37
Winnie, 186, 206
Winnie, Fox, 53, 54
W P.A., 197, 216, 228
Wyman, Mr., 44, 45

Yates Bayou, 125
Yount-Lee Oil Company, 70
Yucatan vireo, 105

Zavala, 45

AUTHORS GUILD BACKINPRINT.COM EDITIONS are fiction and nonfiction works that were originally brought to the reading public by established United States publishers but have fallen out of print. The economics of traditional publishing methods force tens of thousands of works out of print each year, eventually claiming many, if not most, award-winning and one-time best-selling titles. With improvements in print-on-demand technology, authors and their estates, in cooperation with the Authors Guild, are making some of these works available again to readers in quality paperback editions. Authors Guild Backinprint.com Editions may be found at nearly all online bookstores and are also available from traditional booksellers. For further information or to purchase any Backinprint.com title please visit www.backinprint.com.

Except as noted on their copyright pages, Authors Guild Backinprint.com Editions are presented in their original form. Some authors have chosen to revise or update their works with new information. The Authors Guild is not the editor or publisher of these works and is not responsible for any of the content of these editions.

THE AUTHORS GUILD is the nation's largest society of published book authors. Since 1912 it has been the leading writers' advocate for fair compensation, effective copyright protection, and free expression. Further information is available at www.authorsguild.org.

Please direct inquiries about the Authors Guild and Backinprint.com Editions to the Authors Guild offices in New York City, or e-mail staff@backinprint.com.

Printed in the United States
1468700004B/1-3